AMERICA GOES TO THE MOVIES

100 Years of Motion Picture Exhibition

by Barbara Stones

National Association of Theatre Owners

ISBN 0-9638653-0-7

New Hampshire. **On the front cover:** (clockwise from top) 3-D audience stunt, *Norm Levinson*; audience, Garden Theatre, Greenfield, Massachusetts, *John Lowe*; concession counter, *Frank Novak*; El Capitan Theatre, Los Angeles, *Pacific Theatres*; movie palace projection room, *Herb Brown*; Tri-City Drive-in, *Pacific Theatres*; Fox Theatre, Detroit, *Donald Idarius*; children at theatre, *Elliot Cohen*; Delta Theatre, *Roger Rice*. **Inside back cover:** Author photograph, *Michael Spatola Photography*. **On the back cover:** (clockwise from top) Gem Theatre, Kannapolis, North Carolina, *Clyde Scarboro*; concession area, *Act III Theatres*; Roy Rogers, Wisconsin Theatre, Milwaukee, Wisconsin, *Larry Widen*.

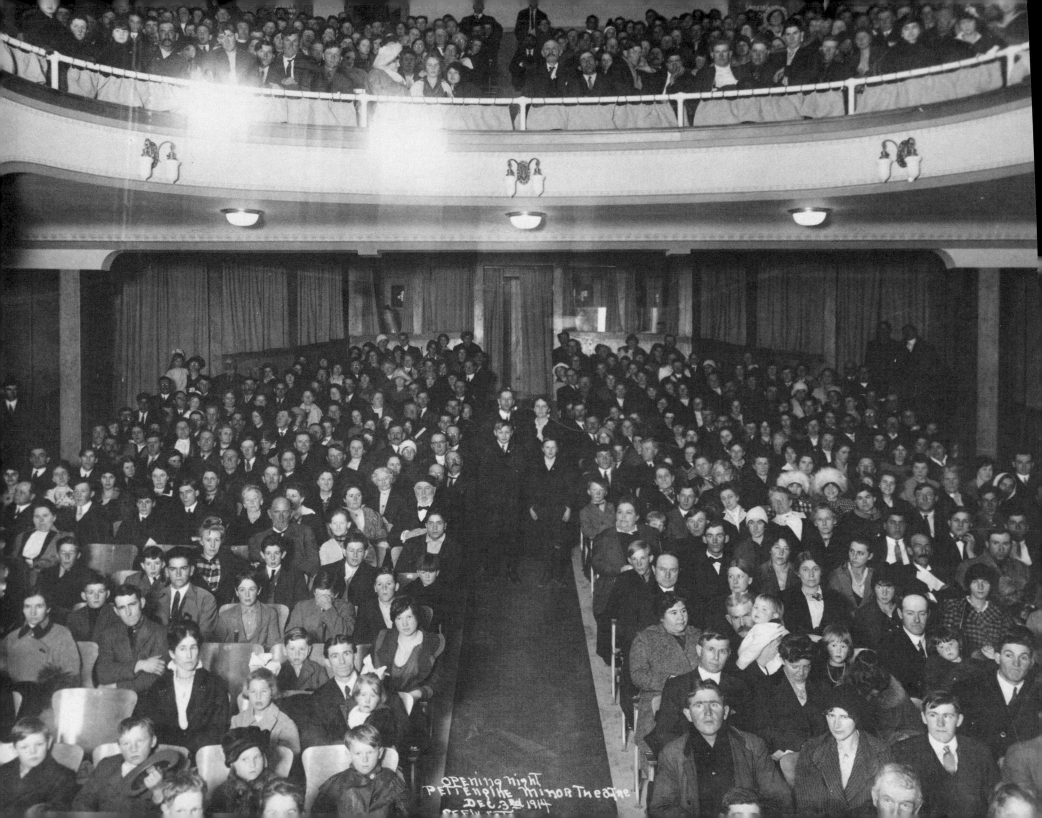

Opening Night
Pettenqine Minor Theatre
Dec 3rd 1914

CONTENTS

Interior of the Minor Theatre on the venue's opening night, December 3, 1914. Arcata, California. *David Jervis*

Madison, Wisconsin, 1930. View of State Street with Christmas decorations and theatre marquees. *Tim Romano, Historic Photo Service*

Chapter 1
THE EARLY YEARS

merica's love affair with the movies began on April 14, 1894 with the opening of the Holland brothers' amusement arcade at 1155 Broadway in New York City. Stepping inside the converted shoe store, patrons found two rows of tall wooden cabinets, each with a narrow viewing slot. The ten motorized contraptions were kinetoscopes, the latest invention of Thomas Alva Edison.

Named after the Greek words for "movement" and "to watch," the kinetoscopes illuminated a revolving film strip to create moving images. Each machine offered a different scene of vaudeville performers or circus acts that lasted a mere 20 seconds. Patrons paid 25 cents to view the films on one row of five machines, or splurged and bought two tickets to see all 10 films. The effect of moving pictures was astounding. Customers had never seen anything like them and were delighted by the startling realism of the tiny moving images. Word of the new novelty machines quickly spread and by the end of the day the Holland brothers had netted a remarkable $120.

So began the commerical history of motion pictures in the United States. The birth of movies shown on a screen would soon follow.

Ever since his highly successful invention of the phonograph, which became a staple of amusement parlors and penny arcades of the 1880s, Edison had sought a way to create a similar device for moving pictures. Impressed with the sequential photographic work of Eadweard Muybridge and others, Edison had commissioned his assistant, William Kennedy Laurie Dickson, to perfect a motion picture camera and viewing machine. The kinetograph camera and the kinetoscope were the result of that research and experimentation. At the same time, Edison began producing moving pictures to supply the peepshows with a constant supply of new images. Within a short time kinetoscope peepshow machines could be found throughout the country in amusement parlors, hotel lobbies, saloons, pool halls, train stations — anywhere that an enterprising businessman could find the space for one or more machines. The kinetoscope soon invaded Europe as well.

The immense popularity of moving pictures pointed

Motion picture pioneers George Eastman and Thomas Edison. *Eastman Kodak Company*

Interior view of Holland brothers' historic kinetoscope parlor at 1115 Broadway in New York City where Amcricans in 1894 first paid to see the marvel of moving pictures. Edison's wooden kinetoscope cabinets can be seen on the right. *John Lowe*

out the commercial flaw in Edison's viewing machine: only one person at a time could use it. The public's enthusiasm for the new novelty, rather than spurring sales of additional units as Edison hoped, prompted interest in modifying the kinetoscope so it could magnify and project moving pictures on a large screen for a roomful of paying customers. The concept was similar to magic lantern shows of the day that projected still photographs and drawings onto a screen and inventors began tinkering with Edison's basic design.

The idea of projected moving pictures made perfect sense from a business standpoint. The use of a single projector meant lower start-up costs to introduce the novelty since only one machine had to be purchased rather than several. As a result of buying only one machine maintenance costs would also be lower. And the obvious plus was that many people could see projected moving pictures at a time and hence more money could be made. By 1895 scientists, inventors and entrepreneurs throughout England, France and Germany were hard at work converting Edison's original technology into projecting machines, a prospect that Edison had unwittingly encouraged by neglecting to secure international patents for the kinetoscope. Edison was convinced that moving pictures were a short-lived fad; so he concentrated instead on selling as many kinetoscopes as possible before the novelty wore off.

After studying Edison's technology the Lumiere brothers of Lyons, France developed a combined moving picture camera, printer and projector called a Cinematographe. The Lumieres are generally credited with being the first to project moving pictures onto a screen for a public audience. That historic event took place at the Grand Cafe in Paris on December 28, 1895. However, three months earlier, American businessman Thomas Armat and inventor C. Frances Jenkins used a

machine they called a Phantoscope to project moving pictures at the Cotton States Exhibition held in Atlanta. Armat and Jenkins exhibited films that were originally produced for Edison's kinetoscope and technically not suitable for projection on a big screen. Despite this flaw the Atlanta Journal gave the Phantoscope a rave review and called it "unquestionably the most wonderful electric invention of the age." Few of the fairgoers, however, saw the film exhibition and the promotional effort was a failure. Soon after, Armat and Jenkins had a falling out and dissolved their partnership. The men then acted independently to exploit the commercial advantages of the Phantoscope. Armat's slightly modified version of the Phantoscope caught the attention of Edison's business partners, who had become aware of European competition. Seeing a chance to expand their moving picture business beyond peepshow machines, they promptly bought the exclusive marketing rights to the projector and arranged for the Edison Manufacturing Company to build it. And so it was that Armat's Phantoscope, promoted to all the world as the Edison Vitascope, debuted at New York City's Koster & Bial's

THE MECHANISM OF THE VITASCOPE

THE VITASCOPE IN THE PROMENADE

FEB OFFICE

Illustration from the New York Herald shows debut of the Vitascope and projected moving pictures at Koster & Bial's music hall in New York City. Note inset with two projectors used so audience would not have to wait while individual film scenes were rewound. *Academy of Motion Picture Arts and Sciences*

Motion pictures earned a single placement on a Keith vaudeville bill at the Academy of Music, Norfolk, Virginia. *Virginia State Library & Archives*

music hall, on April 23, 1896 — marking the start of the shared motion picture experience in America.

What makes going to the movies magical today is the same magic audiences experienced yesterday — the shared emotional experience of watching moving pictures with a group of people. Sitting together in the darkened theatre, the audience cheered with spontaneous delight as the Vitascope projected luminous, large-as-life moving images on the screen. The music hall orchestra played rousing accompaniment to a film program that featured images of two dancers with an umbrella, a strongman flexing his muscles, waves crashing on a pier, a burlesque boxing match, and a military band marching in formation. Each film strip was spliced together end-to-end to form a continuous loop so each

20-second scene could be shown again and again to hearty applause.

The film scenes that so aroused the audience at Koster & Bial's were exactly the same subjects that could be seen in a neighborhood kinetoscope parlor, with one difference. The power of projection magnified the one-inch peepshow film frames into captivating life-size images. The thrilling pictures of realistic movement, now coupled with the audience's shared emotional response, created a powerful new entertainment experience.

It would be years before moving pictures evolved from simple one-shot views to tell fully-developed stories, and years before permanent theatres were built expressly for showing movies. But on April 23, 1896, in that darkened hall off Herald Square, the public's fascination with moving pictures entered an exciting new phase of shared pleasure.

The Edison Company looked at the developing trade of moving pictures as primarily an equipment business. The company's marketing plan concentrated on selling exclusive franchise rights to the Vitascope projector on a state-by-state basis. The state licensees in turn promoted the widespread sale of projectors. Over the spring and summer of 1896 the Vitascope opened in a dozen major cities and resort areas. Promotion centered on the projecting machine itself rather than the films it showed. Treated like a star performer the Vitascope played in vaudeville theatres, music halls and opera houses as part of varied entertainment programs. Some entrepreneurs set up temporary storefront operations where Vitascope exhibitions were put on for weeks at a time. One of the first storefront operations was in Providence, Rhode Island where the public flocked to see screenings of 10 films for 25 cents. The storefront theatre stayed open for four weeks during the summer of 1896. Another early storefront theatre

Traveling exhibitor George Carroll used his car as mobile advertising for his outdoor movie business in 1939. *George Carroll*

The cost of film was another source of frustration. Priced by the foot like so much drapery material, new films could cost as much as $12.50 for less than 30 seconds of movement. Color was not unknown, but films with tinted stock or hand-painted scenes cost more. Early film stock was of poor quality and the emulsion often separated from its base, rendering it useless. Exhibitors were continually betrayed by films that lasted only a few performances, resulting in disappointed audiences and lost revenue.

Within months of the Vitascope's debut, rival projectors appeared on the scene. On June 29, 1896, the Lumiere Cinematographe was presented with great fanfare at Benjamin F. Keith's Union Square Theatre in New York. The Lumiere's Cinematographe was hand-cranked and fully portable, avoiding the frustration of adapting to different electrical standards throughout the country. The engagement was a hit. Keith, the largest operator of vaudeville theatres in the country, was so pleased with this success that he booked the Cinematographe projector into all of his theatres.

Keith's successful introduction of moving pictures prompted other vaudeville theatres to follow his lead. Moving pictures were easily adapted into vaudeville's variety format that consisted of several unrelated acts of singers, acrobats, jugglers, magicians, puppets and magic-lantern presentations. During an evening's performance a collection of film subjects were presented to fill out a standard vaudeville "turn" of 15 to 20 minutes. These early presentations of projected moving pictures generated tremendous excitement and kept audiences returning for repeat performances. Within a short period of time, vaudeville theatres across the country introduced millions of Americans to the novelty of projected moving pictures.

The Lumiere brothers were visionaries in other

opened in New Orleans. After presenting the Vitascope for a month in a nearby summer park, Walter Wainwright and William Rock opened a 10-cent store theatre that ran from July 26 through September, 1896.

The Vitascope was not without problems for budding entrepreneurs. In addition to having to learn the proper set-up and operation of the machine, exhibitors faced the headaches of having to adapt to widely divergent electrical systems. During America's early years of electrification, there were no set standards for currents and voltages. While the Vitascope was designed to run on direct current, many communities were wired for alternating current.

areas of the fledgling moving picture business. They pioneered the concept of the "complete exhibition service"; in exchange for long term contracts, the company provided vaudeville theatres with projectors, skilled projectionists and a complete program of film subjects. The company also filmed scenes of local interest to guarantee higher attendance.

By early 1897 a flood of different film projectors at

competitive prices became available and overwhelmed sales of the Lumiere and Edison equipment. The projectors boasted tongue-twisting names such as Panoramographe, Kalatechnoscope, Kinematographe, Animatographe, Animotiscope and the simpler-to-pronounce Magniscope, Centograph and Bioscope. Some were electric but most were hand-cranked and used portable limelight for illumination. The word "limelight" is used today as a term to describe being in the spotlight, at the center of attention. The derivation of the term comes from a form of brilliant stage lighting produced when a flame is directed at a piece of lime. The light, when condensed through a lens, creates a concentrated beam. Early projectionists adapted the limelight technique to project a bright moving picture.

The high demand for projectors convinced Edison of the advantage of selling equipment outright to all comers and he soon introduced a projector for direct sales. Called the Projecting Kinetoscope or Projectoscope, the projector was priced at $100, an affordable price for even a small business. With a rash of compatible projectors invading the market, all requiring a steady diet of pictures, Edison saw profits from sales of his films exceed those from sales of equipment for the first time.

Exhibitors shared a need to continually update their film collections. Once an audience tired of seeing a particular set of scenes the film strips became useless inventory. Rather than constantly buying new pictures, one group of enterprising exhibition pioneers took to the nation's backroads where they sought to regularly change audiences instead of films. These were the traveling exhibitors.

America of 1900 was still a predominately rural nation with most people living in towns of less than 3,000 with no organized form of entertainment. Recognizing

These 1939 diary entries made by traveling exhibitor J. R. Southard describe good weather for a tent show of movies held at the Beech Creek school grounds, east of Greenville, Kentucky. *Southard Collection, Special Collections, Western Kentucky University*

During the early years of cinema, traveling acting troupes alerted the public that they provided *live* entertainment. Note the phrase "not a moving picture" on the poster. *Museum of Repertoire Americana*

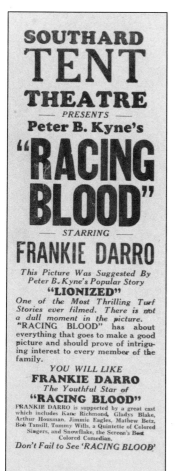

a promising opportunity, the itinerant showman simply loaded a wagon with a projector, a collection of films and a common bedsheet for use as a screen and set off along the country's backroads in search of an audience.

The traveling exhibitor would arrive in a community and arrange to use an empty hall or store, rent chairs from the local undertaker, and offer some of the town's youngsters free admission in exchange for distributing promotional flyers and he was in business. In other cases the traveling showman simply hung his sheet in a public park or projected his films onto the side of a building on Main Street while the townsfolk sat on the ground.

The traveling exhibitor often established regular circuits by stopping in small towns within 20 or 30 miles of each other at regular intervals. Early showman William F. Dalke, rejecting the grocery business in favor of movies, built up a circuit of 12 towns in the Shennandoah Valley west of the District of Columbia. Each town meant a one-night stand. Setting up his projector in a field, or the town hall, Dalke entertained the local audience. At the end of his circuit, Dalke returned to Washington for a fresh supply of films and began his rounds again.

Like a myriad of other traveling salesmen, preachers and medicine shows, hundreds of these moving picture exhibitors could be found touring the country. Their satchels of films brought the world quite literally to the doorstep of the nation's smallest communities. Whether by horseback, wagon or car they traveled to rural hamlets, budding communities, even to the remote mining camps of the Alaska gold rush era, bringing people a respite from their everyday lives. "My daddy was a minister," explained longtime Mississippi exhibitor Juanita "Skeeter" Maxey, "and he always told us that things like that were good for the soul and the mind because people could get away and enjoy a few hours or

few minutes and forget their troubles. He said it was better than medicine sometimes because it just gave people an uplifted spirit."

The itinerant showman traveled America's by-ways as late as the 1960s. Whatever the decade the goal of the traveling showman was the same — to entertain. Recalled Maxey, "The tent shows would come and stay a week at a time. They would have a serial every night. They'd have a western. The shows were just real short, an hour and 15 minutes or something like that. You sat on bleachers, and between reels they'd have somebody selling candy. A lot of times, the candy had a prize in it. We'd beg daddy to get us a box of candy so we could get that little prize. The bleachers were called 'chicken roosts' because they were very much like where chickens go to roost. What it was just plain planks."

"A lot of times you could go in and rent the lodge hall," remembered retired Midwestern exhibitor George Carroll, "The Odd Fellows and the Moose

Lodge, they would rent you the hall for so much a night, and of course it was a pretty nice set-up. They had all their seats and everything, so all you'd have to do is have your portable screen and put it up and set up your portable projector and have someone with you to sell tickets and put the show on."

Wisconsin theatre owner Otto Settele recalled how the traveling show evolved into the "gasoline circuit." "Traveling exhibitors used 16mm equipment and gave shows that lasted about one and a half hours for towns that were not big enough to have a theatre. Small towns typically with 500-600 people. The showman got a print and contacted a tavern. The owner would pay the fee, and the movies were shown free to the public. The owner got his money from the beer or soft drinks that were sold during the intermission. Mainly farm families with kids would come."

It was not only the itinerant, small-time exhibitor who saw the advantages of traveling to find an audience. "High-class" moving picture companies also developed traveling circuits — but these sought out more elite audiences. Most often restricted to travel lectures, these sophisticated, evening-length programs featured elaborate, documentary-style presentations which combined moving pictures of exotic locales with lecture material and illustrated slides. These lecture programs catered to the well-educated, discerning members of the upper class and were typically presented in church halls, music academies or opera houses of larger cities.

In addition to playing vaudeville theatres, temporary storefront operations and traveling shows, the marvel of projected moving pictures thrilled Americans at the amusement parks, carnivals and circuses that operated during the summer months. From 1897 through 1903, motion pictures were a regular attraction at the famed Ringling Brothers Circus. Films were exhibited in black tents or "black tops" which were actually large canvas structures designed to keep the light out. Located along the circus midway, the moving picture attraction was a featured sideshow spectators could experience before they entered the big top for the main circus performance. A series of 15-foot-tall posters lined the front of the black tent and a barker stood outside loudly hawking the pictures to passers-by. The passers-by responded; Americans were definitely developing an appetite for moving pictures.

Whatever the venue, the successful exhibitor was first and foremost a showman who had to develop a knack for maintaining audience interest, or risk losing his patrons to a more imaginative businessman who could. From the early days, these showmen introduced all kinds of embellishments, like voice, music and appropriate sound-effects accompaniment; all to enhance the audience's experience of the screen images. Using a simple phonograph to play recorded sound, the exhibitor could effectively punctuate a film with the sounds of galloping horses or those of a train with rushing steam,

Circus barker attracted a crowd to see film of the Corbett-Fitzsimmons boxing match under a black top tent. *Circus World Museum Baraboo, Wisconsin*

ringing bells and roaring wheels which would inevitably startle audiences as a screen train hurtled toward them. Press accounts were filled with stories of more than one filmgoer who jumped from his seat to get out of the way.

Exhibitors also played a creative role in shaping an evening's program. The use of a story and plot line in films had not yet developed so a showman's program of films usually consisted of a reel of several 20-second views of simple action. Typical film scenes featured a barber shaving a customer, a train arriving at a station, carriages on the Brooklyn Bridge, strolling couples in a park, waves breaking against a pier, and children playing. In the earliest days of moving pictures a varied program of unrelated scenes was enough to hold an audience's attention. Ever mindful of the need to pique the public's curiosity, exhibitors soon began to create sequences of similar or contrasting action to heighten the impact of the scenes, thus creating an early form of film narrative. The efforts of early exhibitors also resulted in evening-length film programs of prize fights and religious passion plays.

During the formative years of moving pictures, Americans from all walks of life had an opportunity to see films in a variety of locations at a wide range of ticket prices. For the middle-class vaudeville patron and opera house fan, moving pictures claimed a spot alongside other vaudeville favorites on the program. Prices at smaller vaudeville houses ranged from 10 to 20 to 30 cents depending on seat location, while prices at premiere vaudeville theatres in the nation's largest cities could run as high as $1.50. Members of the urban working class, looking for inexpensive entertainment, enjoyed moving pictures at dime museums, those affordable emporiums of bizarre and fanciful exhibits, in temporary storefront theatres that popped up in downtown areas, and in the backrooms of amusement arcades where admission was only a nickel. Americans in small rural towns lucky enough to be on a traveling showman's circuit paid between a dime and 50 cents a show.

By 1900, according to some reports, the initial appeal of moving pictures for big-city vaudeville patrons had worn thin. Interest in film subjects had peaked during the Spanish-American War in 1898 when scenes of actual sea battles and clever re-enactments done with miniatures elevated films from a novelty to the compelling status of a moving picture newspaper. The war scenes evoked powerful patriotic sentiments in audiences and demonstrated the tremendous emotional power of screen images. During the war some enterprising exhibitors compiled complete programs of war-related or military footage and traveled from town to town with tent shows of these "wargraph" or "warscope" programs, forerunners of later newsreel theatres. Following the end of the war, however, film shots of everyday scenes and local news failed to excite audiences. The predictable scenes of simple action couldn't compete with dramatic live acts, and films were either dropped from the more prominent vaudeville circuits or relegated to the end of the bill.

Despite a growing lack of interest in films among more sophisticated members of the public, moving pictures remained a regular attraction with small-time vaudeville circuits and other traveling troupes of entertainers. Arcade owners eagerly bought up any used projectors they could find and proceeded to hang curtains across the back of their shops to partition a separate area for projected pictures.

After 1900, the length of films began to increase as more producers moved from "actuality" footage of everyday life to experiment with fictional scenes. Audiences were entranced when the first glimmers of storytelling appeared on the screen. These "stories" were little more than skits with prearranged scenes, but they were enough to refuel the public's interest in moving pictures. Beginning around 1902, films grew increasingly longer, allowing more complete stories to be told. The introduction of special effects, pioneered by French magician George Melies in his whimsical hit, "A Trip to the Moon," ushered in a trend to "magical" story films. Then in 1903, Edwin S. Porter's realistic drama "The Great Train Robbery" burst onto the screen with a full eight minutes of gripping action. Audiences gasped at the close-up of the outlaw's pistol, rooted for the posse during the chase, and cheered the final shootout and annihilation of the gunmen. This wildly successful moving picture marked the birth of the story film. And moving pictures became known as "movies."

The public's rekindled excitement for films prompted a rush to convert opera houses, municipal buildings, church halls and meeting rooms into temporary, makeshift theatres. Programs were supplemented with slide shows, lecturers, minor vaudeville acts and simple stage plays, but movies were the primary draw.

Despite the high level of public interest in story films, it was still difficult to establish permanent storefront theatres to offer pictures on a full-time basis. The cost of film, driven even higher by the advent of longer pictures, and combined with an erratic supply of new films made a movies-only theatre a risky business. Prospects were worse for a storefront operator forced to compete against affordably-priced, small-time vaudeville houses that showed pictures combined with a full bill of live entertainment.

The immense popularity of story films changed the way the film industry conducted business. Once story films caught the public's fancy, film manufacturers faced a backlog of less desirable action scenes that the public had outgrown. When a major manufacturer held a

bargain sale to reduce this inventory, Harry and Herbert Miles saw a business opportunity. The Miles brothers bought quantities of the old films and devised a system of weekly film rentals. The Miles brothers correctly guessed that what was dated film stock to exhibitors in larger cities, would prove attractive to the newly-established arcade owner in small, rural towns where moving pictures had only recently been introduced. While traveling cross country to San Francisco, the enterprising brothers secured enough signed contracts to launch the first formal film exchange.

The Miles Brothers Exchange opened in 1903 and soon grew to include all the films of all the leading producers. The idea was disarmingly simple. They purchased new releases from production companies at full price. They then rented them to exhibitors on a weekly basis for one-fourth the purchase price, exchanging a new film for each one returned. Everyone liked the arrangement. Producers were delighted to deal with one customer who would buy films in quantity, which in turn encouraged the steady production of new films. Rental terms meant exhibitors could afford more frequent changes of program which further stimulated their business. The exchange owners, meanwhile, would continue to accrue rental fees long after the original purchase price was recovered.

The exchange system established distribution as a separate facet of the motion picture business. Even the former exhibition services, which film manufacturers established for vaudeville houses, began to rent a reel of film to theatres for less money than the cost of their full-service packages. Responsibility for projection thus shifted to the theatre. The idea of film rental proved so successful that a dozen rival exchanges were soon in operation. Their numbers would grow rapidly as the number of exhibition sites for movies mushroomed.

The exchange system, combined with the immense popularity of story films, encouraged the growth of permanent "movies only" theatres. Now assured of a steady supply of affordable film, more entrepreneurs began to enter the budding movie theatre business. Nearly a decade after the Vitascope had introduced the wonder of projected moving pictures to American audiences, the permanent movie theatre finally arrived.

Typical film exchange office of the silent era. *Robert Rothschild*

Early St. Louis tent show was operated year-round at the corner of Cherokee and Jefferson. *Ron Krueger*

Chapter 2

THE NICKELODEON ERA

Controversy surrounds the exact date and location of the first theatre that was set up specifically to show moving pictures, but there is general agreement that the boom in storefront movie theatres began after Harry Davis opened the Nickelodeon Theatre in Pittsburgh on June 15, 1905. No stranger to the amusement business, Davis owned the city's Grand Opera House, a stock theatre company, two variety theatres and an amusement arcade. He had already enjoyed success with films as part of vaudeville bills and in a separate movies-only room at his arcade. The small room accommodated 32 people standing and proved an instant hit presenting a film program that lasted four to five minutes. The room cleared and filled up again each time the projectionist rewound the reel. When a competing small-time vaudeville house opened with motion pictures on its program, Davis acted quickly to protect his business. He transferred the continuous all-movies concept to a larger storefront, which he dubbed the Nickelodeon Theatre for its cheap price of admission combined with the Greek word for theatre.

The venue was imbued with an aura of respectability as the exterior of the 96-seat Nickelodeon was graced with classical ornamentation and electric lights. The refined interior featured incandescent lights, comfortable seats, carpeting and a pianist to accompany the films. Davis named his brother-in-law, John P. Harris, manager, and together the two men innovated policies that became staples of the budding nickelodeon trade.

The entire program consisted of one or two reels of motion picture films interspersed with illustrated song slides which ran continuously from eight o'clock in the morning until midnight. The show lasted anywhere from 12 to 20 minutes with a constant turnover of audiences. The theatre's amazing success was measured by an average of 7,000 patrons who flocked to the theatre each day. Those not lucky enough to find a seat could stand behind polished rails in the back — and up to 1,000 people did so daily. The Nickelodeon's winning concept of a short, continuous program with a cheap admission price turned moviegoing into a casual and frequent habit. When the idea took off, Davis and Harris expanded their number of local theatres and launched the concept in other cities. Within two years, Davis and Harris operated 15 nickelodeons in Pitts-

Early movie theatres sought to convey a sense of respectability by catering to women and children. *Decorators Supply Corporation. Catalog courtesy John Lowe*

Classic 1910 Milwaukee storefront nickelodeon. *Larry Widen*

the craze for movies. The nation was caught in the grip of "nickel madness" and attendance soared to as many as 2 million people daily. By 1910, some reports cited as many as 10,000 nickelodeons operating coast to coast.

The word nickelodeon is often used as a generic term to describe small, storefront theatres. In some cases nickelodeons were little more than bare, uncomfortable and poorly-ventilated store rooms converted into theatres with the aid of a canvas sheet for a screen and a collection of hard kitchen chairs. Outside, a noisy barker accompanied by a blaring phonograph exhorted all passersby to enter. The front of the theatre was cluttered with large, garish posters of the day's film attractions. Nickelodeons often attracted the attention of social reformers who found the cramped and shabby theatres alarmingly full of both men and women who mixed freely in the dark.

Other, more refined nickelodeons sported fancy facades, interior lighting and tasteful decorations. While areas of the Midwest and Northeast boasted a profusion of smaller storefront theatres, New England saw a trend

Early Ohio nickelodeon presented a daily change of new pictures. Passers-by saw the projectionist at work through the window above box office. Lyric Theatre, Mt. Vernon, Ohio. *Myron Price*

Ohio's Lyric Theatre featured piano accompaniment to films with the added amenities of gas and incandescent lighting. Lyric Theatre, Mt. Vernon, Ohio. *Myron Price*

burgh alone, in addition to other movie houses in Philadelphia, Rochester, Buffalo, Toledo and Cleveland.

News of the successful "Pittsburgh idea" spread, and entrepreneurs rushed to open similar operations across the country. The word "nickelodeon" quickly became the term for any theatre with a program of continuously-running films at a cheap admission price. Theatres sprang up like wildfire. Estimates vary on the number of nickel theatres that were operating at any given time, but at the beginning of 1907 the trade paper Variety made a conservative estimate of 2,500. In November of that same year, Moving Picture World carried an estimate of between 4,000 and 5,000 nickel theatres and critics warned that the market was becoming oversaturated. And still more theatres opened to accommodate

outside projection booth and a screen up on a wall," Midwestern theatre owner Ronald Krueger explained. "And when it got dark they'd project the picture. But when you operated in conjunction with an indoor theatre you would be running the matinees and then when it would get dark, they would stop the picture and everybody would move from the indoor theatre to the outdoor theatre. This was usually a vacant lot right next door. You would take the film down from the indoor theatre and climb into the booth of the airdome, and start the movie up again from where they left off."

Another popular form of outdoor movies was the tent show. Under a big tent the theatre owner would set up his projector and seating. "In the summertime,"

The Coliseum Theatre in Sitka, Alaska lured audiences with the added attraction of seeing slides of local residents on the screen. *W.D. "Dave" Gross*

Yale Theatre owners Besserer and Marshall pose in front of an eye-catching sidewalk rifle display promoting a Jesse James action film at one of Austin's first nickelodeons. *Film/Harry Ransom Center, University of Texas, Austin*

that converted large vaudeville theatres or legitimate houses into nickel theatres. A nickelodeon's seating could range in size from less than 100 to several hundred, to more than 1,000 seats.

Nickelodeons created the moviegoer, the theatre patron who was specifically drawn to see movies. In bigger cities the working class made up the majority of early nickelodeon audiences. Unlike vaudeville performances that took up an entire evening, or the special day's outing to a summer amusement park, nickelodeons offered affordable entertainment that workers could enjoy on the way to work, on a lunch break, when returning home or later in the evening.

Any space became a potential theatre. "They put together this theatre, just built it on the rooftop, just smoothed it out and made a floor up there," reminisced Texas-based exhibition veteran John Rowley. "Put up a screen at the back and a booth at the front and benches in-between, and that was the theatre." From these rustic beginnings evolved the airdome, an open-air theatre specifically built to woo movie audiences during warm-weather months. "You just had benches in there and an

The public flocked to any location that showed movies, whether it was a dark and dingy storefront, a roofless airdome or a tent. Exhibitors matched the public's enthusiasm for films with frequent program changes. In 1905, programs were typically changed twice a week. By November of 1906, three changes a week were not uncommon. By May of 1907, trade papers reported on theatres that changed programs every day except Sunday.

Once inside a nickelodeon, the mainly working-class audience shared the experience of classless, egalitarian society. Although vaudeville theatres typically offered a range of ticket prices that made them affordable to most everyone, the seats were priced by location; for the working class this meant sitting in the balcony in the lowest-priced seats. However, in the heady world of nickelodeons patrons enjoyed one low price for any seat in the house.

Most theatres advertised that they catered "especially to the ladies and children." It was a comforting

St. Louis' Washington Theatre and adjacent "sky dome." *Missouri Historical Society*

Theatre baseball team poses in permanent airdome constructed next to the opera house in Highland, Illinois. *Herbert Seitz*

San Francisco's former neighborhood Gem Theatre circa 1910. *Jack Tillmany*

noted Krueger, "they'd have big fans running. Then in the wintertime they fired up big pot-bellied stoves. They'd place a fan behind it and that's the way the tent was heated. I heard stories that there would be a snow-storm and they'd have to get up in the middle of the night to knock the snow off the roof of the tent to keep it from falling down."

Arizona exhibitor Dwight "Red" Harkins opened another variation of the outdoor theatre. "Due to the fact that movie theatres did not have refrigeration back then, they would have to close down in the hot summer months," explained son Dan Harkins. "My father would move his operation to the nearby park called the Tempe Beach Park and would show movies outdoors with outdoor seating." The second-generation exhibitor continued, "He built a projection booth tower and had ushers go up and down the aisles spraying mosquito spray and showed movies outside."

slogan that conveyed the idea of a safe and clean environment. Women made up a significant part of the nickelodeon audience. And some reports estimated that children accounted for a third of regular filmgoers — this was an alarming prospect for guardians of the established social order who worried about the effect of movies on impressionable young minds.

The mushrooming number of nickelodeon theatres, combined with frequent program changes, created a tremendous demand for new films. Theatres that changed programs three or more times a week played just about every film released by leading American and European producers. This included a mix of melodramas and "actualities," a term used to describe news footage of current events or interesting locations. All films of this period were silent, so scenes of a French comedy played as well to an English-speaking audience as those of an American-made western. Theatres didn't select their own programming but counted on the film exchange to keep them supplied with regular deliveries of new prints. A valued exchange office was one that had contracts with many producers thus allowing for sufficient films to be kept on hand so that a picture wouldn't repeat at a theatre, or anywhere else in the same town. Exhibitors also sought out exchanges with "quality" films, where scratchy, worn prints were kept to a minimum.

The early days of the nickelodeon era represented a wide-open financial opportunity for anyone with a minimal amount of cash and basic business sense. Former saloon keepers, shoe salesmen, furriers, butchers and cigar store operators became motion picture entrepreneurs during the nickelodeon era. In fact, early theatres were often a family affair. Ron Krueger elaborated, "My grandmother played the piano in the pit. My uncle played the drums. And grandfather ran the projector

and sold the tickets." Third-generation Alaska-based exhibitor W.D. "Dave" Gross recalled, "My dad started as a young man working for my grandfather pushing up seats after the show, because they didn't have springs; they weren't spring-loaded seats. He worked his way through just about every position that was ever in the movie business in those days."

The minimum requirements for a storefront operation meant rent for a space measuring roughly 25-feet wide by 70-feet deep, ordinary kitchen chairs or makeshift benches made from wooden planks balanced on empty barrels, a canvas sheet or painted white wall for a screen, a rented projector and the cost of film rental for two reel changes twice a week. Music would boost expenses by the cost of a piano player and a phonograph to help attract passers-by. A string of electric lights outside also helped. Added to this would be the cost of posters and a sign painter. In an effort to cut down on expenses while offering patrons something extra, one family-owned theatre offered an amateur night complete with props. "My grandmother had amateur nights, and some plays on the stage," reminisced Ron Krueger.

Standing room only crowd at Juneau's Grand Theatre, Alaska. *W.D. "Dave" Gross*

Dwight "Red" Harkins' early outdoor theatre in Tempe, Arizona. *Dan Harkins*

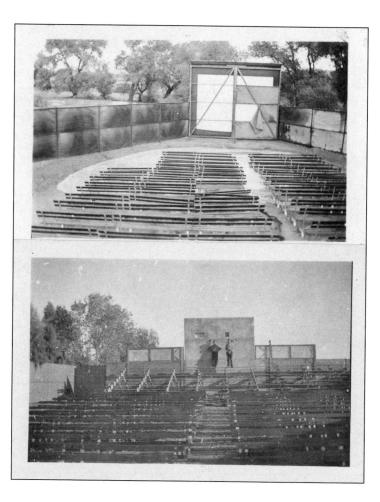

"She would be sitting there, and all of a sudden, the curtain would open and she'd see part of her living room set or dining room set sitting on the stage! They went down to the house when they needed some props and they ended up on stage."

Exhibition practices in early nickelodeons varied widely. During 1906 a survey by the trade magazine Billboard reported that five Baltimore theatres with 110 or fewer seats put on between 40 and 52 shows a day. In Birmingham, Alabama, a 100-seat nickelodeon featured 60 shows a day. Philadelphia's Bon Ton Theater had 1,000 seats and 35 shows a day. The enterprising exhibitor had a favored technique for squeezing in extra shows, explained Illinois-based circuit owner George Kerasotes. "I remember when we had a big crowd, dad says go to the booth and tell the operator to 'speed up the motor.' It didn't make any difference in those days, because there wasn't any sound, they'd just speed up the picture and get the people out faster."

Writing in the Saturday Evening Post in 1907, Joseph Medill Patterson estimated the average expenses of a 199-seat nickelodeon ran from $175 to $200 a week.

St. Louis residents enjoyed movies under the stars at the Delmar airdome located at Delmar and Hamilton. *Missouri Historical Society*

Showing to capacity crowds all day long, seven days a week produced previously unimaginable riches for small-time businessmen in a short period of time.

The pioneers of the motion picture industry, those most closely associated with the founding of Hollywood and its major studios, all got their start in the rough and tumble world of the nickelodeon. Beginning as storefront exhibitors, they parlayed their initial success into the operation of film exchanges and production companies.

Marcus Loew, who gained legendary status by founding Metro-Goldwyn-Mayer in 1924, began his amusement career in penny arcades and, later, nickelodeons. He developed a successful circuit of theatres throughout New York before expanding into other major cities.

Carl Laemmle, founder of Universal Pictures, started his career with the opening of Chicago's White Front Theatre in 1906. He then shifted his attention to operating a film exchange and later entered production. Within ten years he would preside over Universal City, the world's largest film production center.

William Fox entered the movie business with a single 146-seat theatre in Brooklyn. A decade later he was head of Fox studios, one of Hollywood's leading production companies.

Adolph Zukor, destined to become the legendary head of Paramount Pictures, moved from the ranks of nickelodeon owners into production, as did the Warner brothers and Louis B. Mayer.

The phenomenal success of the nickel movie theatre and the public's insatiable demand for films triggered a chaotic period of unbridled competition within the film industry. In 1909, in an effort to stabilize the industry and squelch further competition, nine leading film manufacturers, plus a major importer and distributor of foreign films, formed the Motion Picture Patents Company. Under the leadership of Thomas Edison the member companies, formerly bitter rivals, agreed to drop their differences in return for a greater share of film profits. The companies pooled their patent claims for cameras and projection technology and granted each other exclusive licenses for their use. In a further attempt at control, the Patents Company, otherwise known as the Trust, signed Eastman Kodak Corporation, the largest manufacturer of raw film stock, to an exclusive contract. The Motion Picture Patents Company also moved to control exhibition. Exhibitors were charged a weekly fee which was tantamount to a tax of $2 to maintain the right to use projectors and rent films of the leading film companies. Any theatre owner who dared to show a film made by an "independent," faced the confiscation of his projector and an end to further service. The Patents Company was nothing less than a brazen attempt to exert monopoly control over the entire film industry.

In April, 1910, in a further effort to extend its

Founding members of the Motion Picture Patents Company, commonly referred to as the Trust. Thomas Edison is pictured sixth from the left. *Academy of Motion Picture Arts and Sciences*

Charlie A. S. Smith mans the projection room of Houston's Osis theatre in 1912. *Karl Malkames*

were more than 40 independent producers who nearly equaled the Trust in film output. Leading the independent fight were Carl Laemmle and William Fox, former nickelodeon owners who, as mentioned earlier, would become major players in the Hollywood film industry long after the Patents Company was dissolved by the courts in an anti-trust case.

The legacy of the Motion Picture Patents Company was its success in standardizing film production to supply the nation's growing number of movie theatres with a constant flow of new pictures. Films were produced in one-reel lengths using assembly-line formulas for action pictures, comedies and melodramas. The result was an efficient system to produce short, low-cost films that guaranteed a profit. Members of the Trust insisted that films be kept to a short running time because the mass audience was presumed to be weak-minded and unable to withstand the mental strain of watching a film that lasted longer than 10 minutes. More likely, however, films were kept short so as not to interrupt the Trust's factory-like production schedules.

A growing number of independent producers, many of them former exhibitors, felt that longer, better-quality films could attract an even wider audience. European manufacturers regularly produced multiple-reel classical dramas and those that found their way to American screens enjoyed good success. These longer films were called "features," an industry term that came to mean any picture between two and eight reels in length.

The trend toward feature films spelled the end of the small storefront theatre. Longer pictures disrupted the nickelodeon's successful strategy of short programs with quick audience turnovers. Features meant fewer shows per day, and the small theatre had no way to make up for the missing revenue. When the number of feature films was low, exhibitors played them as specials on

control, the Patents Company created its own national film exchange called the General Film Company. It subsequently bought out rival exchanges or forced most others out of business.

Despite its formidable power, the Patents Company faced fierce competition from independent production companies which managed to survive by using foreign equipment and film stock. They created their own exchanges and found ready customers among exhibitors who were desperate for films and who bitterly resented the Trust's imposition of a weekly tax. By 1912 there

The 1,200-seat Rex photoplay house of Racine, Wisconsin was an example of the trend to build larger theatres. *G. E. Lloyd*

Orchestra of St. Louis' Michigan Theatre. *Ron Krueger*

Sundays only while maintaining a standard policy of short films during the week. As the tempo of feature production increased, nickelodeons became obsolete and exhibitors turned their attention to larger theatres.

Exhibitor interest in longer films and the general trend toward larger theatres resulted from a desire to attract a wide audience, specifically the nation's prosperous middle class. These patrons were already growing accustomed to paying higher ticket prices at vaudeville houses and exhibitors saw them as the key to expanding the movie theatre business. Innovative showmen discovered they could find added success by refurbishing vaudeville theatres and former legitimate houses to present a combined program of movies and live entertainment. Unlike early vaudeville programs that featured moving pictures as a single act within an evening's entertainment, the new small-time vaudeville policy gave movies equal billing with live entertainment. The larger theatres allowed exhibitors to increase both their audiences and their ticket prices while still being cheaper than big-time vaudeville shows.

With business booming, showmen moved beyond converted vaudeville houses and began to build new theatres of 800 seats or more specifically designed for movies. These refined showplaces emphasized patron comfort and ornate design. Floors were sloped for better viewing. With longer programs restrooms became a necessity. Uniformed ushers appeared. Mirrors, beveled glass and polished hardwoods graced interiors. Luxurious carpeting covered the floor. Large and imposing edifices introduced a new "palace" style. As improved new theatres were being built, older theatres were remodeled. Chicago's Decorators Supply offered decorative facades and classical ornamentation to order. The company's catalog illustrated a wide range of prefabricated styles to satisfy the requirements of new theatres or to help transform former nickelodeons into places of greater refinement.

In 1910, the Essanay Company conducted a newspaper contest to select a word that best described "the spectacular entertainment afforded by picture theatres." It was all part of the industry's effort to bestow greater respectability on motion pictures in an effort to attract the middle class audience. The term "movies" was considered a vulgar slang word that came out of the presumably seedy world of cramped nickelodeons. The winning word was "photoplay" and theatres after this time were often referred to as photoplay houses.

The year 1910 also saw the opening of Thomas Saxe's new Princess Theater in Milwaukee, a showplace that heralded a new era in movie theatre elegance. Seating 900, it boasted a seven-piece orchestra and pipe organ, plus mahogany doors, an electric fountain in the lobby and tastefully decorated lounge areas.

Clune's Theatre opened in Los Angeles in November, 1910. It seated 900 and featured an eight-piece orchestra and two singing booths, one for either side of the screen. At a time when high-class movie theatres boasted two projectors, Clune's had three. For the cost of 10 cents, or 20 cents for loge seating in the back, the audience enjoyed five reels of film, two illustrated songs and one specialty song, adding up to an hour and a half of entertainment.

In 1913 the trend toward more "palatial" movie theatres arrived in New York. The Regent Theatre opened in Harlem, then a neighborhood of middle-class German immigrants. Originally built as New York's first deluxe movies-only theatre, the Regent's business suffered from the neighboring competition of a popular Keith vaudeville house. Called to the rescue was an up-and-coming young theatre consultant named Samuel "Roxy" Rothapfel, an exhibitor from the small town of Forest City, Pennsylvania whose exceptional qualities as a showman were recognized throughout the industry. After working wonders with movie houses in Milwaukee Rothapfel was ready for the big time in New York.

Rothapfel had a plan to rescue the ailing Regent Theatre. He doubled the size of the house orchestra and moved it onstage for dramatic effect. He added an electric fountain and dressed the stage with scenery and potted plants to create the effect of a conservatory. He lowered a heavy velvet curtain in front of the screen between pictures and introduced the revolutionary idea that film music accompaniment should fit the action on the screen. The transformed Regent was an instant success and Roxy Rothapfel would soon be summoned to try his hand at bigger things.

In 1913 the Mark brothers, Mitchell and Moe, exhibitors who had developed a successful chain of nickelodeon theatres in Buffalo and other eastern cities, startled the entertainment industry when they began construction of the 3,000-seat Strand Theatre in New York. First envisioned as either a vaudeville house or a possible legitimate theatre, the massive neo-classical venue opened in 1914 as a model for future movie palaces. The Mark brothers had shrewdly hired Roxy Rothapfel away from the uptown Regent Theatre to help fulfill their ambitions to present the most spectacular entertainment in New York. Under Rothapfel's direction the Strand treated audiences to a full evening of varied musical and film entertainment. The Strand Celebrated Concert Orchestra opened the program with a series of popular classical compositions. Next came a newsreel, a travelogue and a comedy short. The evening concluded with the presentation of the feature film accompanied by a full symphony-sized orchestra numbering from 50 to 100 members. The Strand's

Los Angeles' Hyman Theatre pulled a good-sized evening crowd of movie fans. *Allen Michaan*

expanded entertainment policy proved an instant success, as 40,000 patrons streamed through the theatre during its opening week to see the feature film "The Spoilers" along with the entire show.

Rothapfel worked his showman's magic at a succession of other movie palaces on Broadway including the Rialto, the Rivoli and the Capitol, all considered to be among the grandest, most famous movie theatres of the time.

On the West Coast the leading showman was Sid Grauman, who opened the Million Dollar Theatre in Los Angeles in 1918. He is best known for his two lavishly exotic Hollywood theatres, the Egyptian and the Chinese.

As the nickelodeon era came to an end, vast changes awaited the film industry. The public's acceptance of feature films ultimately changed how movies were produced, distributed and exhibited.

Leading the charge for even longer, better-quality films was the former amusement arcade owner Adolph Zukor. Zukor heard about a French production called "Queen Elizabeth" starring the most renowned stage actress of the day, Sarah Bernhardt. It ran for four reels or 40 minutes. Sight unseen, Zukor secured the American rights to the film. Zukor rented one of New York's finest legitimate theatres, the Lyceum, where, in 1912, he staged what is regarded as the first gala movie premiere. The picture's success reinforced Zukor's conviction that audiences would respond to quality films with well-known stage actors. He founded the Famous Players production company which he promoted with the slogan of "Famous Players in Famous Plays."

The following year marked the appearance of "Quo Vadis," a nine-reel Italian film based on the best-selling novel. Imported by George Kleine, a founding member of the Trust, the film was promoted as the equal to a stage play. "Quo Vadis" opened at New York's Astor Theatre on April 21, 1913, at an unheard of $1 admission. Kleine then distributed the feature directly to exhibitors in a technique that came to be called "roadshowing." The film was offered to theatres on a percentage basis, with the distributor receiving 10 percent of the gross receipts. The gamble was rewarded with enormous success and by summer, 22 "roadshows" were exhibiting the picture in large stage theatres throughout the United States and Canada at the same terms.

The roadshow was perfected with the release of D. W. Griffith's "The Birth of a Nation" in 1915. This 12-reel American epic surpassed all production costs of its time and ran for an astounding 2½ hours. When his distributor discussed its release as a 12-part serial, Griffith adamantly refused and arranged for the ultimate in roadshows. He opened the film with a full-symphony orchestra and presented the film with an intermission. The feature played twice-daily with tickets sold in advance on a reserved seat basis. The admission price was the highest fee yet at a full $2. After roadshowing "Birth of a Nation" in the nation's largest theatres, Griffith sold the rights to distributors in different territories known as states righters. Ten years later "Birth of a Nation" was still setting attendance records in large movie theatres. It was the industry's first blockbuster, the breakthrough film that caused movies to be taken seriously.

Even though features cost exhibitors more in film rental, they were so popular with audiences that they produced more profit. Theatre owners learned that a quality feature would have sustained drawing power over several days. Theatres eventually dropped the programs of short films changed on a daily basis in favor of a feature that could be shown from two days to a week. "Shorts" remained on the program in the form of cartoons, comedies and newsreels.

The early days of the feature boom saw significant changes in the film rental system. States rights distributors recognized that a policy of renting the popular films to all theatres that wanted them until the prints ran out actually diluted their profits. The result was likely to be brief runs of a picture at a large number of competing theatres. The rise in the number of larger, more lavish theatres made it obvious that all theatres were not equal and this pointed the way to a theatre-ranking system. During the period of 1914 to 1916, distributors established an elaborate classification system with categories that ranged from the new palatial theatres in prime areas, down to older or smaller theatres in out-of-the-way locations. The system was based on the premise that a picture's release period could be extended and made more profitable if the picture was released in stages. The "first run" would be an exclusive showing at the most prestigious theatre in an area with the highest ticket prices. Then, after a suitable period of time called a "clearance," the picture became available at successively smaller and less expensive theatres within the same area or "zone."

This "run-clearance-zone" distribution system encouraged exhibitors to pay more for the chance to get a new picture first because they were protected from other theatres in their area getting the picture weeks or months later. Theatres that wanted access to features had little

AFTER

BEFORE

Exterior of Milwaukee's
whimsical Butterfly Theatre as
it appeared in 1911. *Larry Widen*

choice but to abide by the system.

Adolph Zukor further refined the system after his company merged with other competing feature production companies and a distribution company to form Paramount Pictures, Inc. in 1916. As the largest producer and distributor of feature films, the company released as many as three or four features a week. Armed with this clout, Zukor established what would become the industry policy of block booking. In order to secure the studio's best pictures with the most popular stars, exhibitors had to agree to rent all of Zukor's other films, no matter what their quality or appeal. Under this plan, money paid for renting a slate of lesser films helped underwrite the cost of the more expensive features. Block booking required theatres to contract in advance to rent a group or block of films within a specified time period. It became the accepted rule for major studios to offer a year's worth of product as a minimum "buy."

At first exhibitors were glad to know that they were guaranteed a steady supply of film from a studio of trusted quality. Block booking helped establish a system of ranking for the movies with prices adjusted accordingly. A popular star or a story from a best-selling novel or hit play would bring more people into the theatres and thus would be worth a higher rental price.

Problems arose when studios tried to adjust their prices after a block of films had been agreed upon. For example, if the popularity of a star (promised in a picture that had been offered in a block) suddenly rose, the producer might then label the picture a "special" to be sold separately on more expensive terms. Exhibitors were given a substitute picture in its place. The overall costs to exhibitors rose as they were forced to pay for a block of often inferior pictures, in addition to paying more for the most desirable films.

When exhibitors resisted the policy of block booking and Zukor's regular attempts to raise prices, the film mogul began to acquire his own theatres. In 1917, in a determined effort to "stop Zukor," and gain greater control of their fortunes, leading American exhibitors decided to pool their purchasing power and deal directly with stars and directors. They formed First National Exhibitors Circuit, representing over 100 theatres in the nation's largest cities. First National's biggest coup was to sign Charlie Chaplin to a $1 million contract, whereby the popular comedian made a total of six films for the new organization. Within a short time, First National controlled up to half the nation's theatres and opened its own production studio.

Within less than three years Zukor's agents managed to buy, build or gain partnership interests in some 600 theatres. While this represented less than five percent of the nation's moviehouses, they included prominent theatres in every major city. Other studios were forced to follow Zukor's lead and begin to acquire theatres to assure themselves of outlets for their films. So while the formation of First National stalled the practice of block booking for a time, the action pushed all the major studios into theatre ownership. This period in the film industry has been called "The Battle for the Theatres," as studio agents scoured the country seeking to acquire prime theatre properties. Intimidation was the chief weapon used against any resisting theatre owners. When an agent of one of the majors approached an independent operator to discuss the acquisition of his theatre, he usually had with him an option to purchase an adjacent theatre site. The choice was clear-cut: sell out or face crushing competition. These were not idle bluffs as scores of theatre owners were forced out of business.

With the acquisition of theatres, the major studios became fully integrated companies that exerted control over all aspects of the production, distribution and exhibition of their pictures. This vertical integration marked the birth of the studio system, a powerful profit-making enterprise that was the hallmark of the motion picture industry until after the end of World War II. The film industry, born as a novelty amusement business open to all comers with some nerve and ready cash had been transformed into a multi-million dollar big business and one of the country's major industries.

Nickelodeons were remodeled or replaced by larger, richly-appointed theatres. Exhibitors concentrated on customer satisfaction and introduced the refinements of comfortable seating, organ accompaniment, vaudeville acts, noiseless projection and a doting service staff. Feature films increased the length of programs to two hours and the public willingly paid 10, 15 or even 20 cents for a evening of entertainment. Theatres began to attract a more middle-class clientele. Huge and luxurious movie palaces began to emerge in fashionable districts. Architects incorporated stylistic gimmicks which added delights for the senses. Now the patron paid 25 to 30 cents to spend time with his or her favorite stars, surrounded by resplendent glamour and style. The era of the movie palace had arrived.

Chapter 3

MOVIE PALACES

"We sell tickets to theatres, not movies." — Marcus Loew

*T*he experience of going to the movies reached an elegant peak during the wondrous era of the American movie palace. And the word "palace" was no exaggeration. Monumental in size and architecturally grand, these extravagantly decorated movie houses defied the limits of description. They were the largest, most luxurious structures ever built for mass entertainment.

Some of the early picture palaces were modeled after the great opera houses of Europe, but in the competitive race to attract the largest audience, big-city exhibitors were soon rushing to build even bigger, even *more* lavish theatres. By the mid-1920s there was no mistaking a picture palace for a legitimate theatre or opera house. The picture palace, with its massive facade, elaborate marquee and blaze of electric lights, dramatically proclaimed its special status as a venue for the exhibition of *motion pictures*.

When audiences entered a movie palace they crossed a magical threshold into a dreamland of extraordinary splendor. Beginning in the mammoth lobby,

every square inch of wall and ceiling space seemed smothered with gilt, glitz or glaze. Architectural styles ran the gamut from Greek Revival, French Renaissance, Spanish Baroque, Italian Rococo and Gothic variations to an astounding hodge-podge of cultural motifs that wove elements of Egyptian, Moorish, Chinese, Persian and Mayan design into dizzying displays of ostentatious glamour.

The public was genuinely awe-struck by the fluted

Smartly-attired staff of New Orleans' Lafayette Theatre stood ready for duty in 1917. *Film/Harry Ransom Center, University of Texas at Austin*

Auditorium view, Grand Lake Theatre, Oakland, California. *Tom Paiva*

Artist's rendering of New York's Roxy Theatre the "Cathedral of the Motion Picture." *Motion Picture News. Courtesy of Allen Michaan*

Well-dressed theatre patrons were the rule in an earlier era. These Virginia movie fans are lined up at Richmond's Byrd Theatre. *Frank Novak*

Loews' palatial Kings Theatre in Brooklyn promotes "selected motion and talking pictures" in addition to its own symphony orchestra. *Bernard Diamond*

marble columns, hand-carved woodwork, finely-woven tapestries, mirrored arcades, rich velvet draperies, classical statuary and original art. Grand staircases rose to the heavens, huge crystal chandeliers hung from enormous dome ceilings, and delicate cove lights and electric torcheres imbued theatre auditoriums with a sensuous glow. Plush carpeting cushioned the audience's every step as attentive, smartly-uniformed ushers escorted patrons down expansive aisles to wide, welcoming and elegantly-upholstered seats.

Movie palaces exemplified the golden age of Exhi-

bition. Deliberately-overdone, the purpose of these theatres was to attract and entertain large audiences. The theatre was part of the show — and every bit as entertaining as whatever appeared on stage or screen. From the earliest days of the movies, audiences looked to the screen and its illusionary dreams to find a welcome escape from everyday cares. The advent of the lavish picture palaces guaranteed that patrons would be transported into fantasy realms and far-off exotic locales, regardless of what film was playing. Movie palaces showcased an astonishing world of art and luxury to a public eager to embrace it. Day after day, week after week, audiences returned to experience these privileged realms of wealth and grandeur for the modest price of a movie ticket. "Everything was done in grandeur," remembered Irving Ludwig, a veteran of both motion picture exhibition *and* distribution. "You didn't have a white sheet in front of you, you had a presentation. The house would darken, the curtains would open, the subject would be on the screen. People were escorted to their seats. The Rivoli Theatre had a policy in those days that if you didn't have a jacket, you wouldn't be admitted to the theatre. In other words, going to the movies on Broadway was an event. And you just didn't decide at the last moment, you planned for it."

The movie palace era extended from 1913 to 1931, during which time the majority of these deluxe theatres were built. As defined by film industry historian Douglas Gomery, the classic movie palace is a luxury theatre with a minimum of 1,500 seats that presents movies in conjunction with some form of stage entertainment. This type of palace or "deluxe" theatre, as described by the trade, was characteristically found in cities with populations of 100,000 or more. On the other hand, many *theatre* historians would characterize *any* large, ornate theatre — whether it has more than 1,500 seats or as few as 900 seats — as a picture palace.

Although palace theatres were concentrated in the nation's largest cities of New York, Chicago and Los Angeles, palace theatres also appeared in mid-size cities like Seattle, San Francisco, Denver, Buffalo and Minneapolis, all of which boasted 10 or more of the luxurious movie houses.

Construction of a movie palace required more than a design representing some architectural flight of fancy. The architect had to incorporate all the demanding technical requirements of a venue presenting motion

LOEW'S KING'S THEATRE
Front Detail

Pipe Chamber for Lobby Organ, Fox Theatre, Detroit Michigan. *Donald Idarius*

Los Angeles' exotic and world-renowned Chinese Theatre. *Cinamerica, L.P.*

Lobby art, Grand Lake Theatre, Oakland, California. *Tom Paiva*

exotic, foreign motifs.

The architectural firm of Rapp and Rapp was most closely associated with the Balaban & Katz circuit in Chicago. Renowned for a trademark style of intense opulence, C.W. and George Rapp were responsible for the ornate splendor that marked such local landmarks as the Chicago and Tivoli theatres. Captivated by their designs, and following his circuit's merger into Paramount's Publix chain, Sam Katz recruited Rapp and Rapp to design a new set of distinctive movie palaces that stretched from coast to coast.

Among the most enchanting of movie palace designs was the "atmospheric" theatre, pioneered by John Eberson. Its essential charm was based on the fanciful illusion of being outdoors. The auditorium of an

atmospheric theatre was designed like some grand European or Near Eastern courtyard complete with rock garden walls, twining vines, fountains and an assortment of imitation trees and birds, all presented under a huge

pictures and elaborate stage shows without sacrificing the luxurious palace motif. A handful of architects and specialty firms were responsible for designing the majority of the American picture palaces. Thomas Lamb was among the best known of these premiere architects, first recognized for his work in New York for the Regent, Strand, Rialto, Rivoli and Capitol. His early work followed a neo-classical style embroidered with ornate floral patterns, while his later work embraced more

Metropolitan circuit's most spectacular theatre, the Los Angeles was home of the star-studded MGM musicals from 1943-1949. *Metropolitan Theatres*

domed ceiling that was variously lit to resemble a daytime or evening sky. As the lights dimmed to reveal the violet sky of dusk, miniature lights appeared overhead like so many twinkling stars. A special machine called a Brenograph was located in the projection booth. It cast the image of gently floating clouds against the ceiling, thus completing the illusion of being outside. All that was missing was real weather.

The grand palaces flourished during the 1920s. March 11, 1927 heralded the opening of the world's greatest silent movie palace, New York's Roxy Theatre. Described as the "Cathedral of the Motion Picture," the 6,214-seat theatre was the crowning achievement of legendary showman Samuel "Roxy" Rothapfel. Conceived by architect Walter W. W. Ahlschlager and designer Harold W. Rambusch, New York's Roxy exceeded all previous standards for opulence and luxury. The extraordinary structure featured a mammouth rotunda and towering marble columns, as well as its own hospital, barbershop, and gymnasium. Other palaces offered playrooms for children and glass-walled "crying rooms" for mothers with young infants. Some deluxe theatres also maintained separate seating areas for children patrolled by stern-faced matrons who maintained quiet order.

Movie palaces offered audiences a remarkable experience quite apart from whatever picture was playing. Patrons regularly came to the theatre for the sheer enjoyment of its grand environment and musical entertainment. A typical 1920s program began with the orchestra's 10-minute overture, which set the tone for the movie that would follow. Next came 20 minutes of live entertainment which consisted of soloists and some form of stage presentation. Veteran West Coast exhibitor Morton Lippe recalled palace acts from his backstage vantage point: "Well, I'll tell you. We had monkeys. We had elephants. We had tigers and lions. We had dogs. There was always Bob Williams and his dog. 'Come on darling roll over.' The damn thing would sit and look at you. That was the act. Bob Williams and Red Dust his dog. We had all kinds of acts. We used to have a loading platform in the alley and it was huge. Two doors that swung open so you could get the sets in and also the equipment of the performers and the animals."

These elaborate stage presentations replaced the vaudeville acts of earlier "combination" houses of the post-nickelodeon era and were a hallmark of the movie palace experience. Following the stage entertainment the audience enjoyed a comedy short and newsreels. The feature film presentation would complete the standard two-hour program.

Pictures changed weekly. The names of major stars on the marquee combined with an exhibitor's clever stunts and advertising alerted the public to each new feature. There was little time for word of mouth, good or bad, to affect the box office; the public came regardless. Weekly program changes of both films and stage shows proved a continuous challenge for the theatre's music department. The musical accompaniment of a silent film reflected the talents of the house conductor-arranger, the orchestra, and, in smaller theatres, the piano player. "I can remember," said veteran Portland projectionist and theatre owner Harry Moyer, "that the highest-paid man in the theatre was the organ player. He could look at the picture and play any kind of tune that fit the picture. He had a very good memory of songs and stuff. He had all kinds of contraptions to make noises like trains and horses running. And when he'd take his 15 minute break or so, the picture would fall flat. It wasn't the same picture. It was just so different."

"The organist decided what to play during the picture and their job was sort of at stake in the sense, if they

LOEW'S JERSEY CITY THEATRE
General View from Stage Looking S.E.

didn't do well, didn't get favorable reaction, the theatre would have to find someone else," noted Southern California exhibitor Art Sanborn. "In other words, the organist determined what to play; they lived or died by their job, by how they performed, what they came up with to play."

Palace theatres maintained large libraries of sheet music. The music was heavily indexed to help the conductor quickly compose a score matched to a film's changing moods and types of action. Scores were patched together using stock melodies and well-known

Auditorium view Oakland's Grand Lake Theatre. *Tom Paiva*

Auditorium view, Orinda Theatre, Orinda, California. *Tom Paiva*

Movies are still experienced in an atmosphere of grandeur at the Mount Baker Theatre in Bellingham, Washington. *Ruth Shaw*

Santa Barbara's Arlington Theatre opened in 1933 and was completely restored in the late seventies. Classic example of an atmospheric theatre. *Metropolitan Theatres*

classical pieces that became the "musical vocabulary" for the action on the screen. A completely original score was extremely rare. More common were semi-original scores that mixed stock melodies with the conductor-arranger's original themes. Movie producers supplied

Portland's Egyptian Theatre is a blend of architectural influences that are best-described as "exotic." *Act III Theatres*

View of lobby and staircase of the Loews Paradise Theatre in the Bronx. *Bernard Diamond*

gested musical selections and gave the approximate time and a short description for each film scene. With careful study of the cue sheets, a conductor could prepare an orchestration in advance based on the music library's stock selections and without screening the film first. In addition to accompanying the feature film, movie palace orchestras were also called upon to accompany short subjects, play an overture, support any soloists and musically animate the elaborate stage presentation of the week.

One popular performer during every movie palace show was the organ soloist. On proper cue the great organists of the day would rise majestically along with their gleaming consoles from the depths of the organ pits. Thrust heavenward by hydraulic lifts and bathed in brilliant spotlights, the organists proclaimed their ascension with the thunderous tones of the grand organ. As the air vibrated throughout the mammoth auditorium, the communal pulse of the audience quickened with anticipation. Such was the power of this stirring music that for the next 10 to 12 minutes, the organist held the room captive under a spell of magnificent music.

The organist earned his place in the annals of exhibition history. In addition to several solo performances a day, the theatre organist often pulled yeoman's duty during those times when the house orchestra did not perform. During the less-popular morning and early afternoon shows, it was the organist who was called upon to provide full accompaniment to the feature films.

The most renowned of all movie palace organs, the Mighty Wurlitzer, was a combination pipe organ, symphony orchestra and sound effects generator. Invented by Robert Hope-Jones and initially dubbed a "unit orchestra" by the Rudolph Wurlitzer Co., the organ was a marvel of musical tones, harmonies and odd noises.

film scores only with the occasional high-profile special release. Some films arrived with a selection of appropriate musical selections comprised of well-known standards that an orchestra could quickly work up with a minimum of rehearsal time. In other instances, the house orchestra used their own selections. As a result, audiences in New York experienced a film somewhat differently than those in Chicago, Los Angeles, or Cleveland.

Music cue sheets also proved a popular approach to movie music during the 1920s. Cue sheets listed sug-

LOEWS PARADISE THEATRE
Inner Lobby Looking West from Right Promenade

sleigh bells, rain on the roof and smashing crockery. "Silent" movies became a thrilling auditory feast when a quick-witted and agile organist took command of the Mighty Wurlitzer.

Movie palaces were graced by the mighty organs of other respected manufacturers such as Kimball, Robert Morton, Moller, Page or Barton, but it was the name "Wurlitzer" that became synonymous with grand movie palace music and delightful sound effects.

Every movie palace promoted its own organist with as much fanfare as any screen idol received. The most

Interior Grand Lake Theatre, Oakland, California. *Tom Paiva*

Interior detail, Paramount Theatre, Oakland, California. *Tom Paiva*

The Wurlitzer enabled the organist to reproduce the sounds of a full orchestra in addition to a wide range of individual musical instruments, including tom-toms, chimes, tambourines, castanets, triangles, gongs, cymbals, marimbas, a xylophone, a glockenspiel, a grand piano and a battery of drums. On proper command, the Wurlitzer also mimicked the sounds of car horns, canaries, cuckoo clocks, galloping horses, train whistles, airplanes, hurricanes, ringing telephones, door bells,

Paramount Theatre where they delighted audiences from twin consoles.

Live entertainment had been a hallmark of movie palace programs ever since 1913, when Roxy Rothapfel wowed the Regent's uptown audiences with his striking innovations of putting the house orchestra on stage and adding singers to the accompaniment of the film program. This tradition continued as the stage portion of the picture palace shows kept expanding and audiences came to expect imaginative off-screen pageantry to be

Twilight view of Oakland's Grand Lake Theatre. *Tom Paiva*

Second-floor promenade, Paramount Theatre, Oakland, California. *Tom Paiva*

famous of all was Jesse Crawford, billed as the "Poet of the Organ" at New York's Paramount Theatre. Crawford appeared at some of the most sumptuous of all the movie palaces. Having begun his career at Grauman's Million Dollar Theatre in Los Angeles, he was lured away by Balaban & Katz for a five-year run at the Tivoli and Chicago theatres. While in Chicago Crawford married fellow organist Helen Anderson, featured performer at the Roosevelt Theatre. The couple's succession of on-stage duets made "Mr. and Mrs. Crawford" one of the most popular and well-paid teams in show business. The Crawfords moved to New York's huge

talking mynah birds. Somebody got backstage and was teaching them dirty words. The woman says 'say good evening to everyone' and someone had taught them dirty words and the birds were yelling four-letter words all over the stage. They had to bring down the curtain and the poor woman was in a state of shock. Another time we had a chimpanzee act. The chimp was named

Fanchon & Marco's "Exotique Idea" at the Chinese Theatre, Los Angeles. *Alice Lomas Collection, B'hend & Kaufmann Archives*

Famed movie palace organist Jesse Crawford at the console. *John Fergeson Collection, B'hend & Kaufmann Archives*

An elaborately-decorated proscenium arch and the splendor of an Arabian castle motif highlight this typical atmospheric theatre. *Harley Lond*

served with the film program. "So you would get for your money a top, first-run picture, you'd get the orchestra in the pit, you would get two organs, Mr. and Mrs. Jesse Crawford, and you would get a stage presentation," remembered longtime Chicago theatre manager Jack Belasco. "Well, you can't ask for more than that, can you?"

By 1925, movie palace stage presentations had become quite elaborate. Changed on a weekly basis just like the movie, stage shows presented large-scale musical revues, dazzling costumes, spectacular sets and intricate lighting. There were ballet companies, tap dancers, chorus lines, animal acts, and singers of every stripe. Some acts were better than others. "There is a famous story," noted Morton Lippe, "about a lady and her

Toto. The trainer said, 'Toto, take off your hat and say good night to the audience.' Instead, Toto turned around, pulled down his pants and did you-know-what all over the Orpheum stage. These are funny things that happened."

A theatre's stage presentation followed a number of formats devised by the great showmen of the era. In Los Angeles, Sid Grauman introduced the idea of "prologues" at his Million Dollar Theatre where each act and setting related to the motion picture that it preceded. He later expanded his idea into grandiose productions at his Egyptian and Chinese theatres in Hollywood.

Other stage shows revolved around a "personality" band leader such as the phenomenal Paul Ash and his "Merry Mad Musical Gang." Still other palace theatres featured vaudeville headliners and chorus lines.

In smaller, outlying cities where access to headliners and other major entertainers was more limited, the prologue approach to stage shows was widely imitated. Unfortunately, few theatre managers had the creativity or financial resources to consistently pull off such an undertaking week after week. The results were often disappointing and reflected poorly on the feature films they were intended to imitate. Some studios supplied prologue designs to help middle-size theatres with their productions.

A far more workable approach to stage shows was something called the "unit show," a musical stage production built upon a single theme that was independent of the feature film. Typical examples of unit show themes are "Way Down South," "Alpine Romance," and "Opera vs. Jazz."

The unit show was pioneered by Frank Cambria for the Balaban & Katz circuit and later adopted by Paramount's theatres after the studio merged its theatres with the Chicago circuit to form the Publix chain. Produced at a cost of $20,000 to $50,000 each, the visually stunning unit shows ran as long as 60 to 75 minutes. The touring unit shows became a powerful inducement for regional theatre circuits to partner with Paramount; having access to the Publix unit shows provided them a decided edge over the competition.

During the late 1920s a former brother-and-sister ballroom dance team named Fanchon & Marco began to produce musical revues for theatres that lacked the expertise to produce a lavish stage show using local talent. Fanchon and Marco's "Ideas" toured the coun-

try on a rotating basis and brought the style and spectacle of deluxe moviehouse shows to the masses. Themes like "Fan Fantasy," "Skirts," "Dangerous Curves," "Nile Nights" and "Eskimamas," made it easy to see why audiences delighted in a Fanchon & Marco show.

Children's playroom at the Los Angeles Theatre, Los Angeles, California. *Jim Lewis Collection, B'hend & Kaufmann Archives*

Gentlemen's Smoking Room at Loews Jersey City Theatre, New Jersey. *Herb Brown*

Movie palaces had nothing on Southern California's El Monte Theatre that featured the added bonus of a glass-walled crying room, upper right. *Arthur L. Sanborn, Jr.*

Massive columns graced the auditorium of the Loews Jersey City Theatre. *Herb Brown*

Each of the touring "Ideas" featured elaborate staging, whimsical costumes and the versatile talents of the Sunkist Beauties.

To the dedicated movie palace showman, the goal of a theatre's program was a "balanced presentation," a performance that delivered equal parts music, film and spectacle (with just a dash of reality added in the form of newsreels), all presented in a two-hour format. For many theatres that two-hour time limit was sacred, in a bow to the filmgoing habits of regular patrons, as well as to keeping an eye on the bottom line. "You started off with usually an introduction of some kind, maybe a short subject and then you went into the picture and then after the picture you usually had a newsreel or a cartoon, and then after that the stage show and that was a routine," remembered longtime Roxy Theatre manager William Miller.

If a popular stage act or soloist threatened to push the program into overtime, the house manager rarely lengthened the entire program's running time. Instead, he often resorted to shortening the films or projecting them at an faster speed, thereby shaving minutes off the total running time of the show. Miller continues, "Now the one that was the most difficult to work with on a stage was Danny Kaye, because he would come out and do his first show and you had him scheduled for 55 minutes and he'd do 40 minutes, so you ran 15 minutes early. You had to fill in time to get back on schedule. Well, that was fine. You could do that with an added short subject of some kind and maybe add some more music. Then he'd come on the next show and he'd do 50 minutes. Then you had 5 minutes to get back on time. Then when it came to the last show at night you'd go in on time and he'd do 75 minutes. When you had a full house and a big audience he would really carry on."

A distinctive feature of the deluxe moviehouse was its uniformed staff. Upon arrival at the theatre, patrons were met by a succession of attentive staff members whose goal was to help assure total comfort and satisfaction. Each and every member of the massive audience was treated as an honored guest if not outright royalty. "Yes, we were steeped in courtesy to the patron," recalled exhibitor Ludwig. "This was a must. From the time that the doorman would open the door and the person would walk up to the cashier, everything was done to make them feel as though they were an honored guest. And there were 'thank yous' and ushers were dressed immaculately from the time that your ticket was taken. You were directed to the next usher. The next usher would take you to the aisle, ask you where you wanted to sit, and you were seated."

A footman opened car and taxi doors, and in rainy weather came armed with a welcome umbrella. The doorman served as a keeper of the portals, on the alert for drunks or gate crashers. "Oh you would meet the people," recalled veteran Alabama exhibitor Harry

Curl of his early career as a doorman. "They would come in and you would tear their ticket and speak to them and hope they enjoyed the show. And then when they came out, if it was cold, you helped them put on their coats, thanked them and told them to 'come back to see us.' Just being real friendly."

Streetmen supervised milling crowds in the outside lobby and on the sidewalk. A young female box office cashier was typically dressed in an evening gown to set the tone for the upcoming movie palace experience. Inside the lobby, page boys made note of the seat locations of doctors and others on call and stood ready to deliver important messages to them during the show.

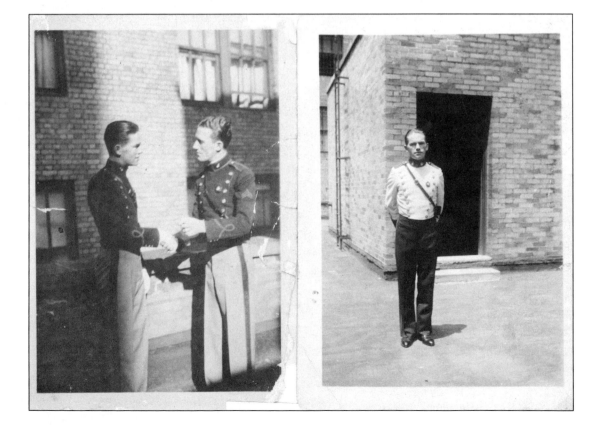

Page boys also directed visitors and assisted in the checkroom.

It was the smartly-uniformed usher, however, that was the pride of the theatre staff. Young men, often college students, were recruited to man the front line of courtesy, tact and service for the expectant throngs of movie patrons. Ushers were trained with strict military style and discipline and the position was held with honor. Usher jobs were highly competitive and carried with them the best prize of all, free movies!

The most famous usher corps of them all was that of New York's famed Roxy Theatre. Training was conducted by the head usher and began with instruction in house rules and regulations. Ushers were drilled in the proper way to address patrons — "Yes, sir," "Yes, ma'am," — and how to make a request: "This way please; kindly pass down the aisle," or "Stairway to the right, please." When asked about the current film, ushers would respond automatically with a well-rehearsed standard line: "The comments have been very

favorable, sir. I believe you will like it."

Ushers were also trained in flashlight etiquette. When guiding a patron to an empty seat, the cardinal rule was that the flashlight was never shone above a patron's ankles and was to be extinguished as soon as the patron entered the seat row. "The theatre was what we called 'dressed.'" explained Ludwig. "You dressed the theatre. In other words you didn't put everybody in one spot. You dressed so that it started as a small circle and became bigger and bigger so that there was a togetherness."

Ushers were also trained to deal with noisy patrons, amorous couples and the intoxicated. In the event of an especially difficult or unruly patron, the usher summoned a member of the executive staff.

Roxy ushers were trained in discipline and drill formations by a former Marine Corps drill instructor. Each morning ushers met in their upstairs quarters to change from street clothes into the honored uniform. Then it was time to face a rigid daily inspection of locker, uniform and self. The usher ideal called for a close shave, neatly trimmed hair, an immaculate uniform, polished shoes and narrow flashlight hanging from a belt clip. Each usher also carried an emergency pouch filled with smelling salts, pencil and note paper, accident reports and a personal supply of breath fresheners. Promptly at 11:10 a.m. a bugle sounded and the Roxy corps of ushers, or attaches as they were called, marched in close formation down the Grand Staircase to the Rotunda where they received the day's orders. Flashlight batteries were checked. Fire drills were conducted and first aid techniques were reviewed. At 11:35 sharp, a bugle sounded again, the house lights came up and the ushers marched to their respective posts in the grand auditorium. Each inspected his territory, on the alert for broken seats or burned-out aisle lights. At 11:45 the

lobby doors opened and, as a bugle sounded first call, the Roxy ushers — 125 strong — snapped to attention, ready for the day's work ahead.

Sharply at 6 p.m., the Roxy's daytime ushers, outfitted in smart dress blues, surrendered their flashlights and emergency kits to the evening corps dressed in white ties and gold-braided jackets. This was done in a crowd-pleasing precision drill ceremony akin to the changing of the guard at Buckingham Palace, all accompanied by the military strains of the lobby pipe organ.

Staff uniforms were an important component of the movie palace experience. Uniforms bestowed a sense of authority on young men and conveyed to the audience that their needs would be properly addressed. The military look and demeanor of the Roxy ushers was emulated by scores of other movie palaces. No less formal but certainly less intimidating was the tuxedo look that was also popular at many picture palaces. "The men all wore uniforms," recalled veteran exhibitor Lippe. "The girls all wore beautiful usherette uniforms, satin slacks, wide slacks and beautiful brocade blouses. In the evening, the head girl would change into an evening gown to be on the spot, to direct everybody in the big houses. The cashiers always wore red satin blouses, with white piping on them and big handkerchiefs. We had a head cashier that would walk around to make sure everybody's nails and hair were done."

To become an usher was not an easy task. There were house rules to learn, hand signals to master, plus training in fire drills, first aid and proper etiquette, in addition to "other duties as required..." "As a doorman, just to catch tickets we had to wear an Egyptian robe and a little round Egyptian hat," noted Virginia-based veteran exhibitor Jerry Gordon, who early on in his exhibition career worked at a number of Los Angeles theatres, including the Egyptian. "Had to put on makeup so that your cheeks were rosy and you looked nice, and you were almost like a fixture. And then when I got off and took my robe off, and got into my clothes, then my job was to get in and clean the monkey cage. I would do that before I went home. I liked the business enough that I didn't mind, and the monkeys didn't care either."

An usher's formal training might stretch from one to four weeks before a new recruit was "ready for the floor." "If you worked at the Paramount Theatre in Springfield for example," recalled longtime Loews executive Herb Brown, "which I did for a short time, you couldn't even get on the floor until you practiced for almost a week. I mean you had to drill and you had to really know what you were doing. Then they would let you go up on the floor and let you usher." When the San Francisco Fox opened in 1929, ushers received a minimum of 100 hours of intensive instruction.

Despite their star role on the theatre staff, ushers were among the lowest-paid employees. Typical wages were $20 a week for full-time, $10 for part-time. Despite the meager salary, it was not difficult for theatre managers to recruit ushers because of the good prospects for promotion. Ushers could advance through a military-style ranking system that started with a post in the balcony and moved to lieutenant and then shift captain. These moves could be followed by promotion to head usher, assistant manager and, finally, house manager. "I think I was making $40 a week as a manager," mused Gordon. "I was a real big-shot. The living was cheap and it was a great experience. We worked seven days a week, wore tuxedos every night. The manager tended to be on the floor of the theatre to greet the people all the time. Any book work or anything, you had to find time to do it. We would start in the morning and the manager would close the theatre at night, which was

about 1 a.m. Being young we didn't care a lot about sleep."

The theatre usher served as a kind of traffic cop who helped maintain a smooth flow of patrons throughout an enormous theatre. Even a moderately-sized movie palace faced the crucial challenge of crowd control. And crowds there were, seven days a week. Once a theatre's morning program started, the day's schedule of performances ran continuously until closing time near midnight. Patrons of an earlier era saw no problem arriving at the theatre in the middle of a performance; they simply stayed over to the next show to see what they

Hand signals were the trademark of movie palace ushers and usherettes. Seen practicing are smartly-uniformed usherettes of the Palace Theatre in Canton, Ohio. *Ralph Russell*

had missed. "You played continuously," recalled veteran New England exhibitor Carl Goldman. "Once the picture went on the screen (let's say for example on a Sunday when you started at one) people filed into your theatre until every seat was taken. Then people continued to come in and stood in the lounges waiting for seats. We kept what we called a 'spill' card that was done in 15-minute increments. You would check that with your box office ticket numbers, of course, so that you would know that approximately at a certain given time, how many people would actually leave. Then we'd seat the new patrons." During the booming box office years of the 1920s, a capacity audience in the largest movie palaces also meant hundreds or even thousands of other expectant patrons waiting in the lobby and adjacent areas.

The palace usher corps took control of the situation with a practical yet unobtrusive system of hand signals that alerted the staff when an empty seat became available. "We used to give hand signals to show how many seats were available," noted Brown. "If you were down an aisle and you wanted to let the man at the head of the aisle know how many seats you had, you would hold your arms akimbo for example. Or if you had a couple of singles you'd hold up two fingers and swing them around. You had all these signals, but these were the things you had to learn."

The Roxy's plush lobby carpeting, with its distinctive rug pattern, was also used to best advantage. Designed with a bold, decorative border, the rug pattern served as a guide for waiting crowds who wound around the carpet's edge while keeping the central lobby clear for good traffic flow. "The Roxy had a great oval-shaped rug covering most of the lobby," recalled exhibitor George Aurelius. "It had a distinctive six- or eight-foot border. When seating became limited, and a 'hold-out' was developing, the very ample and courteous uniformed staff would converge to line up the incoming patrons six or eight abreast on the border area of that lobby rug, extending the lines out to the ticket lobby and beyond with hundreds waiting in the street line."

The successful development of a national theatre chain comprised of hundreds of first-run theatres required a centralized business strategy much like that employed by nationwide chain store operations like Sears-Roebuck, and Woolworths. During the movie palace era a number of regional theatre circuits pursued business policies that foreshadowed those of the country's first national theatre circuits. These regional circuits included: the famous Loews circuit headquartered in New York City, which would soon have a guaranteed supply of films through its ownership of Metro-Goldwyn-Mayer; The Stanley Company of Philadelphia with theatres stretching from New Jersey to Washington, D.C.; Harry Crandell in Washington, D.C.; the Saxe brothers in Milwaukee; the Skouras brothers in St. Louis (brother Spyros would later ascend to the presidency of 20th Century Fox); the Blank circuit based in Des Moines; Rubin and Finklestein in Minneapolis; John Kunsky based in Detroit; the Saenger Amusement Company of Louisiana; and the Turner and Dahnken chain centered in San Francisco.

Yet another regional chain, Chicago's Balaban & Katz, is credited with establishing a nationwide standard of excellence for movie palace operations. Starting with a handful of theatres, the circuit faced rapid expansion after its successful opening of the Windy City's Central Park Theatre. Within ten years Balaban & Katz would come to dominate Chicago exhibition and move into surrounding states to own or control a total of 500 movie theatres.

In 1925 the circuit merged with Adolph Zukor's

Madison, Wisconsin's Orpheum Theatre combined a military and bell hop look in their usher uniforms. *Tim Romano, Historic Photo Service*

Paramount Theatres to create Publix Theaters Corporation, also known as the Paramount-Publix theatre circuit. Under the guidance of Sam Katz the circuit quickly grew in size and prosperity, which guaranteed that the chain's policies would be widely imitated throughout the industry. Balaban & Katz perfected a system of theatre growth based on creating an image of

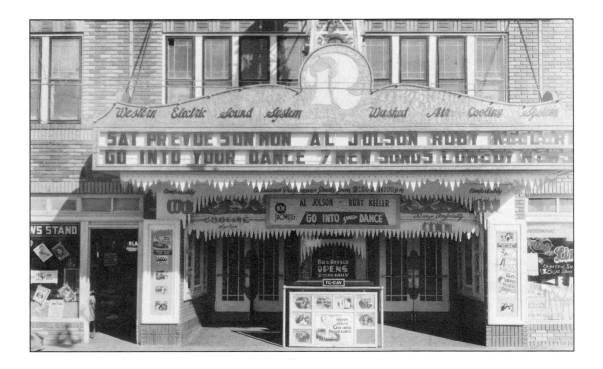

The Rig Theatre in Wink, Texas used multiple icicle cutouts to promote its washed air cooling system. *Roger Rice*

Paramount's Publix theatre circuit was renowned for its well-trained staff and elaborate picture palaces. *Ralph Batschelet/Beverley Carlson*

the individual theatre as an institution that was vital to the community. They developed a five-point policy for success: location, superior architectural design, service, a live stage presentation of consistently high quality which could be easily duplicated throughout the circuit, and, finally, air-conditioning.

Hot weather — historically the bane of theatre owners everywhere — brought with it the most dismal

business of the year, forcing many theatres to simply close during the summer. But Pennsylvania-based theatre owner Ted Manos remembered that there *were* ways to beat the heat. "Tell you what we used to do in the summertime. All the theatres had great, big enormous fans that were on the roof. And what we would do, we would open the doors going out of the theatre and we would blow that air through there at pretty high velocity. And that would have a tendency to make you feel cool. Now it was not like air conditioning, of course not, but that's the best we had at that time."

"You got to remember there wasn't any air conditioning," added Maryland-based industry vet Paul Roth, "so theatres were cooled by a variety of things. From the kind of paper fans that you hand out at the funeral parlor to electric fans that blew air on people to complicated things like hauling blocks of ice up on the roofs of theatres and then blowing air over the ice and the cooled air would go down through a duct into the building."

"When air conditioning came, that was almost as good as sound as a business booster, because not many people had air conditioning when the theatres had it early," explained Jerry Gordon. "People would just leave their homes and not necessarily care about the movie, but come in to stay cool." Paul Roth concurred: "I think that you'll find out that among the very, very first buildings that were air-conditioned were movie theatres."

Eager audiences flocked to theatres that offered air-cooled comfort. After 1926, most movie palaces either installed air conditioning or saw patrons defect to the competition that had.

"I used to have to come along in the beginning of the summer and we would post all kinds of banners and signs and what have you and start putting in our newspaper ads that [the theatre] was either 'delightfully air-cooled' or when we really had it, 'delightfully air-conditioned,'" remembered Roth. "These signs were always green and white, green being a cool color. We used to be instructed to go into the auditoriums where during the winter the running lights on the side walls and perhaps the ceiling would be reds and blues. In the summer we would take out all the reds and go to greens, because green was a cooler color. This made people think they were cooler and let them know the air cooling or air conditioning was on."

The movie palace was the place to go for an evening of bountiful entertainment. Situated in the best locations of the nation's largest cities, the downtown movie palace boasted abundant seating, wonderful amenities, the newest films with Hollywood's top stars, and top-notch live entertainment.

The palaces garnered the bulk of film industry revenue and by 1930, were in the hands of Hollywood's major studios. Mini-palaces or deluxe theatres with 600 to 1,000 seats emerged in outlying business and residential areas. These theatres also put a premium on audience service and satisfaction but they were not as large or ornate as their luxurious cousins. If stage presentations were offered at all, they were not the elaborate presentations of the palaces. Even so, audiences seemed not to mind; going to the movies still seemed to eclipse all other entertainments, and would become even more popular with the introduction of sound.

Chapter 4

BIRTH OF THE TALKIES

"Wait a minute, wait a minute. You ain't heard nothing yet!" — *Al Jolson in "The Jazz Singer"*

Silent movies were rarely presented in absolute silence. Because early clattering projectors tended to annoy audiences, exhibitors quickly learned that they could cleverly mask the noise with the welcome strains of a piano. The noisy projector was soon exiled to a separate booth, but the accompaniment continued. Theatres treated audiences to music, sound effects, and talkers, all to enhance their enjoyment and understanding of the film.

Attempts to mechanically link sound with moving pictures are as old as cinema itself. As early as 1887 Thomas Edison had commissioned W. K. L. Dickson to develop a moving picture camera and viewing machine to provide a visual accompaniment to his hugely successful invention of the phonograph. By 1894 Dickson's efforts to synchronize separately-recorded sound with moving pictures proved inadequate and the kinetoscope debuted with silent film. While some early models offered non-synchronized music that patrons could hear through stethoscope-like rubber tubes connected to a phonograph, the majority of kinetoscopes were sold as silent peepshows.

For the next 20 years inventors and entrepreneurs throughout the U.S. and Europe labored to fulfill the promise of sound movies. Most research focused on the phonograph and attempts to keep recorded discs "in synch" with a film projector. When moving pictures made the leap from a peepshow box to the screen, scientists faced the added challenge of amplification; how to make sound audible to a roomful of people. While scientists labored over the technical challenge of synchronization, theatre owners made do with non-synchronized sound, playing records to match the screen action as best they could. "We used sort of canned music behind the silent pictures," recalled Jerry Gordon. "This was a little two-turntable machine with a volume control in the center which could go from one to the other. We would cue the pictures the night before they opened with records. We had a full cabinet of records, full of all types of records. We even had sound effects, sound-effects records of the train coming into the station, and the train leaving the station. While the music was playing we could put a sound-effect record on the

Make no mistake, Vitaphone sound has arrived at the Metropolitan Theatre in Mitchell, South Dakota. *Jeff Logan*

The movies begin to speak. *Allen Michaan*

other turntable and then turn the volume control to that one and cue it."

As movies gradually grew longer and evolved from simple skits to more complex stories, filmmakers began experimenting with new techniques for cinematic story-telling — quick cuts, dissolves, close-ups and flashbacks — and the audience often got lost in the action. In an effort to eliminate audience confusion, theatre owners began providing narrators or "talkers" who stood alongside the screen and explained what was happening. Other theatres advanced to employing actors who stood *behind* the screen and provided makeshift dialogue for

The Bijou Orchestra accompanied the theatre's silent films. *Virginia Historical Society*

the film. English-speaking audiences weren't the only ones to benefit from this technique, according to St. Louis-based circuit owner Ron Krueger. "We were in some German areas and we would have a talker that would stand next to the picture screen and explain what was going on in German."

A movie presented with actors became known as a "talking picture play" and the practice reached wide popularity between 1908 and 1912. Acting troupes, working under names such as Actologue and Huma-novo, typically consisted of two men and a woman who traveled a circuit of theatres with a collection of films for which they had pre-rehearsed dialogue for all the roles. After staying in one town for a week they moved on, to be replaced by the next acting troupe. There are some reports of production companies that filmed actors reciting silent dialogue that they would later read from scripts behind the screen in a reverse form of lip-synching.

As films grew longer the idea of these acting troupes became more and more impractical and interest was revived in mechanical devices that would link recorded sound with film. During the mid-1900s a number of such devices were marketed under important-sounding names such as Cameraphone, Chronoscope, Synchron-scope and Theatrephone. Despite the exaggerated claims of their inventors, the devices achieved only hit-and-miss sound synchronization with the screen's moving images. When all else failed the projectionist was enlisted to hand-crank the film faster or slower until sound and picture matched. Sound quality was another matter altogether. Audiences complained of low volume, sharp and nasal sound, and often-undistinguishable voices.

Small storefront theatres that couldn't afford expensive sound equipment and professional talkers improvised their own talking pictures. It was not unusual for the theatre manager, his wife or child, or even the piano player to be called upon to provide some running commentary for a film. Some theatres took to posting plot summaries in the lobby to help acquaint their patrons with the film story in advance. In time Hollywood gradually developed a narrative screen style that was widely understood by audiences and assisted by the use of on-screen title cards.

By the early 1920s advances in technology hastened the development of dependable sound systems using sound-on-disc and sound-on-film technology. Despite these technical breakthroughs, Hollywood was in no hurry to introduce talking screens. Sound was a costly gamble for studios that enjoyed healthy profits with the current mode of production. A switch to sound meant the complete overhaul of production and the expensive conversion of all theatres to sound with no guarantee of added success. Acutely aware of the long string of failures associated with synchronized sound, the majors were content to let others take the risks and develop the technology and market for sound.

In 1923, American inventor Dr. Lee DeForest introduced a sound-on-film system that he called Phonofilm. One of the distinct advantages of the system was that it completely eliminated the problem of sound synchronization. DeForest began producing short films with vaudeville performers to showcase his invention for exhibitors and producers. The public saw and heard these musical novelties for the first time in April 1923, at New York's Rialto Theatre. Audience response was positive and over the next year 34 movie theatres were equipped for Phonofilm sound — a scant number that hardly represented a breakthrough trend for the nation's estimated 15,000 full-time moviehouses. DeForest continued to produce short musical films in an effort to

Typical musical cue sheet of the movie palace era. *B'hend & Kaufmann Archives*

market his invention. By 1927 DeForest had amassed as many as 1,000 sound shorts yet he failed to convince any film companies to adopt the Phonofilm technology. He also lacked the necessary financial backing to convert his invention into a mass-produced system. As a result,

METHOD OF SETTING RECORD AT STARTING POINT ON WESTERN ELECTRIC REPRODUCER SET

Detail of synchronized sound-on-record system from a Western Electric Training Manual. *Bob Tankersley*

Theatre marquee promises romance you can "See & Hear" at New York's Warner Theatre. *Allen Michaan*

any studio showing an interest in his system faced the daunting prospect, and expense, of tooling up to manufacture the sound equipment that would be required for both movie production and the nation's theatres. It was hardly the kind of financial risk the studios were willing to take for the sake of what might be some passing fad.

As DeForest worked to sell his sound-on-film system, salesmen representing one of the world's largest corporations, American Telephone and Telegraph, were marketing a competing sound-on-disc system to the Hollywood studios. AT&T engineers, working for the

research subdivisions of Bell Laboratories and Western Electric, overcame the technical problems that had long plagued sound-on-disc recording and playback systems. Initially developed to monitor and test the corporation's new long-distance telephone network, the sound system was soon adapted for movies. Technical improvements included enhanced recording techniques and the development of the first true loudspeaker as well as an electronically-synchronized film projector and phonograph that operated off the same motor. As the division charged with marketing the system, Western Electric approached the Hollywood studios as early as 1922 — and met the same resistance that DeForest faced.

Prospects for sound movies languished until 1925, when Sam Warner of Warner Bros., then a modestly successful film company, saw a demonstration of the Western Electric system and convinced his brothers of its potential.

The Warner brothers — Harry, Sam, Albert and Jack — had entered the movie business in 1906 at the start of the nickelodeon boom.

Moving into production, the Warner Bros. company was determined to join the ranks of the major studios. In 1925 the company expanded into feature film production, the operation of worldwide film exchanges and the ownership of a small number of theatres. Faced with intense competition from the major studios, Warner Bros. desperately sought a way to expand its business. The novelty of sound movies seemed like a promising gimmick to convince theatres to book their films. After several months of conducting tests with the sound equipment, Warner Bros. in April, 1926 entered a partnership with Western Electric to exploit the sound system named Vitaphone. "Vitaphone was a system of big records. I think they were, if I remember correctly, 16-inch records," noted Jerry Gordon. "A turntable was attached to and synchronized with the projector. You would put the needle on the record and start the projector. The main problem was the synchronization. It just didn't last. The needle could jump a groove and you would have a man's voice behind a woman and you never could get the needle back in the right place again."

"They never thought the talkies would go over," said veteran Illinois exhibitor George Kerasotes. "My father did not think so either. I said, 'Dad, I don't think you're right about that; this is not a novelty. People want to see Rin Tin Tin bark.'"

Warner Bros. for its part, never intended to produce talking features. The studio's strategy focused instead on boosting the appeal of the studio's silent features by offering them with a package of recorded vaudeville acts. Warner targeted smaller theatres with the idea of "canned" stage shows. The studio reasoned that exhibitors who couldn't afford to pay the excessive weekly salaries of major entertainers would jump at the chance to offer their audiences celluloid facsimiles of the same acts for the modest price of a film rental.

Poised to break cinema's sound barrier, Warner Bros. planned an elaborate premiere for its first presentation of vaudeville shorts. As part of the gala evening, the company also planned to present the first feature film with a recorded film score. The company had recently completed production of the silent feature "Don Juan," starring John Barrymore and Mary Astor. Under a cloak of secrecy the studio contracted with the New York Philharmonic to record an original movie score which would include sound effects of cathedral bells, knocking, galloping horses and clashing swords. The recorded score was given special attention since it had to demonstrate Vitaphone's superiority over a live orchestra during a feature film presentation. The Philharmonic orchestra was also filmed during the recording of the

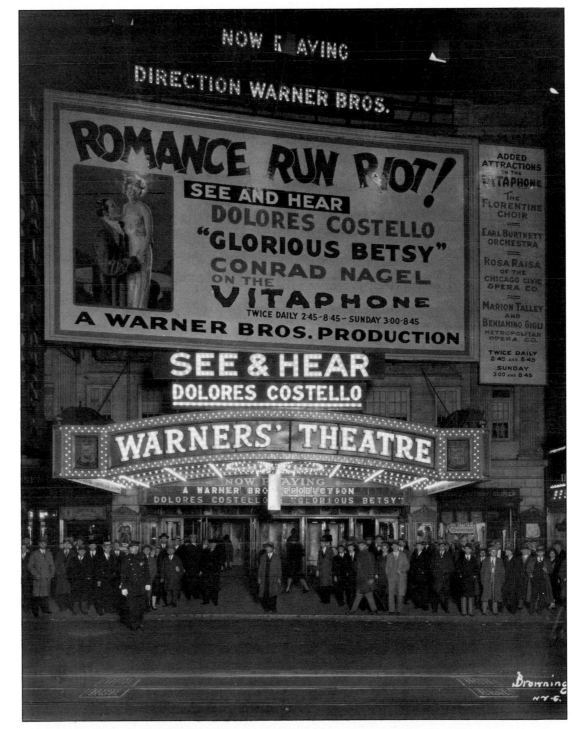

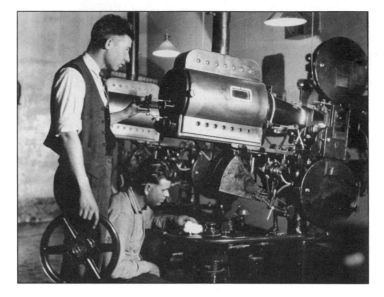

overture so the audience would enjoy the customary sight of a conductor and musicians playing the overture before the start of the feature film. The key difference, of course, was that this time the orchestra would be on the screen instead of in front of it. Popular artists from the Metropolitan Opera were also captured on film to be screened during the opening segment of the all-Vitaphone program.

While filming took place at Manhattan's Opera house, workers labored to wire Manhattan's Warner Theatre for sound. As described by author Harry Geduld in "Birth of the Talkies," the theatre's projection booth had to be equipped with amplifiers, a monitor "horn" to enable the operator to judge the sound level in the vast auditorium, a disk attachment for the projector, and various control gears. To insure a guaranteed power supply for the performance a separate room was set up with a generator, transformer, battery charger and generous supply of batteries. Sound speakers described as four 12- and 14-foot long horns were placed on stage behind a special screen.

By the night of the premiere, Warner Bros. had invested so heavily in the success of Vitaphone that the system's failure could have meant the studio's bankruptcy. On August 6, 1926, however, Vitaphone lived up to its advance hype as dignitaries, studio chiefs and the cream of New York Society came to cheer the thrilling display of synchronized sound. The evening's presentation began with a filmed introduction by movie industry czar Will Hays, whose startlingly lifelike on-screen remarks caused the audience to erupt in applause. The audience was then treated to a prelude of musical films of classical and popular performers. After a 10-minute intermission; "Don Juan" then appeared on screen in all its recorded musical glory. Vitaphone's debut was a success and the influential trade paper Variety devoted a special issue to the new marvel of sound pictures.

The initial results of Warner Bros. gamble on sound looked encouraging. The Vitaphone program drew huge audiences that punctuated each performance with sustained applause. The New York run lasted nearly eight months during which time it was seen by more than 500,000 people. "Don Juan" proved equally successful in Chicago, Los Angeles, Boston, Detroit and St. Louis. Critics were uniformly positive with some reviews bordering on the ecstatic. Theatre owners took notice of the public's reaction and more than a hundred moviehouses signed up for Vitaphone during the following year including those owned by such major circuits as Stanley in Philadelphia and Rubin & Finklestein in the Midwest. The industry took special notice when famed impresario Roxy Rothapfel ordered Vitaphone for his Roxy Theatre.

Warner Bros. initially offered Vitaphone to theatres under a licensing agreement that charged for the sound

equipment and installation, charged a royalty on every foot of sound film screened, and charged 10 cents per seat per week for the privilege of having access to sound films.

Proceeding cautiously, Warner Bros. stuck to its original strategy of producing a regular schedule of entertainment shorts. The company embarked on an ambitious plan to record all the leading vaudeville performers of the day. The Vitaphone plan was an undeniable bonus for theatre owners who, regardless of their operation's size or location, could offer patrons the same entertainment on film as that presented on stage at the grandest movie palaces.

Seeking to further expand Vitaphone's appeal, Warner Bros. planned to insert brief musical segments into otherwise silent features. Their first attempt involved a sentimental story about a cantor's son who

The talkies invade the Midwest.
Metropolitan Theatre,
Mitchell, South Dakota, 1932.
Jeff Logan

preferred jazz to religious music. The result made cinema history.

Were it not for a dispute over salary, the historic "The Jazz Singer" would have starred leading vaudeville entertainer George Jessel. Unable to come to an agreement with Jessel, Warner Bros. turned to Al Jolson, one of the most charismatic stage performers of the day. The movie's production plans called for Jolson to sing three songs during the film. According to Hollywood legend, the irrepressible Jolson ad-libbed some dialogue during the recording of the musical scenes and Sam Warner convinced his brothers it should stay in the film. Jolson's memorable first lines, a signature phrase from his stage act spoken between songs — "Wait a minute, wait a minute. You ain't heard nothing yet!" — proved prophetic.

"The Jazz Singer" premiered on October 5, 1927 at Broadway's Warner Theatre the same venue that hailed the premiere of "Don Juan" some 14 months earlier. Audiences were electrified by Jolson's realistic dialogue and natural delivery. "It was just about the most wonderful thing I had ever seen in my life," remembered Mississippi exhibitor Juanita "Skeeter" Maxey of her first encounter with the film. After completing a successful two-week New York engagement, "The Jazz Singer" moved on to extraordinary success as a road show presentation in other cities. During a time when big hits were held over for two week runs, the "The Jazz Singer" and its accompanying package of musical vaudeville shorts was drawing crowds for up to four weeks. The public's reaction pushed "The Jazz Singer" into profit even though only about 100 of the nation's theatres were equipped for sound. The film's success prompted hundreds of additional theatres to sign up for Vitaphone. Seeking to take advantage of the public's interest in sound, Warner quickly added talking sequences to silent films that were nearing completion. Theatres equipped for sound ballyhooed these pictures as "part-talkies," a surefire way to win audiences away from the competition.

In 1928, Warners released "Lights of New York," marking the first "all-talking" feature film. The success of sound movies was assured with Warners' release of the Al Jolson musical "The Singing Fool" in September, 1928. Tickets for the premiere went as high as $11 and scalped for prices in excess of $25. The film broke box office records across the country. While the major studios withheld their immediate support of sound production, many of their theatres didn't. Theatres owned by Paramount and Loews joined the scramble to sign up with Vitaphone so they, too, could share in the box office bonanza of "The Singing Fool." The rush for sound was on.

While Warners was trailblazing the way for talking features, William Fox was innovating the use of sound with newsreels. Fox acquired the rights to an improved version of the DeForest sound-on-film Phonofilm system and christened it Movietone. Weekly installments of the Fox Movietone News debuted in 1927. In a fortunate happenstance, a Movietone crew was on hand to capture the only sound recording of Charles Lindbergh taking off on his historic non-stop flight to Paris and his triumphant welcome back in Washington.

This major publicity coup prompted hundreds of theatres to equip their houses to exhibit the popular Fox Movietone News. Encouraged by the success of Warner Bros., Fox expanded into the production of talking features in 1928. Theatres now faced two competing choices of sound equipment, Warner's synchronized sound-on-disc Vitaphone system and Fox's sound-on-film system. Not wishing to limit their options (or profits) by selecting one system over the other, many theatres

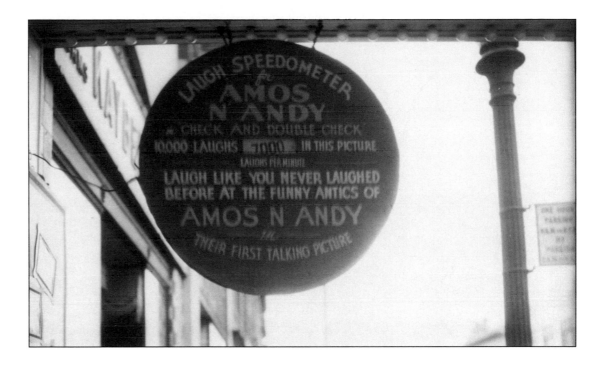

simply decided to install both.

Impressed with the success of Warners and Fox, Hollywood's other major studios decided to take sound seriously. Recognizing that it would be in their best interests to standardize sound production and exhibition, the majors formed a committee in 1927 to gather information and to recommend the best system for the industry to adopt. Over the course of a year, representatives from Paramount, MGM, First National and United Artists met secretly to review the technical merits of a growing number of competing sound systems and to anticipate any problems involved with converting to sound. Film-industry historian Douglas Gomery explained that the studios, seeking to assure their total success, wanted to align themselves with a quality system produced by an established manufacturer, a company that had sufficient resources to manufacture and install

Promotion for radio favorites Amos and Andy's first talking picture. *Tim Romano, Historic Photo Service*

Hobart, Oklahoma welcomes the talkies at the Kiowa Theatre. *Roger Rice*

Portland's Oriental Theatre marquee boasts "Where the Sound Is Better." *Act III Theatres*

sound equipment on a massive scale. In the end the competition narrowed to two communications giants: the Radio Corporation of America, promoter of sound-on-film technology with its Photofilm system; and AT&T's Western Electric, with the Vitaphone sound-on-disc system. Seeking to gain further advantage with the studios, Western Electric terminated its partnership agreement with Warner Bros., giving the studios an opportunity to deal directly with the manufacturer. After months of complicated negotiations, the final vote was decided by which system charged the lowest royalties. The final nod went to Western Electric and the sound-on-disc Vitaphone system.

Although RCA lost out to Western Electric when the major studios decided to adopt a single sound system, the company remained enthusiastic about its sound system's applications for the motion picture industry. RCA merged with the Film Booking Office production company and the Keith-Albee-Orpheum vaudeville theatres to form an instant major studio and theatre circuit that would use the RCA Photofilm system. The new venture was named Radio-Keith-Orpheum or RKO.

When the full-scale changeover to sound finally came, Hollywood moved rapidly and smoothly. The big studios continued to thrive while smaller producers who couldn't afford to convert to sound were either acquired by the majors or simply forced out of business.

Theatres affiliated with the studios enjoyed a big advantage during the transition period to sound. As part of negotiations between the studios and Western Electric, the studios won the concession that their theatres would be wired for sound ahead of their independent competition. The initial cost of converting a theatre to sound in 1927 ranged from $8,500 to $20,000 depending on the size and acoustical needs of the theatre. Smaller, independently-owned theatres had to wait their turn, a wait that sometimes lasted more than a year. Many smaller theatres were doomed by the high cost of converting to sound. Unable to compete against theatres that offered talkies, many theatres went out of business.

The cost of converting theatres to sound eventually decreased as the necessary equipment became more readily available. By 1928, when the other Hollywood studios joined Warner Bros. and Fox on the sound bandwagon, the conversion cost dropped to between $5,000 and $12,000, amounts that studio-owned circuits began to recoup as soon as they unspooled their enthusiastically-received sound pictures. The following year the price fell to between $5,000 and $7,000, an affordable range for even smaller, independent theatres.

During the transitional movie season of 1928/1929, audiences witnessed the amazing transformation of silent films into "talkies." As the majors geared up for sound they hastily added musical scores to previously produced films awaiting release. Dialogue sequences were clumsily-inserted so that a picture could qualify for promotion as a "part-talkie," ensuring it greater box office success. For a time, studios released pictures in silent and talking versions to accommodate those theatres not yet ready for sound.

Sound films rapidly replaced live stage presentations in theatres. By the end of 1929 only the largest movie palaces still offered live music, an expensive and suddenly "old-fashioned" practice.

The public was wild about talkies and marched to the box office in record numbers. In 1929 business at the nation's theatres jumped 30 percent. Enjoying its newfound prosperity, Warner Bros. promptly moved to expand its theatre holdings by purchasing the Philadelphia-based Stanley circuit. They also acquired the production facilities and theatres of First National, an organization that had been founded by a group of leading exhibitors. Through a series of other mergers Hollywood evolved into the Big Five (the major studios that owned theatres: Warners, MGM/Loews, Paramount, Fox and RKO) and the Little Three (the three leading studios without any theatre holdings: Columbia, Universal and United Artists).

Sound was introduced just a year before the Great Depression. Had sound not been introduced when it was, American audiences might have had to wait a full decade to experience the wonders of the talking picture.

Chapter 5

DEPRESSION YEARS

*T*he Depression years are filled with images of bank closures, Dust Bowl farmers and businessmen reduced to peddling pencils on the street. A time when people had everything but money. It was during these years of hardship that movie theatres became an even more inviting refuge than they had been in the past. Money may have been scarce, but there was always 10 cents for a movie.

The public's continued enthusiasm for the talkies defied the gloom of the stock market's Great Crash of 1929. More than a year later moviegoing reached a new high of 80 million patrons a week. Despite early indications that motion pictures were somehow "Depression-proof," the trend didn't last. Theatres began to see a significant slump in business in 1931. By 1932 theatre admissions had dropped by 25 million people a week and 4,000 theatres were forced to close.

Studio-affiliated theatre circuits faced the crisis burdened with millions of dollars of newly-acquired debt as the result of a battle to control the nation's theatres during the 1920s, and the high costs of converting to sound. Bankruptcies and receiverships awaited RKO, Fox, Paramount and Universal.

Demonstrating the adage that everything old is new again, the studio circuits turned to vaudeville to revive their sagging fortunes. Scaled-down stage shows and vaudeville acts were introduced in smaller towns. RKO

The lure of a free set of dishes and a movie were often too much to resist for the Depression-era moviegoer. *Ron Krueger*

Bridge and coffee during intermission at Florida's Mayfair Theatre, 1933. *Arthur Hertz*

Depression-era car give-away at St. Louis' Cinderella Theatre. *Ron Krueger*

temporarily kept grosses up by presenting four-acts with its pictures. Warner enlisted band acts, chorus girls and comedians to travel its circuit for one-to-three day stands. Paramount-Publix added live acts to its theatres in New England, Pennsylvania and the Southwest.

By 1933 the appeal of small-time vaudeville had lost its effectiveness and the circuits dropped the touring entertainers. The lingering Depression eventually forced movie palaces in the nation's largest cities to cut out their big-budget stage presentations and headliner

acts. By 1934, with the exception of the Radio City Music Hall, the Capitol and the Roxy Theatre in New York, most of the country's deluxe theatres had switched to an all-movies policy.

Ticket prices were slashed as low as they could be. First-run theatres cut ticket prices by as much as 15 cents, bringing them to within a nickel of the neighborhood subsequent-run theatres. In the modern economy this may not seem like an impressive drop but in the Depression era it could constitute a 40-percent price cut. Theatres that charged 25, 30 and 35 cents before 1931 lowered their ticket prices to 10 cents and 15 cents by the end of that year. More than 2,000 theatres became dime houses.

Times were tough and more and more Americans stayed home to find their entertainment on the radio. Certain nights boasted popular radio stars and movie

Deluxe Country Store Night at the Bluebird Theatre, Denver, Colorado. *Ralph Batschelet / Beverley Carlson*

Was it the chance of winning $309.00 or Penrod's "Double Trouble" that brought patrons to San Francisco's Rialto Theatre? *Jack Tillmany*

Live poultry promoted a grocery giveaway in this theatre's lobby. *Eric Levin*

Bank Night at the Princess
Theatre , Bristow, Oklahoma.
Roger Rice

The winner yelled "Screeno!"
at the Key Theatre, Wewoka,
Oklahoma. *Roger Rice*

In testament to the success of
Bank Night a crowd gathers in
1937 to hear the winner's name
at the Academy of Music
Theatre, Northhampton,
Massachusetts. *Julian Rifkin*

theatres felt the impact. "I recall one particular thing," said movie industry vet Irving Ludwig "The night that Milton Berle was on was deadly for theatres. Business just went to pot, Whether you were in a neighborhood operation or even on Broadway, you were very, very careful in scheduling your evening attraction so that you'd start your feature after the radio broadcast."

"I can remember in the late' 30s when Amos and Andy were on the radio, it just killed the movie business," remembers longtime East Coast circuit owner Paul Roth. "Everybody stayed home to listen to "Amos and Andy"; you might as well have closed the theatres."

As losses continued to mount, showmanship became the order of the day. Enterprising exhibitors in cities and towns across the country devised an astonishing array of gimmicks and giveaways to lure patrons back to theatres. While an atmosphere of economic gloom settled over the country, the neighborhood movie house crackled with ballyhoo and hoopla. A ticket to the movies promised a much-needed diversion along with free dinnerware (moviegoers could often collect a dish a

Derby Night, another chance to win cash. *Allen Michaan*

Main Street of Forester, Arkansas boasted a movie theatre on the left. *Arkansas History Commission*

The Rayette Beauty School promotion drew a full house in Denver, Colorado. *Ralph Batschelet/ Beverley Carlson*

week), plus the chance to win free groceries, glassware, puppies, permanent waves, automobiles — or anything else a shrewd exhibitor could get free from local merchants in exchange for a promotional plug. "'The Country Store' was like a raffle," said Oregon-based exhibition vet Emma Moyer Kane of one early promotion. "We'd have sacks of groceries and, believe me, that really brought them in right at first. Because a bag of groceries meant so much to people then. They'd line up clear around the corner to buy a ticket for this raffle." Emma's brother Harry remembers it the same way. "We'd give away about six baskets of food, and I can remember what we put in those: we used to put bacon,

eggs, oatmeal, bread, potatoes and celery, coffee, sugar — and that was about $2.50 or $3.00 for one of those baskets."

Free cash awards were another immediate draw. SCREEN-O, an on-screen version of bingo, proved popular as did talent contests, beauty pageants and fashion shows. The ingenuity of exhibitors seemingly knew no bounds as theatre patrons found money, gifts, contests and prizes dangled at the end of their movie tickets. Biggest of all was the prize offering of a new automobile. But the lucky winner wasn't always so lucky, "Well, you see, when they came up to collect their car," recalled veteran West Coast exhibitor Morton Lippe, "you had to tell them they would win the car but it was around a couple of hundred dollars for tax and license. These people just didn't have that. It was too hard in those days. We would give them a cash settlement instead."

The most popular of all Depression-era theatre promotions was Bank Night. Bank Night promised visions of newfound riches with its weekly cash drawings. The idea first occurred to Charles U. Yeager, a Fox circuit theatre manager who tried the idea in the small moun-

During the Depression years people didn't always go to the movies to win groceries; sometimes they went to the movies and made food donations to charity. Collection of food for the Salvation Army at the Strand Theatre, Madison, Wisconsin. *Tim Romano, Historic Photo Service*

was not present, the cash amount rolled over into the following week's drawing. By 1936, more than 4,000 theatres had adopted the game. Some theatres, in an effort to avoid paying a licensing fee, substituted their own form of cash giveaway. Promoted under such names as Pirates Night, Klondike Night, Treasury Night and Movie Sweepstakes, the gimmick worked wonders to revive attendance at the box office. For many theatres, Bank Night spelled the difference between staying open or closing during the Depression years.

The promotion with the biggest impact on the film industry was the move to "double features" or two movies for the price of one. Independent exhibitors in New England began the practice in 1930 and the idea caught fire with the public. Within two years, 40 percent of American movie houses had adopted double bills. The practice grew in popularity and by the end of the decade an estimated 60 percent of the nation's theatres showed double features on a daily basis or during part of the week. In time, even the studio-affiliated theatres relented and offered double bills. After dropping live entertainment from their stages, these first-run theatres found it hard to justify their higher ticket prices for a single feature when theatres around the corner showed two for the price of one. The only real complaint about double features came from the parents, teachers and other social guardians who worried about eye strain and other ill-effects a double bill might have on children.

The trend toward double features meant that an average theatre with three program changes a week now required more than 300 films a year to fill its screen. The second half of a double bill was usually filled by a low budget "B-movie," although some theatres offered two "medium-budget" pictures or even two Bs. In desperate cases, exhibitors turned to triple bills. Low-

tain town of Montrose, Colorado and its adjacent communities. The idea may have remained a purely local phenomenon had he not shared it with Frank H. "Rick" Ricketson, the successful force behind the Fox Inter-Mountain circuit. Ricketson envisioned the full possibilities of Bank Night and copyrighted the idea under a hundred different names. The enormous success of Bank Night made Ricketson and Yeager a fortune and proved a lifeline for struggling theatres. With cash awards of up to $500, few people could resist entering the weekly drawing. The rules stipulated that a contestant had to be present to win so exhibitors shrewdly offered Bank Night on a theatre's slowest night of the week, typically a Monday or Tuesday, to help build attendance. Entries were placed in a drum and once a name was pulled, the person had to appear on stage within three minutes to claim the prize. If the winner

budget B-movies had been part of Hollywood's film output for years. The switch to double features necessitated a sharp increase in film production and by 1935 all the major studios had opened B-movie production units. The studio output was supplemented by well-known independent producers such as Republic and Monogram and scores of "quickie" production companies. B-movies were shorter than their A-list counterparts and lasted anywhere from 45 to 85 minutes. Audiences enjoyed them as reliable, formula entertainments filled with western shoot-outs, singing cowboys, gangsters and mystery sleuths. "Because the Depression was on a lot of the pictures were made with a happy ending, like a Horatio Alger picture," said Harry Moyer. "The hero would always come out ahead and things were always good in the end. It was tough in the beginning and people enjoyed those kind because the Depression was on and you know things weren't so good. They liked to see a happy ending."

In rural areas some theatres were forced to change their double bills daily. In large cities smaller theatres functioned as "grind houses" screening a continuous program of action films with little regard for schedules or film quality. exhibitors often referred to these theatres as "shooting galleries," as much for their long narrow design as for the relentless onslaught of flying bullets on screen. "They called them the shotgun houses," said Kansas exhibitor Paul Kelly. "They were action, that type of thing." Pennsylvania exhibitor Don Woodward remembered the theatres were referred to as "ranch houses, where they played nothing but westerns, and serials and so forth." These smaller theatres operated outside the run-clearance system of major producers and distributors and featured the quickie-production companies, lowest-budget films.

A variety of strategies and promotions helped keep

theatre owners in business during the Depression years. Movie attendance increased in 1934 and rose steadily thereafter. Some observers credited the industry's adoption of a Production Code and the release of better-quality pictures for the box office upswing. "It was clean action, you know what I mean," remarked Pennsylvania-based circuit owner Ted Manos. "The hero always won, the good man always won. When people went to a movie in those days they always left inspired. The bad people were always punished. The cowboy always kissed his horse, he never kissed the girl. You never had pictures where you had a double-bed. They

A crowd waits to hear the name of the $400 Pirate Night winner at the Roxy Theatre, Mitchell, South Dakota. *Jeff Logan*

PIRATE NIGHT ~ ROXY THEATRE
MITCHELL ~ S.D. ~ SEPTEMBER 17 ~ 1935
~ HARSEY PHOTO SERVICE

were always twin beds and they had to be separated by so many feet too. So, they were very, very zealous of what went on that screen and what people would see."

Whether it was better-quality pictures or a need to escape the Depression, the industry breathed a collective sigh of relief at the rebounding box office. The Film Daily Yearbook, an industry almanac, stated that average admissions rose in 1934 from 60 million to 70 million a week. According to the same source, moviegoing climbed to 80 million patrons a week in 1935 and upward to 88 million the following year.

The decade ended with a banner year for movie

classics. In 1939 audiences flocked to theatres to revel in the cinematic riches of "Gone With the Wind," "The Wizard of Oz," "Wuthering Heights" and "Stagecoach," to name just a handful of that year's most memorable pictures.

The last remnants of the Depression evaporated with the coming of World War II. The United States transformed itself into a full-time, full-employment war economy. Americans went back to work and looked to the movies for entertainment in record numbers as the nation faced the prospect of war.

Chapter 6

BOOM-BOOM AND BALLYHOO

"Get 'em in, get 'em out, get 'em back next week" — *George Aurelius*

What follows is a celebration of the showman's art. All that hype, hoopla and hucksterism that's thrown into the pot to stir the public's imagination. The goal — pack 'em in!

Promotion is the lifeblood of the motion picture industry. Whatever a film's attributes, whatever superior elements a film might possess — from its well-crafted story to its spectacular special effects — it remains just so much exposed celluloid in a film can until promotion gives it the aura of a "must see" coming attraction.

Today's audiences are familiar with previews, posters, radio, television and newspaper campaigns which tout the coming of Hollywood's newest attractions on a weekly basis. Movie reviewers and entertainment editors discuss the movies from every angle — story, direction, acting and cinematography. We live in a movie-savvy world.

This has not always been true. The novelty of early moving pictures was their own best advertisement. Crowds flocked to the nickelodeon on a daily basis eager to experience the phenomenon of moving pictures. As

audiences became accustomed to movies and competition among theatres increased, showmen found themselves relying on a variety of sales techniques to reach their audience.

Storefront operators borrowed the crude advertis-

The personal touch in movie theatre ballyhoo. *Eric Levin*

Dramatic example of an oversized marquee cut-out at the Sooner Theatre in Norman, Oklahoma. *Roger Rice*

Aggie Theatre in Stillwater, Oklahoma showed a dramatic flair for promoting "Boom Town." *Roger Rice*

ing techniques used by traveling carnivals and circus barkers. Theatre fronts were awash in brightly-colored, bold, hand-lettered posters. When electricity became widely available it was immediately put to use. At night, the facades of many theatres were draped in strings of incandescent bulbs which punctuated the darkness and beckoned all within range to come inside and see the show. Prominently positioned outside the theatre, the barker barked his come-on while a phonograph blared rousing music in the background.

Children passed out heralds or throw-away flyers door to door. In the days before film manufacturers distributed posters of their films, theatre owners painted their own, or sensibly found a quick sign painter to create daily sign changes. "Today you don't hear anything about heralds," said veteran Iowa exhibitor Don Bloxham. "But they used to be put out on every prac-

Hand-painted signs and a blaring phonograph welcomed all passers-by to the Bijou, Grinnell, Iowa's first nickelodeon. *Jim Emerson*

Movie posters nearly obliterated the front of Austin's Texas Theatre. *Film/Harry Ransom Center, University of Texas, Austin*

tically every picture that was released. It was an advertising piece that had a blank backside for the theatre's imprint. Kids pedaled them around to houses and put them in the door to advertise a show. We would go to towns 20, 50 miles around, and maybe once a week put those in doors of houses in these neighboring towns that either didn't have theatres or else had one that played behind our town."

The theatre itself became a prime merchandising tool, a focal point of attention. Early photoplay houses boasted elaborate neo-classical facades in an effort to create an aura of respectability. The theatre owner thus tempted the reluctant middle class, which previously associated movie theatres with "rowdy low-class amusement." The facades, which could be purchased by mail order, sported fake columns, pilasters, cherubs, and elaborate curly cues.

By 1914, custom-made electric signs changed the

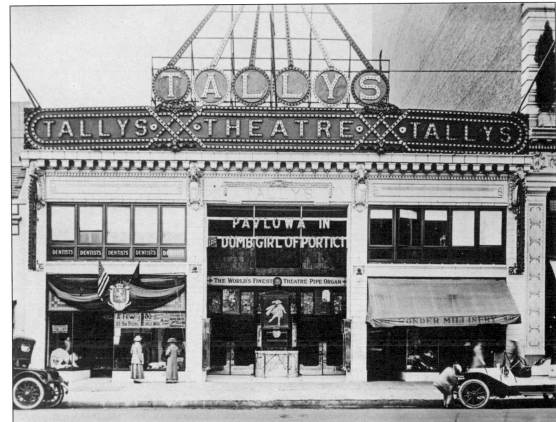

face of theatres. No longer limited to a simple row of bare light bulbs, or stock signs, theatres could now design imaginative electric displays. Formal display signs emerged in 1916, featuring plain copy board and changeable letters. The enduring movie marquee had arrived.

Theatres developed "house mottos" to convey a sense of hospitality and quality on which patrons could count. The mottos emphasized refinement and commitment to service as a way to convey that an evening spent at the movie theatre would prove a rewarding experience. The mottos, which ranged from the playful "House

Thomas Tally's Los Angeles theatre reminded audiences it had the "World's Finest Theatre Pipe Organ." *Allen Michaan*

Before the advent of radio and television advertising, exhibitors pasted movie posters right down on the sidewalk in front of their theatres. *Otto Settele*

lobby, be given another coin and routed out by an exit door with the others to regroup out front to form another buying line. After a couple of hours of this, the activity had served its purpose and was discontinued for the day."

Unlike today, newspapers of an earlier age refused to carry movie theatre advertising. The only way a theatre could promote a picture, and get press coverage,

Sign shop at Miami-based Wometco theatre circuit during the 1930s. *Arthur Hertz*

Stilt-walker attracted a crowd at Madison, Wisconsin's Capitol Theatre. *Tim Romano, Historic Photo Service*

of Hits" to the grandiose "Cathedral of the Motion Picture," helped establish the personality of the theatre in the public's mind.

When all else failed, exhibitors created their own long lines of expectant moviegoers which then became a self-fulfilling prophecy. "Occasionally, especially on an opening-day matinee, a dozen or so 'stooges' or 'silent claques' would be recruited from employment offices to help create 'buying lines' at the box office," remembered veteran exhibitor George Aurelius. "Each was given the price of one admission and told to proceed leisurely with the others to the box office, buy a ticket, enter the theatre

was to make it news. Thus movie ballyhoo was born. The public witnessed a succession of sidewalk stunts, street parades and outlandish feats all designed to get people talking about the movie or the theatre. According to Bill Hendricks and Howard Waugh, authors of the Encyclopedia of Exploitation, "Every stunt should call attention, and definitely favorable attention, to the theatre and its attractions to justify use, and should be reasonably sure of sufficient box office returns to justify the expense." It was a prescription designed to guarantee results without limiting the showman's imagination.

Exhibitors are showmen. First and foremost, they dedicate themselves to their featured attraction with all the verve, flair and dramatic presentation they can muster. "The best promoters did the best business, " explained veteran New England exhibitor Julian Rifkin. "We did not have the national advertising as we do today. The advertising was up to the local theatre. We used to have stunts and gags and every week you'd have a promotion of some kind for some picture. You'd see a picture in advance and you'd build a campaign. Some were semi-legal. For instance, at midnight you'd start going out with a stencil and stencil all the sidewalks with the name of the picture. The next morning you would have to go and take them off but it got a lot of publicity." "My dad used to say to me, 'Now look, you do this street bally (and that's what it was called, ballyhoo), you go right ahead and do it and attract all the attention you can," remembered Maryland-based circuit owner Paul Roth, who got into the business through his family. "If you get arrested, it's all right, but I won't bail you out unless the newspaper carries the name of the picture and the name of the theatre along with the story of your arrest. If you get credit in the paper we'll come bail you out. If you don't, that's your problem.'"

It was okay to get arrested but it was not okay to get shot. "I got a guy and dressed him in a loincloth and put him up in a tree on Mamaroneck," explained Loews publicity veteran Ted Arnow. "I don't know if you are familiar with the area, but it is a very exclusive upgraded avenue in Westchester. This guy was supposed to let out a shriek or the Tarzan yell at 5 a.m. He did not have a watch so at 3 a.m. he let out this yell and there were all kinds of complaints. They had the police department there. They had the fire department. At one point, they threatened to shoot the guy out of the tree if he wouldn't come down."

Classic example of movie theatre street stunt, Orpheum Theatre, Phoenix, Arizona. *George Aurelius*

"Now this may sound humorous to you," Arnow continued, "but unbeknownst to me UPI and AP and radio stations they all picked the thing up. As a result the following morning, or that evening, the papers and the radio stations were loaded with this stunt, which was my first claim to fame. From that point on I was classified as a publicist."

"Every element of a program was booked for value and was expected to be publicized. This is where the promotional instincts of the showman materialized and rose to the challenge," noted Aurelius. "When one realizes new programs were presented weekly, sometimes twice weekly, one can better appreciate the achievements and pressures on those responsible for getting the word out. Just how they did it many times remain their secret. Maybe that is where we learned to "get 'em in, get 'em out, get 'em back next week.""

"When we opened 'Guys and Dolls' at the Capitol Theatre I and my crew staged a wedding in Times Square," said Arnow. "I had the Goldwyn Girls. There were 12 of them, the most gorgeous lovelies in their full regalia as bridesmaids." The promotion, said Arnow, was a part of a newspaper write-in contest where actual engaged couples were invited to compete. The prize was an elaborate wedding, staged at high noon on 43rd and Broadway. The theatre worked with local merchants and obtained furniture for the couple's new home as well as the honeymoon trip. "All the papers covered it and radio stations covered it, exclaimed Arnow. "It was unbelievable. Really unbelievable."

"I remember we had a gorilla picture one time, 'Mark of the Gorilla'," said Georgia-based circuit owner Carl Patrick. "We fixed up a searchlight on a truck and had a man dressed in a gorilla suit go all over the circuit. We just had more people in the squares looking at that and they couldn't figure out if it was a real gorilla. Those things wouldn't go today but this was in the late '40s and early '50s." Industry vet Irving Ludwig recalled a similar type of stunt: "We once played a picture at the Rivoli called the 'The White Zombies', an exploitation picture. The publicity department built a catwalk on top of the

"Frame job" transformed Phoenix' Rialto Theatre with a prison facade. *George Aurelius*

Towering gunslinger looms in front of Kansas City, Kansas' Granada Theatre. *Chuc Barnes*

Streetcar banners were highly effective advertising for movie theatres. *Tim Romano*

theatre and they had so-called zombies walking around in a trance."

Theatres found it in their own best interest to maintain an on-site sign shop. Staff artists and sign painters could quickly create posters, lobby displays, advertising layouts, whatever was needed. They could even temporarily transform the front of the building with something called a "frame job" with the express purpose of promoting a film. A frame job, as it is known in the business, was a removable false front affixed to the building. It could be painted to resemble a frontier fort, a jungle outpost or a brick jail cell. It could be decorated with huge cut-out letters, figures or even animated displays. The only limitation was the artist's imagination, his talent, and — of course — the budget.

"Almost all of them had their own sign painters and artists on their payroll who did elaborate cut-outs," said

Seductive "Madam Satan," draped in garments made from sterling silver and solid gold, beckoned patrons in the lobby of Phoenix, Arizona's Orpheum Theatre. *George Aurelius*

An oversized image of Elvis greeted moviegoers at the Gem Theatre in Kannapolis, North Carolina. *Clyde Scarboro*

Merchants' free movie night drew a big crowd to Park Lake, Iowa's State Theatre. *Otto Settele*

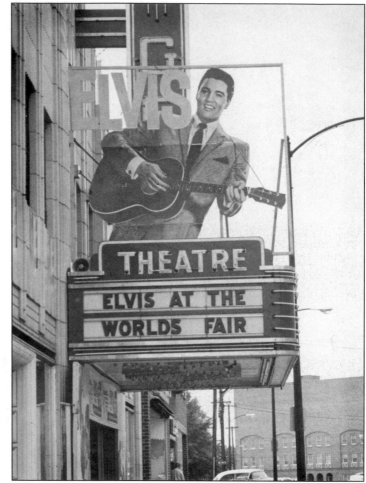

Roth of the showmen of the era. "The big marquee pieces that you've seen and the blow ups of stars that were cut out and pasted on the boards. They were rear-lit and back-lit and front-lit. Even these little jerkwater towns in the Shennandoah Valley in Virginia had a sign painter. My father had a sign painter and they'd be painting these covers for spare tires and I'm pretty sure my dad used side boards on cabs, like they now have on buses." "The ad people were very clever but there were many unsung heroes around the country who made the advertising people and the managers look great," explained Aurelius. They were the local ad artists who executed the ideas for newspaper display ads and the sign artists who created the "lobbies" and "false fronts."

"If we had a western picture, we'd have a western front," remembered Pennsylvania-based circuit owner Ted Manos. "If we had a picture that had to do with any other field, we would try to bring that spirit into the theatre through our promotions. In those days you didn't have national promotions like we have today on TV. We had to do a hard selling job locally in order to sell the pictures."

"For a picture like 'The Great Ziegfeld' they'd have big, big musical notes," recalled Loews veteran Herb Brown. "They'd have a lot of cut-outs of the stars of the picture. They had what they called a lot of glitter, which they sprinkled on, and it would be all shiny. They were very, very impressive. They were overwhelming, some of those displays."

Cooperative efforts with local merchants yielded successful promotions called retail tie-ins which allowed local store windows to become tools of the theatre's promotion department. The store became a "prop" to promote the theme or locale of a picture. For example, a jewelry story could adorn its windows with diamonds to promote "How to Marry A Millionaire," or a travel agency could be tapped for a free trip to Hawaii to promote "Blue Hawaii." Merchant tie-ins also included free prize and contest possibilities. A theatre, in cooperation with a local merchant, could offer a raffle that not only provided the patron with a prize but also promoted the picture and the merchant. These give-away promotions included everything from cash to groceries, housewares, even automobiles.

usual; the audience enjoyed a movie "on the house" and merchants enjoyed an opportunity for extra sales.

The excitement of seeing Hollywood stars on the screen was often exceeded only by the excitement generated when those stars actually came to town. Film company executives and theatre owners alike understood the promotional value of having a celebrity promote a picture, and both parties worked together closely to use this effective tool to its best advantage. Today it's done on talk shows; but in an earlier time, stars would

This advertising sound truck rolled through the streets of Oklahoma City, Oklahoma promoting movies and the moviegoing experience. *Roger Rice*

Shimmering backdrop alerted moviegoers to the arrival of the next featured attraction, Paramount Theatre, St. Paul, Minnesota. *George Aurelius*

A traveling billboard display mounted behind a sound truck like the one shown here at San Francisco's El Capitan Theatre, was a common advertising device during the 1930s and 40s. *Jack Tillmany*

All-too-willing to make use of the tried and true advertising technique of associating products with Hollywood glamour, merchants were eager to participate in cooperative promotional campaigns. "We had press books at that time," remembered Julian Rifkin. "The press books had stories of the actors and the show and promotions they could do and tie-ups with different jewelry stores. Every star would wear jewelry of some kind to be manufactured by some company. You'd go to that company and you'd have the stills and they'd put them in the windows of their stores showing the star wearing this particular piece of jewelry or clothing or what have you — they even used automobiles." Another example of merchant-exhibitor synergy was the Merchant Free Show, an evening of free movie entertainment sponsored by one or more of the local merchants. On Merchant Free Show days, the stores also stayed open later than

rities, and who better to attract a teenage crowd than the local radio disc jockey? "With the realization that rock & roll was the most contagious entertainment trend," reminisced Wisconsin theatre owner Otto Settele, "we jumped on the bandwagon. In this campaign we gave nothing away except good entertainment. We invited a popular deejay to appear on our stage to simulate a radio broadcast. We convinced the disc jockey we would be enlarging his listening audience and he obliged us for a very small fee. The feature film was

Celebrity endorsement promoted the picture, the theatre and the product. *George Aurelius*

Personal appearances by leading celebrities such as Barbara Stanwyck were a tried and true way to promote a film. *George Aurelius*

Nothing beat the excitement of a celebrity-packed premiere, especially if it was in your home town. *Jack Belasco*

visit a series of communities on a "junket." All the attendant hoopla reserved for a visiting dignitary or politician couldn't match the flurry of activity bestowed on visiting Hollywood royalty. "In the old days," recalled Illinois-based circuit owner George Kerasotes, "Gene Autry came to Springfield. Roy Rogers came, Buck Jones, another cowboy star. They all came there too. People came out to see them, like they were a circus. They came out to see the cowboy stars."

Personal appearances could also feature local celeb-

aimed at teenagers. It was a sure draw."

The height of Hollywood glamour and promotion reached its pinnacle with the premicrc. Nothing could match the excitement generated by the red carpet treatment of a klieg-lit movie premiere. Crowds, search lights, fancy dress and limousines, all enhanced by invitation - only guest-lists, helped to make the "premiere" the ultimate expression of "Hooray for Hollywood." It didn't hurt the box office either. "I remember many world premieres in small town theatres," recalled industry veteran Bernard Diamond. "I remember Kentucky, where we had Rosemary Clooney in her first movie. We had 'Drums Along the Mohawk' in upstate New York. We had some horse picture in Lexington, Kentucky."

Contemporary motion picture promotion is marked by national advertising campaigns with saturation TV advertising and mass market merchandising. Everything from television talk shows and movie entertainment programs to T-shirts and fast food drink cups are pressed into service on behalf of a film. The days of the grass-roots theatre campaign, however, are far from over. Imaginative theatre managers, encouraged by their circuit headquarters, still create hand-lettered signs, promote merchandise from local retailers, give away prizes, stage stunts, and decorate their theatre lobbies and marquees with false fronts. Somctimcs the more things change, the more they stay the same. It's all part of the show.

Animated lobby display featured star-studded wheel which revolved behind Shirley Temple cut-out at the Palace Theatre, Canton, Ohio. *Ralph Russell*

Chapter 7

CONCESSIONS

A colorful, brightly-lit, well-stocked and well-staffed concession stand shines at the center of the modern American movie theatre. Every week millions of moviegoers respond to its tantalizing aromas and visual charms and find themselves happily chewing, munching, sipping and slurping their way through the screen's featured attraction.

The pleasurable combination of moviegoing and snack treats was introduced during the early nickelodeon days soon after the turn of the century. Cramped storefront theatres with few amenities willingly allowed patrons to carry in small bags of roasted nuts or candy from the local confectionery store. "The people I worked for had no concessions whatsoever," recalled retired Iowa exhibitor Don Bloxham. "They allowed people to bring things in. They had a sub-rental in one of the store fronts right next door to the theatre that they owned that sold candy and things like that." Street vendors with horse-drawn popcorn wagons discovered that moviehouses, with their continuous audience turnovers every 20 minutes or so, were prime locations for steady sales of freshly

popped corn and roasted peanuts, so it was not unusual to see them parked near the local movie show. Early reports of food sold in theatres describe neighborhood children running down the aisles and hawking small bags of peanuts, adding to the general commotion in the rowdy nickelodeons.

During the 1920s, some small neighborhood theatres began to sell wrapped candies in their lobbies as a way to augment their income. In larger cities moviehouses adopted a technique from burlesque theatres and began offering boxes of chocolates to their patrons. Selling was done by a vendor or "candy butcher" who roamed down the aisles and tossed candy samples to the patrons. The vendor then mounted the theatre's stage and loudly announced the price of his treats before returning to the aisle to fill requests with the candy gathered in his apron. "Now before the picture would start, after the stage show, you used to have vendors that would walk through the theatres and sell candy and cotton candy and things like you generally see at a fair," remembered Iowa-based circuit owner Myron "Mike" Blank. "There wasn't a concession stand. You couldn't go out to the

Smartly-attired concession staff stood ready to serve soft drinks from the fountain dispenser. *Coca-Cola USA*

Fox Mayan Theatre, Denver, Colorado, 1958. *Ralph Batschelet/Beverley Carlson*

lobby and buy something; you had to buy at the time that these vendors walked through the theatres."

Towards the end of the 1920s, some of the larger movie houses installed coin-operated candy boxes attached to the back of the seats. For the price of a nickel patrons could enjoy a serving of chocolate drops.

Interest in concession sales perked up during the hard years of the Great Depression. Theatres experimented with small portable candy stands and vending machines to help boost income. New York's Rivoli Theatre had a specific policy regarding vending machines. "The instructions to the cashiers were, 'when you give change don't give half dollars or dollar bills,'" explained industry vet Irving Ludwig. "'Give small

change so that you're tempted to buy candy from a machine for five, 10 and 15 cents.'" The independent street popcorn vendors found themselves displaced from their choicest locations when movie theatres set up their own portable popcorn carts out front.

"When I started as a small boy, working in the theatre in Winchester, Illinois, a lady would come before showtime with her little popcorn machine," remembered theatre-supply company and former circuit owner Bob Tankersley. "She would stand out front of the Lyric Theatre and sell popcorn for a nickel a bag and the people would either eat it outside or after they came out of the theatre. She used the old P.T. Barnum way of selling it too. She started popping it before showtime and then just before the end of the movie she would crank it up again, having the smell permeating the street and the air around. And people would buy it." The tempting aroma of freshly popped and buttered corn, coupled with the machine's constant pop-pop-popping sound and the visual display of dancing kernels, proved

an irresistible attraction for many passers-by and arriving theatre patrons." "I used to like the popcorn," said veteran exhibitor Paul Roth, "where the noise could be heard by the people in the auditorium and where the wonderful, wonderful smell would immediately get out into the auditorium and encourage you to come buy popcorn. When we stopped popping it on the back rail in the auditorium we sure as hell put it out in the lobby where you had to pass it coming in."

The popcorn trend grew fastest throughout the South and Midwest, where theatre owners eagerly embraced any idea that contributed to the patron's satisfaction. While Depression-era gimmicks and giveaways kept audiences in the moviegoing habit, overall attendance was down and credit is given to popcorn sales for keeping many a theatre's doors open. "Other theatre owners teased our father saying, 'old Moyer was going into the peanut and popcorn business.' But he told them, 'well, you guys will all be in this too,'" remembers veteran Oregon-based exhibitor Harry Moyer. "And sure enough that's what happened. Then we used to have candy bars. We'd buy our candy and sell candy bars on the counter there, where the popcorn machine was."

The nation's opulent movie palaces were among the last to introduce snack food into their hallowed halls. Theatre owners and managers were aghast at the prospect of candy bits or greasy popcorn kernels falling onto luxurious mohair seats or being trampled into exquisite, hand-woven carpeting. "They were very fussy about it and, remember, when you went to one of those theatres you were stepping out; you went with a tie and a jacket," remembered veteran exhibitor Don Baker. "We put in a temporary popcorn stand and sold popcorn in the theatre. I remember getting a telephone call from our division manager who told me he would personally

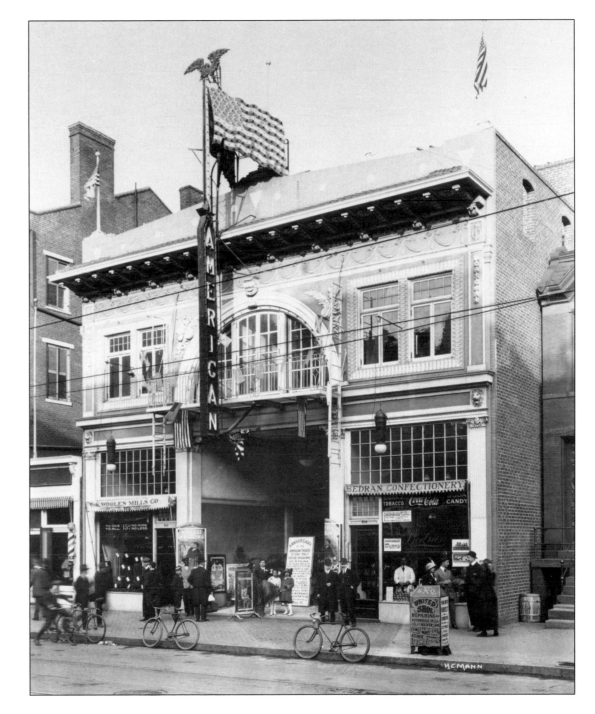

come down and strangle me. . . If he found one popcorn kernel in my theatre I was dead." And then there was the smell. The whole idea of selling food to movie patrons smacked of vulgar burlesque houses, tawdry amusement parks and cheap carnivals.

As the nation's economic slump wore on, however, even the movie palaces, the grande dames of exhibition, experimented with candy sales. Retired Loews executive Herb Brown once overheard his manager say, "You're going to be getting a candy machine here pretty soon. We don't know what to do with the damn thing, but let's find a place to put it." "And they looked for a place where the patron would have to have a seeing-eye dog to find it," remembered Brown. "It was their pur-

pose to hide it as much as possible. It was almost as if they felt embarrassed to have a candy machine in the lobby. I say embarrassed because theatres like these beautiful palaces, they just felt it was out of place." It would be some time, in fact, before deluxe theatres allowed patrons to carry their snacks to their auditorium seats.

In 1933, Detroit's Fox Theatre began selling candy as a courtesy to patrons who repeatedly made requests to leave the theatre to buy candy, gum or popcorn. The public's positive response to concessions was enough to overcome the fears of hesitant theatre managers. At first, portable candy stands were the rule, since they were quick to set up and easy to locate in small spaces. By the end of the 1930s, theatres began installing vending machines and permanent concession counters. Most palace-type theatres, although enormous, had not been built with room for snack counters in mind. Early snack bars in these exquisitely-designed venues featured streamlined, fold-out cabinets that could be tucked in alcoves, lobby corners or walkways. As the popularity of snack items grew, theatres remodelled lobby areas to accommodate larger concession stands and a staff of attendants.

Theatres that allowed patrons with popcorn into the auditorium soon faced complaints about the noisy bags. "A big revolutionary item for the industry was noiseless popcorn bags," noted Tankersley, recalling the annoying rustle of early paper popcorn bags. "I think it was developed by Rex Paper Bags in New York and it was somewhat like a paper towel that you see on the market today." This led to the development of the cardboard popcorn box, forerunner to today's familiar popcorn tubs.

The popularity of sugary treats and salty popcorn hastened the introduction of thirst-quenching beverages

Dunkin Theatre, Cushing, Oklahoma. *Roger Rice*

into theatres. The first drinks were non-carbonated fruit drinks that swirled in bubble-topped drink dispensers, followed by the introduction of carbonated soft drinks during the 1940s. Patrons at the Texan Theatre in Hamilton, Texas concocted their own house speciality, explained current theatre co-owner Lambert Little. "Mollie Dalton remembers that right after the war the pickel juice concoction became popular. They would mix all of the carbonated drinks (except orange because it was too sweet) with a little bit of pickle juice. The drink was called a 'suicide.' Apparently it was quite popular because lots of folks around here still remember it. In fact a few still order them and we dutifully serve them up."

When "Gone With the Wind" opened in Norfolk, Virginia, the enterprising theatre manager arranged for Coca-Cola to be served during the film's 15-minute intermission as a benefit to a local charity. Theatre operators everywhere took notice when more than 800 bottles of the popular soft drink were sold. The promo-

tional idea spread to other roadshow presentations of the film and helped introduce the idea of cool, refreshing soft drinks as part of the moviegoing experience.

Coca-Cola became widely available in theatres after its successful July, 1947 debut at New York's famed Roxy Theatre, and paved the way for the introduction of other soft drinks into moviehouses. The Roxy's circular drink counter graced the theatre's main lobby, where attendants poured individual bottles of Coke into paper cups. Patrons were free to enjoy the small, seven-ounce drinks during intermissions or when leaving the theatre.

Hand-poured bottle service proved time-consuming

Plaza Theatre, Milwaukee, Wisconsin. *Larry Widen*

Movie theatre vending stand, Oakland Theatre, Milwaukee, Wisconsin. *Larry Widen.*

As soft drinks at the movies grew in popularity, theatre managers faced the twin problems of bottle storage and units that required constant restocking. Beginning in the early 1950s, the familiar clank and rumble of bottle machines gave way to high capacity cup vending machines. "Do you know how cheap they were in those days? They would always hook up the soda machine to the drinking fountain because it was cheaper to hook it up to that water because that water was already refrigerated, it was cold to begin with. So you came in, and you had your choice of a free drink of water or a soda," remembered New England exhibitor John Lowe. "Later on they smartened up and moved the drinking fountains behind somewhere, in some corner or underneath the stairwell going up to the balcony. You couldn't find the drinking fountain, but you'd see the soda machines."

The contents of a theatre's automated vending machines were not limited to the typical assortment of candy, beverages and cigarettes. Many movie houses

Concession stands were abundantly stocked to accommodate overflow crowds. Byrd Theatre, Richmond, Virginia. *Frank Novak*

Early fold-out candy stand. *Ralph Batschelet/Beverley Carlson*

Fold-out candy counter and self-serve drink dispenser were tucked away in hallway of Portland's Hollywood Theatre. *Act III Theatres*

and required extra concession staff. Before the advent of fountain service, theatres switched to refrigerated vending machines to provide quicker service for their thirsty patrons. "We started out selling bottled Coke for about five or 10 years," recalled Montana exhibitor Jess Armitage. "They made so much noise rolling down the seats that we finally went to a fountain type dispenser." Early coin-operated models lacked a change-making feature yet provided patrons with as many as three bottled drink selections for a nickel apiece. The welcome introduction of change-making machines in the late 1940s boosted theatre vending sales as much as 25 percent.

installed profitable penny amusement machines to entertain waiting patrons. A 1941 issue of Theatre Catalog, a widely-read industry trade magazine, devoted a major section to the potential success of various vending machines. The magazine detailed how coin-operated scales that measured weight and dispensed fortunes and

counter and performed regular maintenance for a percentage of all sales. The system was a sweetheart deal for theatre owners who could offer patrons an expanded array of treats with no out-of-pocket costs. The theatre's percentage of concession profits was a healthy dose of "found" money that helped theatres survive tough times.

The successful snack bar operator developed a sixth sense about popular sales items. Some even went so far as to match their candy stock to audiences for particular pictures. According to one trade article a "class" picture that appealed to the occasional moviegoer did good business with Life Savers. Theatres playing the leading man dramas of Robert Taylor, Clark Gable and Tyrone Power found success selling chocolate mints and Bon Bons. Comedies spelled good sales of rolled candies and fruit gums, while hard candies were the top choice for audiences of westerns and the blood-and-thunder action pictures. And kids, well, they bought the biggest candy bars available. "I used to say I think I'll review a picture by Jujyfruits," recalled veteran East Coast concessionaire Elliot Cohen. "It's a one-Jujyfruit picture, I used to make fun. Or a two-Jujyfruit picture. A ten-Jujyfruit picture was a great, good action movie. They ate like crazy. And the best one was the horror shows. They used to get scared. Run back out into the lobby and eat again."

The late 1940s saw a surge in expanded concession operations. Counters became bigger and brighter and offered a growing array of treats. Fast-flowing fountain dispensers gradually replaced drink vending machines. Snack counters made room for self-service ice cream bins that offered a chilled selection of ice cream varieties. Soft ice cream machines joined the counter, poised to deliver a cone's worth of ice cream with a distinctive swirl top finish. But with all these choices, popcorn

Self-serve soft drink dispenser.
Coca-Cola USA

fortunes and horoscopes earned as much as 100 extra dollars a week. Machines that dispensed grooming aids and items for personal hygiene also appeared in theatre rest rooms and lounges.

Theatres typically contracted with independent concessionaires or concession companies that serviced a theatre's vending machines, stocked its concession

ing the movies they would just walk up and down the aisle. They wouldn't say anything. If anybody wanted anything they would motion to them and they would give it to them."

Concession sales took off when exhibitors used the razzle dazzle of showmanship to catch the patron's attention. Concession counters grew in size with colorful displays of stacked candy bars and packaged treats. Simple counters grew extension wings and wall units. Accent lighting and mirrors fixed the wandering eye on the mouth-watering wares. And finally, posters of coming attractions and displays of movie-star photos surrounded the snack bar with celebrity smiles and the allure of Hollywood glamour.

Theatre operators often provided weight machines and other coin operated novelties. Agnew Theatre, Oklahoma City, Oklahoma. *Roger Rice*

Early Coca-Cola bottle service. *Coca-Cola USA*

remained the most popular snack choice by far, followed by soft drinks and candy.

Some of the larger circuits took full control over this lucrative business and established their own confectionery companies to service not only their own concession needs but also those of smaller, independent houses. Despite the wholesale drop in movie attendance following the postwar peak of 1946, word spread about the healthy profits enjoyed by the larger circuits that had enhanced their concession operations. The reports spurred exhibitors to take a second look at snack counters.

The popularity of concessions took off as soon as theatres recognized that the snack bar was part of a theatre's total entertainment experience. One theatre capitalizing on the audience's desire for concessions harkened back to earlier practice of aisle sales, with one refinement: "We had concession girls that sold popcorn and candy up and down the aisles of the theatre," explained Mississippi theatre owner Paul Maxey. "Dur-

Managers launched seasonal promotions that regularly transformed the look of snack counters with holiday decorations, spring colors and Halloween monsters. If a theme picture was playing, the concession staff might be costumed to match, adding to a special level of interest at the concession stand. Some theatres hid movie passes in boxes of popcorn to create excitement and spur extra sales.

The trend of continuous movie shows gradually faded in favor of an intermission break. By the late 1940s, most theatres, whether they showed a single or double feature, scheduled a 15-minute intermission between shows to help the audience take full advantage of the snack bar. Beginning in 1948, snack food manufacturers supplied food trailers to theatres without charge. They were ideal screen fillers for the intermission period between features and left no doubt as to how a patron should spend the typical 10- to 15-minute break.

As theatres braced against the 1950s plummeting box office revenues, they raised the level of concession

service. Beginning in 1953, soft drink vending machines added ice to the cup. Within another two years fountain service expanded to offer the thirsty public drinks in small, medium and large cup sizes.

Movie refreshments reached an apex in drive-in theatres. During their heyday, outdoor theatres offered full menu service with hot dogs, hamburgers, french fries, fried chicken and pizza to compliment the traditional choices of popcorn, soft drinks, ice cream and candy. Drive-ins became family social centers with playgrounds, baby-bottle warmers and a chance for parents and children to enjoy a complete meal together.

Fox Venetian Theatre, Milwaukee, Wisconsin. *Larry Widen*

Concession stand with self-serve soft drink vending machines, State Theatre, Sioux Falls, South Dakota. *George Aurelius*

Movie palace concession stand. *Elliot Cohen*

Beginning in the 1960s, theatre concessions reflected the new youth-oriented, image-conscious world and offered low-calorie diet soft drinks. Theatre owners installed new multiple-drink dispensers that served as

Capitol Theatre, New York.
Ralph Batschelet / Beverley Carlson

many as six different types of soda two of which were usually low-calorie.

During the 1960s and 1970s snack counters continued to expand even as theatre auditoriums shrank. Multiple-screen theatres were designed to give central importance to the colorful and well-stocked refreshment stand.

During the 1980s, Americans became more health-conscious and theatre owners looked for ways to capitalize on the trend. "We call them alternative snacks," explained veteran Virginia-based circuit owner Sam Bendheim, "because there are a lot of people who just don't want to eat candy anymore, they don't want the syrupy soft drinks. So in a lot of our theatres we've gone into SoHo sodas and those kinds of drinks." Snack counters also began offering low-fat frozen yogurt and "air popped" popcorn cooked with low-fat canola oil. The upscale patron was tempted with premium ice cream, espresso and cappuccino. "We began a program," remembered Arizona-based circuit owner Dan Harkins, "of bringing in baked goods, baked brownies and, as an alternative, healthy products such as fruit juices, carbonated waters, coffee, trail mix, granola and imported candies." Southern California-based circuit owner Bruce Corwin, on the other hand, acknowledged the continuing appeal of traditional theatre snacks. "I thought we would be on the cutting edge out here in California by going to less sugar, less salt, more of a health-conscious concession item," said Corwin, "but I have come around to believe that, for the most part, theatres are a safe haven to cheat on your diet at the concession counter. By cheating, I mean buttered popcorn, Milk Duds and a Coke. Nobody can see you. You can go on your diets at home. But the movie theatre is the great escape." Health foods weren't the only items widely introduced during this era. Warm and salty nachos turned out to be the most popular new snack entry of the decade.

The modern concession stand has come full-circle since the days of folding candy carts and vending machines as theatres saw, late in the century, a return to such old stand-bys as portable carts and self-service.

"The multiplex created another situation," longtime East Coast exhibitor Tom Elefante explained. "Often the concession stand was quite a distance away ... so we tried several ways to overcome that. We tried filling carts with pre-packaged popcorn and soda and bringing them up and down the aisles, and actually selling to people after they got to their seats. Then I had an idea that maybe the answer was to develop auxiliary concession stands and locate them closer to where the people were going to ultimately end up. So I began putting in these little auxiliary stands and locating them as near as possible to the entrances of the auditoriums. That worked out very well."

A typical theatre operation of the 1990s might boast a 30-foot concession counter with seven or more individual work stations. The efficient design put the entire menu of drinks and treats reach of each counter person, with the goal of friendly service and no waiting. Some theatres began experimenting with self-service areas, recalling the cafeteria service of drive-ins some 40 years

earlier. And, despite all the changes, the familiar standbys of popcorn, soft drinks and candy continued to maintain their popularity with generation after generation of moviegoers.

"May I help you, please?"
Ralph Batschelet/ Beverley Carlson

These exuberant children "paid" for their Saturday matinee admissions with Pepsi-Cola bottle caps and found plenty of ice cold Pepsi to drink in the theatre lobby.
Pepsi-Cola Entertainment Group

Chapter 8

HOLLYWOOD GOES TO WAR

In this time of stress and anxiety, wholesome amusements can play a big part in upbuilding and maintaining the public morale. — Franklin D. Roosevelt

The outbreak of World War II ended a decade of economic depression as America geared up for an around-the-clock war effort. By 1942, virtually every adult American not in the armed services was working, bringing a wave of economic prosperity to the country. Restrictions on travel and gas rationing forced people to look for entertainment close to home, and there was no better value than the neighborhood cinema. And there seemed to be no bad time to see a movie. "In those days," former New England exhibitor Bernard Levy explained, "they were working around the clock in the factories. These people would come in at different hours to kill time."

Americans flocked to movie theatres. Going to the movies brought welcome relaxation during a time of crisis while newsreels satisfied the public's craving for information and held the promise of a possible glimpse of a loved one at the front. "Don't forget you had no television then; there was no competition for the dollar," noted veteran East Coast exhibitor Bernard Myerson. "People wanted to escape the radios and the newspapers, you know, with stories about what was happening in

Europe. They went to the movies for escape."

The nation's movie theatres enlisted in the war effort through the motion picture industry's War Activities Committee, organized under the government's Office of War Information. More than 16,000 movie houses were pledged to exhibit government-produced war in-

Films of the Second World War helped rally public sentiment against the Nazi peril in Europe. Mecca Theatre, Enid, Oklahoma. *Roger Rice*

Celebrity appearances bolstered local war bond drives. *Ron Krueger*

In order to accommodate throngs of war workers, swing shifters and service personnel involved in the war effort, theatres stayed "Open All Night." Paramount Theatre, San Francisco, Autumn 1944. *Jack Tillmany*

formation films and to serve as venues for their communities' patriotic activities.

With throngs of ticket buyers in line, theatre owners dropped the promotional gimmicks and giveaways that were necessary to fill theatre seats during the Depression. Exhibition's talent for showmanship was instead redirected in support of the war. When the government commissioned movie theatres to sell war bonds and stamps, exhibitors responded with banners, lobby displays, sales booths and special promotional campaigns to encourage public participation. National theatre circuits set bond drive quotas for individual theatres, and theatre managers were quick to turn their publicity talents to the cause. From marquees to theatre programs, exhibitors spread the message, "Buy Bonds."

War bond premieres proved a highly-successful way to promote bond sales through the war, as were honor-roll promotions and the industry's "bond-a-scat" campaigns which sought to ring up one bond sale for every theatre seat in the nation. Hollywood's War Activities Committee netted close to $37 million from motion

picture audiences.

Capitalizing on their positions as important community centers, movie theatres became the focal points for scrap metal drives and inventive "rubber matinees" designed to gather much needed raw material for the war effort. Collection drives were often aimed at children who joined the cause with all the enthusiasm they would typically devote to an old-fashioned scavenger hunt. Scrap drives culminated on weekends with special matinees during a theatre's off-hours where one pound or more of rubber was the price of admission. Selected films were available from studio exchanges free of charge to theatres participating in war-related campaigns. Collection drives were promoted at the theatre and with announcement cards in store windows. In

Illinois-based circuit owner George Kerasotes (third from left) hosted celebrity Marlene Dietrich as she toured Springfield, Illinois on her buy-a-bond campaign. *George Kerasotes*

Even prior to America's entrance into the war, U.S. theatres supported the European allies. The Roxy Theatre in Mitchell, South Dakota collected aluminum for the British "defence" effort. *Jeff Logan*

War bond premieres proved popular with movie audiences. RKO Orpheum Theatre, St. Louis, Missouri. *Ron Krueger*

many instances local merchants contributed prizes that were awarded to the children who brought the greatest poundage to the theatre.

Theatre lobbies periodically took on the appearance of junk heaps as scrap and rubber drives grew in popularity. A well-positioned display of cast-off items was an ideal reminder to patrons to keep on the lookout for similar scrap. Theatre "rubber matinees" typically yielded a bounty of water bags, golf balls, rubber-soled shoes, rubber balls, gloves, and old door mats, in addition to car and bicycle tires.

During the industry's first organized rubber matinees in 1942, five theatres in Arizona's leading cities produced four tons of scrap rubber in one day. In Los

Angeles, eight theatres combined their efforts for a yield of 15 tons. Proceeds from the sale of the rubber went to various government war relief funds.

Candy Shows for the USO were also conducted as special events during a theatre's non-operating morning hours. Using the theme "Buy a Bar for a Buddy," theatres offered free tickets to patrons who purchased two or more candy bars for the theatre's USO "buddy barrel." Citizens were invited to "do their share" by making bulk purchases in return for extra tickets that could be given to friends or donated to charity.

Patriotic ceremonies were commonly conducted on a theatre's stage before the film presentation for these special wartime matinees. USO officials, civic leaders, Boy Scouts and local military personnel would lead the ceremonies with the presentation of the flag and the Pledge of Allegiance, followed by special tributes to General Douglas MacArthur or other military commanders, and concluding with the "Star Spangled Banner." Then it was time for the kiddie feature or all-cartoon program.

Going to the movies was a popular respite for service personnel stationed at home or overseas — regardless

This is a 1942 style theatre foyer — not a junk heap! Scenes like this were played out across the country as theatres sponsored collection drives to support the war effort. *Truman Schroeder*

Using the theme "Buy a Bar for a Buddy," theatres offered free tickets to patrons who purchased two or more candy bars for the theatre's USO "buddy barrel." *Truman Schroeder*

of where they were they always found their way to the nearest theatre. "There was nothing else to do," remembered Mississippi theatre owner Paul Maxey. "There was an army base nearby and of course they were coming and going all the time. If they had a couple of hours to kill, they would go to the movie. It didn't cost but a nickel for service men. Other people, they were a dime."

The movies also went to the front as former ushers, projectionists, theatre managers and assistants found themselves operating military base theatres and temporary "foxhole cinemas." Hollywood films were a welcome diversion at U.S. military sites around the world. Movies were the ideal "two-hour furlough" that helped take a soldier's mind off the war and provided an important emotional link to the folks back home.

Years before the advent of television news coverage and decades before the dawn of the instantaneous satellite feed, a concerned nation counted on motion picture newsreels to capture the sights and sounds of war. Public interest in newsreels began during 1898's Spanish-American War and continued interest in world events made newsreel featurettes a moviehouse staple. They reached a new level of popularity, however, during World War II by serving a nation hungry for information from the front.

Newsreel theatres , having first come onto the scene in the late 1920s, also reached a new plateau of popularity during World War II. Theatres devoted exclusively to newsreels began appearing in the U.S. soon after a number of local newsreel companies that mixed local news with coverage of specialty topics sprang up. Before long there was enough newsreel footage consistently available each week to fill a theatre's entire screen program.

The Fox Film Company, already the owner of a group of theatres, was the first to experiment with the idea of an all-news theatre. On November 2, 1929 Fox opened the Embassy Theatre in New York City at 46th and Broadway, in the heart of Times Square. The 600-seat venue debuted with standing-room-only

crowds for all of its 11 daily shows. Modeled on the concept of quick audience turnaround, the Embassy offered patrons an hour program of not only worldwide political news but also the daring feats of aviators and other adventurers, all for the price of a quarter. Other theatres were quick to adopt this kind of all-documen-

When the government commissioned movie theatres to sell war bonds, exhibitors responded with banners, lobby displays and special campaigns to encourage the public's participation. *Ron Krueger*

tary programming, and this specialized form of film exhibition experienced wide popularity during the 1930s and 1940s.

Three newsreel theatre circuits emerged to control most of the all-news theatres in the U.S.: Trans-Lux, Newsreel Theatres, Inc., and Telenews. The Trans-Lux system of rear-screen projection was ideally suited to newsreel theatres because, according to Trans-Lux circuit head Richard Brandt, "They wanted to have a lighted auditorium where people would be moving in and out all the time."

"When newsreel theatres started there was no television, so the only way you got to see pictures of what was happening around the world was through newsreels," noted Brandt. "Newsreel theatres would be a one-hour show that would allow people to come in any time they wanted to. There was no beginning of the show."

By the time the U.S. entered the war in 1941, there were 25 operating newsreel theatres. Many were former second-run downtown theatres that could be cheaply converted to the newsreel format. The typical newsreel theatre was small, with upwards of 160 seats. The largest theatres, similar to the Embassy, held 600 seats. Admission was typically a quarter for a continuous 45-minute to one-hour program that showed newsreels from the major services, along with an assortment of sports, travelogues and comedy shorts that filled out the bill during slow news times. The public's desire for late-breaking news led newsreel theatres to tie-up with radio stations and print sources. Whenever late-breaking news occurred, patrons could count on the newsreel theatre's management to stop the show and read from the news wire. "Every hour it changed," remembered exhibitor Morton Lippe. "Every hour except Friday when the old shows changed at 4:00 p.m. Everyone

would rush in and you'd see the old show and the new show. Businessmen would come down and spend an hour on their lunchtime."

Opening a newsreel theatre was an economical way to enter the movie theatre business during a time when the major studios controlled most first-run theatres in the country. "I had discovered that the industry was dominated by the major producers of films who owned the major exhibition circuits, either in partnerships or individually," remembered Michigan circuit owner Jack Loeks, "and so the opportunity to get into exhibition was highly restricted. I had been told there was a downtown theatre in Grand Rapids that was just sitting for the asking. I discovered what they called a newsreel theatre, which was a one-hour news format. So I did some checking with film companies and said, '...if I can't get feature films on any kind of current level, can I get newsreel films?' and they said,'... news is like newspaper, it's here today, gone tomorrow.' Fortunately, I found a market in Grand Rapids of people who wouldn't go to regular movie theatres but *would* go to newsreel shows. So I opened the theatre as a one hour news format and this market supported it until the war ended."

Newsreel theatres satisfied the public's craving for information from the front and held the promise of a possible glimpse of a loved one. This Trans-Lux twin theatre, at 49th and Broadway, New York City, showed newsreels in one auditorium and short subjects in the other. *Richard Brandt*

The Blaine Theatre in Henryetta, Oklahoma supported the war effort. *Roger Rice*

The Newsreel Theatre in New York's Rockefeller Center. *Theatre Historical Society*

By 1950 many newsreel theatres had closed. The nation's postwar shift to the suburbs had robbed downtown theatres of the audiences they needed throughout the day. More significant was the encroaching growth of television news and televised sports. The newsreel theatres that survived often did so by converting to art house programming.

While Americans insisted on keeping abreast of news from the front and around the world, the American mainland never suffered the direct consequences of war. The public, however, remained braced for imminent attack. Along with rationing and air-raid drills, brownouts became a part of everyday life. "The theatres were 'browned-out' every night," recalled Lippe. "In other words, instead of seeing the lights of Broadway, all the lights were turned off. Under the marquees, there were usually great floodlights and bulbs of lights and what have you. During the war you were only allowed three or four lights under the marquees, but there was no overt lighting at all."

But even the browned-out marquees attracted throngs of moviegoers.

Hollywood's wartime films mixed welcome escapist fare with patriotic stories that helped rally support for the war. The public increasingly turned to movie theatres for a welcome retreat and a source of encouragement during a time of national crisis. Movie attendance during the war years grew to record levels.

"It's Over!" V-E Day in Norfolk, Virginia. *Virginia Historical Society*

Trans-Lux newsreel theatre, New York City, New York. *Theatre Historical Society*

Interior of Trans-Lux newsreel theatre, 58th Street and Madison Avenue, New York City, New York. *Richard Brandt*

Chapter 9

SATURDAY KID SHOWS

For many children Saturday morning often meant the start of a cherished day-long adventure at the movies. The weekend might begin with a check of the piggy bank for nickels or a search for soda bottle caps often good for admission during special soft drink promotions. In any event it meant making quick work of any household chores that needed to be done before joining the rest of the neighborhood kids at the local movie theatre. Best of all it meant sharing the adventures of such popular screen heroes as Tarzan, Hopalong Cassidy and Flash Gordon.

Saturday movie clubs, children's matinees and variously-named kiddie shows became a staple of theatre programming in moviehouses across the country. Evoking something not unlike a giant tribal rite, neighborhood theatres allowed countless numbers of children to give full vent to their youthful enthusiasm as they laid claim to the theatres as their very own clubhouse for the day.

The programs were popular with theatre managers who saw the chance to utilize a few of their theatre's off-hours for a profitable weekly enterprise. "We used

to buy pictures flat rental for Saturdays," explained Georgia-based circuit owner Carl Patrick. "Back then we charged nine cents for kids and 35 cents for grown ups. You'd pay 30 dollars for two pictures and take in $1,000 at the box office. It was only on Saturday that you could do that. The rest of the week, your grosses

Cowboys and horses appeared onstage during children's matinees across the country. *Elliot Cohen*

Clutching small change, a horde of neighborhood children, jockeyed for position at the candy counter. *Elliot Cohen*

There was no doubt when it was time for the Saturday Matinee at the Rahway Theatre, Rahway, New Jersey. *Elliot Cohen*

Warners Regent Theatre in Newark, New Jersey, sponsored five weeks of prizes galore. *Elliot Cohen*

Free collie pup to the lucky winner helped promote a theatre's "Lucky Dog" cartoon program. *Chuc Barnes*

Tom Sawyer look-alike contest at the Rialto Theatre, Phoenix, Arizona. *George Aurelius*

Exhibitors Otto and Sophie Settele surrounded by eager Saturday matinee film fans. *Otto Settele*

were way down."

Even as they generated enormous profits, Saturday matinees also served an even more important purpose: the weekly pilgrimage to the theatre was grooming a new generation of movie fans. Children who had fun at the movies could be expected to maintain their movie-going habits as adults.

For children, the coming Saturday at the movies gave shape to the entire week. It was the focus of growing anticipation and excitement as the school week

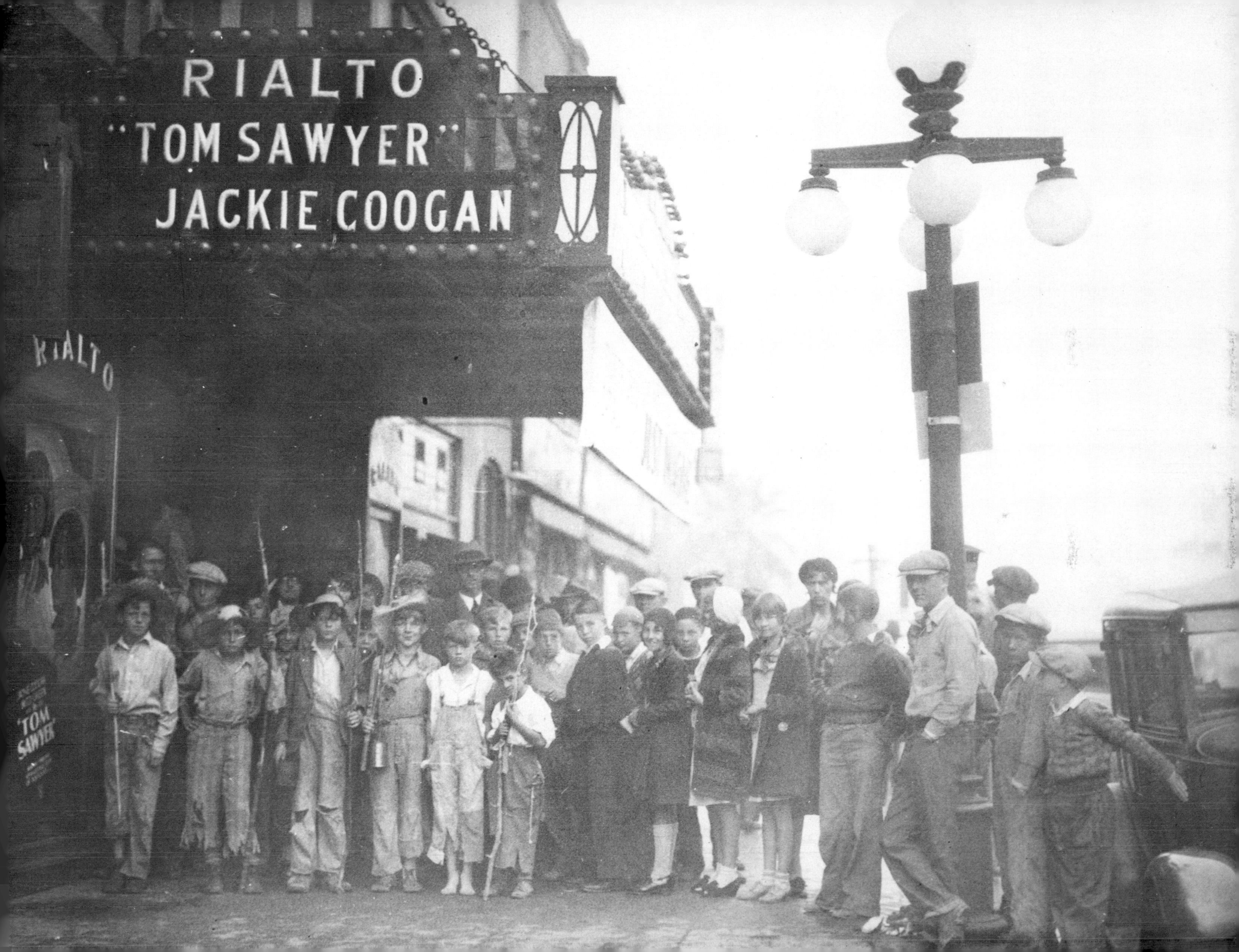
RIALTO
"TOM SAWYER"
JACKIE COOGAN
RIALTO
"TOM SAWYER"

ground to an end. As any member of an older generation still young at heart can remember, it was simply one of the best times a kid could have.

Children's shows proved enormously popular with kids, parents and even theatre managers. On Saturday mornings theatre managers transformed themselves into masters of ceremonies, climbing the theatre stage to face packed auditoriums full of giggly, squirming, rambunctious children. Rising to the occasion, the seasoned theatre manager would often take to the microphone like an accomplished nightclub pro, alternately stoking the kids' excitement and attempting to subdue their youthful enthusiasm. Theatres often opened the program with the Pledge of Allegiance. Those with organized movie clubs might feature a reading of the club's credo or messages from elected officers.

The main point, however, was the show itself: a full program of cartoons, short subjects, newsreels and a feature. As the house lights dimmed and the curtains parted, an audience of children soon fell under the magic of the silver screen. Young cowpokes rode the range with their cowboy heroes Ken Maynard, Tom Mix, William S. Hart and Hopalong Cassidy. When it was time to laugh, nothing could be funnier than the antics of Buster Keaton, Laurel and Hardy, and the beloved members of "Our Gang." The "Bowery Boys" and the "Dead End Kids" brought images of tough New York street life to the nation's more rural areas, and Dick Tracy, with his amazing two-way wrist radio, waged war with the meanest crime bosses. "People loved serials," remembered Virginia theatre owner Jerry Gordon. "They were very popular. You'd have the movie and you'd have a serial. It ran about 20 minutes, 'The Perils

of Pauline' and different things. It would end up in such a way that the hero or heroine couldn't possibly live, so you'd have to come back the next Saturday to find out what happened, and they'd get out of it somehow or other and go into another adventure. They'd run about 10 or 12 weeks and then you'd start a new serial. It was very popular."

Veteran theatre managers recall the distinctive nature of kiddie shows. Some describe intermission's mad race of children up the aisles to the rest rooms, or their dash to be first in line at the drinking fountain, the kids sounding for all the world like a herd of thundering shetland ponies. Enthusiastic youngsters would replay the just-completed screen action, brandishing cap pistols while staging an ambush behind theatre seats.

Many theatres added live entertainment for kiddie shows, ranging from singers to magic acts, talent shows,

Amateur magic tricks delighted young audiences at the Saturday matinee. *Elliot Cohen*

Every kid in town showed up for the Christmas Show in Orville, Oklahoma. *Leonard Mishkind*

contests and prize drawings. A street parade might be called to herald a personal appearance by a star or as sure-fire ballyhoo for an upcoming feature.

Children's programs always meant good business at the snack bar. As an integral part of the moviegoing experience, young moviegoers could be counted on to buy their weight in popcorn, grape drink, licorice, and Milk Duds. As frantic theatre employees can attest, it was not unusual to see long lines of boisterous youngsters, eager to spend their allowance money on treasures from the concession stand.

Saturday at the movies provided long hours of good, clean, escapist fun and it also served as a kind of moral schoolhouse for developing young minds. The movies carried powerful assurances that crime didn't pay, that the good guys always won, and that even in the depths of personal calamity rescue was just around the corner

— even in outer space (Just ask Flash Gordon).

Perhaps most exciting of all, the movies showed that there was a whole wide world beyond Main Street, wherever a child's Main Street happened to be. "The theatre was showing 'the Mikado,'" recalled veteran Mountain States exhibitor Ross Campbell. "I was still an usher and I said, 'Do you mean I've got to handle 500 kids through an operetta?' It was the original version, and I just dreaded that day. And do you know that we ran that whole movie, and the kids were so fascinated we didn't even hear any noise."

Saturday at the movies showed there could be more: more adventure, more excitement — and more problems to be sure, but problems that always had solutions. Saturday matinees offered a safe haven of fun and a chance to learn all about life; those matinees spawned many a dream about new horizons.

"Robinson Crusoe in person!" Actor Dan O'Herlihy at the world premiere held at the Palms Theatre, Phoenix, Arizona. *George Aurelius*

The Paramount Theatre, Oakland, California's leading downtown movie palace, hosted a special kids show, 1959. *Jack Tillmany*

Annual Kiddie Show, Rialto Theatre, Phoenix, Arizona. *George Aurelius*

Chapter 10

FILM BUYING AND BOOKING

"The distributor's trying to sell it and the exhibitor's trying to buy it. You try to cut down all the trees in between that are creating the problem." — M.W. "Bud" Saffle on film buying.

Whether attending a mega-multiplex, a drive-in or a surviving single-screen theatre, the moviegoer has only to purchase a ticket to enjoy the distinctive shared pleasure that is "going to the movies." Behind the scenes, however, is the business side of exhibition and the story of how a picture makes the journey from the distributor to the screen. The process known as "film buying and booking" has undergone fundamental change over the 100-year history of motion picture theatres. And that process determines what pictures are playing at the neighborhood cinema tonight.

In the earliest years of the film industry, moving pictures were purchased outright by the foot. Individual pictures lasted less than 30 seconds and, despite a wide variety of subject matter, they were considered of equal value like so many feet of fabric, drapery or carpeting. Film manufacturers sold their "products" directly to exhibitors who assembled collections of short films to create moving picture programs of 15 to 20 minutes in length. These were played over and over again to the delight of early audiences. But, like yesterday's news, the novelty of moving strips of film soon wore off and soon

became useless inventory. The exhibitor was forced to continually replenish his stock of "fresh" films to hold the audience's interest. Moving pictures were priced at an average of 10 to 12 cents a foot, with tinted or hand-painted films costing much more. With projection speeds running from 60 to 120 feet per minute, the exhibitor's film costs could run as high as $120 for a mere 10 minutes of programming.

The expense of buying films that soon became outdated slowed the early growth of the motion picture industry. Although illegal, exhibitors soon began swapping films among themselves as a way to hold costs down while still introducing constant variety to their programming. It was a haphazard system at best that was resolved with the formation of formal film exchanges in 1903. Film exchanges introduced a system of renting films for less than the cost of purchase, thus establishing distribution as a separate business apart from either production or exhibition.

During the time when popular "story" films developed from three to eight minutes or longer in length, the exchange system helped to keep film costs affordable.

Standard film booking contract of the 1920s. *Bill Stembler*

Double features drew a crowd at the Chakeres Warner Fairbanks Theatre, Springfield, Ohio. *Michael Chakeres*

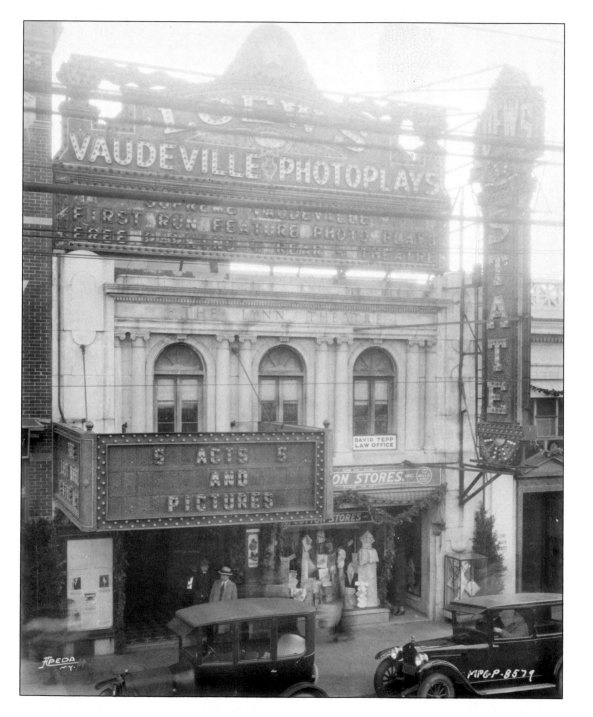

The system of film rental remains to the present day, although in industry parlance it is still referred to as "buying" film.

Competing among themselves for a manufacturer's product, film exchanges sought exclusive access to a producer's films. In the days before national distribution organizations, a system called "states rights" distribution emerged. An independent producer would lease the rights to a film to independent exchanges in each territory of the country, typically by state. The states rights distributor would then promote the film, and those of other independent producers, to exhibitors.

The states rights system of distribution had its drawbacks for producers. First, exchanges that were operated by exhibitors would not aggressively promote films to competitive theatres. Secondly, the exchanges, representing films from several producers, could not give priority attention to any one film. And third, when films were leased to exchanges on a percentage basis, distributors were always suspicious that exchanges under-reported rentals, or cheated them by "bicycling" a print to unlicensed exhibitors and keeping the rental fee. The term "bicycling," or "railroading," refers to the actual method of distributing prints to an unlicensed exhibitor.

In the 20th century's second decade extended-length feature films of two or more reels prompted exhibitors to start running longer programs in larger theatres. Soon after, American distributors would introduce audiences to the "spectacle" film of eight or more reels and one to two hours in length. Early pioneers of feature films inaugurated the "roadshow" form of distribution for these specialty pictures. Similar to the road companies of legitimate theatre productions, a roadshow picture was a special event booked into large, legitimate theatres for extended periods of time at higher-than-usual ticket prices. The first roadshow pictures were licensed with 10 percent of the gross going to the distributor.

As the popularity and length of feature films grew, producers looked for a faster way to recoup their investment as well as a way to make more features for an enthusiastic public. After Adolph Zukor established himself as the leading producer of feature films, he merged with competing production companies and Paramount Pictures, the first national distribution company, to form Paramount Pictures, Inc. Zukor transformed film distribution with a system known as "block booking." Simply put, an exhibitor who wanted to rent the best feature films with the biggest stars also had to agree to rent up to a year's worth of the studio's lesser pictures. It was an all-or-nothing proposition. Other producers adopted the block booking system to be sure of a market for their films.

Production companies first tried to compete with each other by monopolizing star talent. Studios that held the services of Mary Pickford, Douglas Fairbanks or Charlie Chaplin were assured land-office business with theatres. When competition for stars set off bidding wars and skyrocketing contract terms, the leading stars recognized the extraordinary value of their names on the marquees and proceeded to set up their own distribution companies. United Artists was formed to control the financial destinies of Pickford, Douglas, Chaplin and the famed director D. W. Griffith. When producers lost the leverage of having these leading stars under exclusive contract, they began to exert control over the film industry by buying theatres.

The system of block booking continued as a way of insuring a steady return of profits from theatres to finance continued feature film production. In 1921 the Federal Trade Commission filed suit against Paramount for restraint of trade and unfair business practices.

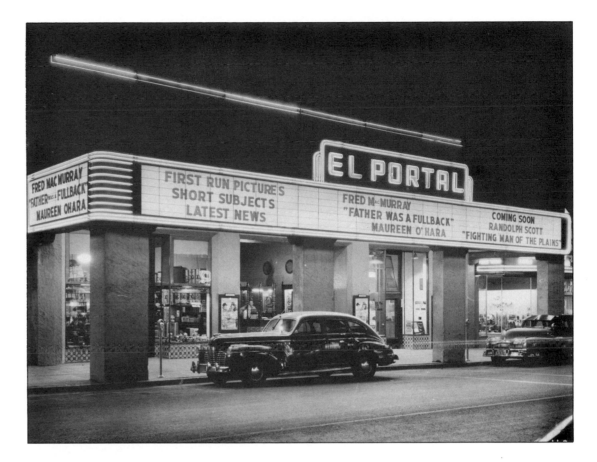

Block booking was banned along with other unfair business practices although the ban was overturned by the U.S. Circuit Court of Appeals in 1932. The major studios continued the practice of block booking until 1948, when the Supreme Court outlawed the system for good.

For audiences at America's first-run and second-run theatres, block booking meant a steady diet of films from Hollywood's leading studios. By "buying" pictures sight unseen, theatre owners were assured of a certain number of quality pictures mixed with more mediocre fare. Theatre managers and bookers bargained as best they

Marquee at the El Portal Theatre promised audiences a full evening of entertainment and news. *Wagner Zip-Change Inc.*

Loews State Theatre, in White Plains, New York featured movies and five acts of vaudeville. *Bernard Diamond*

could, seeking a guarantee of so many "Gables" or "Crawfords," top films with top stars. These "A films" were rented for a percentage of the total box office gross. "B films" were rented for a flat fee.

Unlike today, many movie theatres during the 1920s, '30s and '40s changed pictures two or more times a week. This meant a change in the feature film as well as its full complement of cartoons, newsreels and short subjects. The advent of double features during the Depression years effectively doubled a theatre's film requirements. With single bills alone, theatres needed access to a minimum of 100 pictures a year, more than any individual studio produced. Exhibitors of the era, therefore, had to negotiate block booking arrangements with at least two different studios. Happily for the film fan, theatres were awash with movies, movies and more movies!

"Many theatres played two shows a week," explained veteran Boston-based exhibitor Malcolm Green. "They would play a Sunday-Monday-Tuesday change and a Wednesday-through-Saturday change. Strange as it sounds today, the strongest day of the week was Sunday. You only had three days on that change but you did have the strongest day. And Wednesday to Saturday was the second best. Now that would vary from town to town; everybody had different patterns. There were patterns where there was a Sunday-Monday change, a Tuesday-Thursday change and a Friday-Saturday change."

A theatre running a double bill with three changes a week required an extraordinary 300 films a year to fill its screen. "In those days, you had relationships with companies where you had a commitment for all their product," remembers veteran East Coast exhibitor Bernard Myerson. "It was like a franchise, which you can't have today. You sat down for a day or two days or three days with the sales people at the film companies and worked your deals out for the year. So that if you agreed to play six pictures on percentage, of the six you would pay 40 percent for two, 30 percent for two, and 25 percent for two. The film company had the choice of naming the six pictures and the rest of them were bought flat. Some of the titles were just titles, they hadn't even started the pictures, but we knew what the cast was, and the director and the producer. That's important. If Columbia sold us their product for a year, which they did, we knew Frank Capra was going to make four pictures. We knew we had four good pictures."

"We would screen pictures but not before we bought the annual product," remembers long-time New York-based exhibitor Bernard Diamond. "We went by press notices, by the books, by the brochures. Usually you left yourself a cancellation privilege of a certain amount. It was a completely different form of buying. You would have so many pictures at percentage, so many pictures flat. If the company misjudged the picture you would make a killing."

Knowing a year's slate of film titles was one decided advantage of block booking films. Theatre managers had ample time to plan elaborate promotional campaigns for each picture. The results of that planning could be seen in the lobby displays, "frame jobs" and publicity stunts that were the hallmark of movie theatres everywhere. Distinctive facades and neon-lit marquees typically made the hometown cinema the most prominent building in town. When operated by an enterprising showman, the theatre was the community's centerpiece for excitement. "Theatre managers, they were the unofficial mayors of Main Street. That's where all the action was. They were king of the heap," enthused Maryland-based circuit owner Paul Roth. "They dealt with the great world of entertainment and

la-la land. Bright lights and movie stars, the whole works."

The practice of block booking went hand-in-hand with a staggered release pattern that ranked all theatres in the country. Theatres were designated "first-run" or "second-run," down to "fifth-run" or lower in the nation's largest cities. The system assured the studios that their affiliated theatres received the latest Hollywood films before the competition.

Studio ownership of theatres accelerated following the unqualified success of the talkies. With immense profits in hand, the leading studios went on an extended theatre buying-spree. As a result, the nation's largest

Two shows for the price of one, at the Mecca Theatre, Enid, Oklahoma. *Roger Rice*

A double feature at the Orpheum Theatre. *Eric Levin*

highest tickets prices to see the best films first. Other theatres were ranked in the order in which they received the film after its release, from second-run to third- or fourth-run or lower. Any theatre other than a first-run theatre was also often referred to as a "subsequent-run" or "sub-run" theatre, terms that survive in the industry today. Ticket prices fell at each level of the run system.

The studios protected the run status of a theatre by giving it the exclusive right to a film within a certain run and within a specific zone or territory. To minimize competition between runs, meaning to keep most patrons from waiting to see a picture at a cheaper price, the studios fixed a certain lag time or "clearance" period between runs. An individual clearance period could range from 14 to 42 days or longer. The major studios

regional theatre circuits came under control of the Big Five — Fox, Warners, Loews/MGM, Paramount and RKO. The majors controlled the majority of first-run theatres in 92 of the largest cities in the country, and thus controlled the majority of industry profits. Independent, non-affiliated theatres were forced to submit to the rigid exhibition policies of the studios or risked losing access to Hollywood's top films.

The studios guaranteed themselves the largest share of profits from any individual picture through what is called a run-clearance system of distribution and exhibition. A first-run theatre was first in line to receive a studio's newest releases with top stars. In exchange for this favored position, first-run theatres paid the highest film rental. Similarly, patrons of these theatres paid the

cooperated with each other to designate runs, zones and clearances for theatres in all cities and towns in the country. Depending on a theatre's imposed ranking, an exasperated independent theatre owner might have to wait anywhere from a month, or in big cities up to a year, before he could offer his patrons the "latest" from Hollywood.

Independent, subsequent-run theatres that did not have access to the leading studios' films turned to independent producers for a reliable stream of lower-cost "B movies." Studios such as Republic and Monogram turned out a constant flow of westerns and gangster pictures. These films found a welcome home in the nation's "grind houses," theatres with a low admission price that treated patrons to continuous showings of action films and exploitation fare. "A grind house is a house that would open up at 10 o'clock in the morning," recalled veteran Wyoming theatre owner Ross Campbell, "and the admission from 10 to five was 15 cents and then it went up to a quarter. It would operate till about one o'clock in the morning running double bills just continuously. That was the last place you could see a movie. If you missed it all over town, you could go there."

Exhibitors needing to book independent films found a varied selection of films produced in the broadly-defined "exploitation" genre. Exploitation has been a niche market for filmmakers since the arrival of the slightly-risque moving pictures that were produced for early peepshow parlors. The 1940s saw the emergence of so-called "educational" or "hygiene" films that were thinly-disguised attempts to introduce sexual themes to a conservative mainstream audience. "Mom and Dad" was a low-budget morality play about the dangers of pre-marital sex. It contained what was considered at the time to be sensational footage of the birth of a baby.

The Mecca Theatre changed its film program three times a week. Stillwater, Oklahoma. *Roger Rice*

Truth in advertising at Oakland's Rialto Theatre, 1943. *Jack Tillmany*

Distributor Howard W. "Kroger" Babb took the film from town to town as an exploitation roadshow and sold "marriage manuals" during intermission. Some theatres offered the film at gender-segregated showings as a way to bolster its "shocking" appeal. It was not uncommon for theatre managers to enlist the services of a nurse, or someone merely dressed like a nurse, and station her prominently in the lobby, supposedly so that she could attend to the faint of heart. An ambulance parked out front was another familiar promotional ploy. Such was the lot of independent theatre owners unable to obtain "A" product. Or, at least, such was their lot prior to 1948.

By far the most significant changes to visit the history of film buying and booking came with the 1948 Supreme Court-issued "Paramount Decrees," which banned block booking and other unfair trade practices

in the motion picture industry. Distributors now had to offer their films for rent on a picture-by-picture, theatre-by-theatre basis. The court's prohibition against unreasonable clearances led to an abbreviated system of first-runs, neighborhood-suburban-runs and drive-in-runs, although drive-in theatres were later upgraded to play simultaneously with downtown and suburban theatres. Film industry historian Tino Balio has compared a movie's release patterns to those of other consumer goods — first, the exclusive shops; next, the general department stores; and, finally, the close-out sales.

The decisions and resulting consent judgements in the Paramount case transformed the patterns as well as the methods of movie releases. Required to relinquish control of their affiliated theatres, the studios no longer had the same incentive to maintain a steady flow of product throughout the year to keep the nation's screens full. "When you took away the film company's ownership of theatres," noted Georgia-based exhibition veteran John Stembler, "they lost one of the motives for making pictures, which was to supply their theatres." When the emphasis shifted to the marketing of individual film titles, the Hollywood majors made fewer, more expensive films that could stand on their own merit. The wide-screen, epic pictures of the 1950s were rented on a percentage basis. In order to maximize their profit potentials, the studios began to release a disproportionate number of their films during those periods when audience attendance was highest, namely the Christmas holiday period and during the summer.

Premium films were first released to select theatres in major markets for extended runs after which they eventually went into wide release. The most prestigious films were the "roadshows," those high-profile, star-filled pictures that played exclusively in one theatre in each major market. Roadshow pictures were typically scheduled for just two showings a day and featured both reserved seating and higher ticket prices. Sometimes lasting three hours or longer, roadshows usually played with an intermission. The films were typically shortened for their general release so that heartland exhibitors could present at least two shows each evening.

Hollywood studios released as many as six roadshow films a year during the 1960s. Exhibitors faced the highest rental terms to date for roadshows during this period, with standard terms calling for 90 percent of gross ticket sales to be returned to the distributor, after the deduction of agreed-upon expenses referred to as "the house nut."

A roadshow picture was usually launched in Los Angeles and New York and later released in other cities throughout the country. "The roadshows were valuable to distributors because it was in their best interests to have the feature play for as long a period of time as possible," explained Green. "They could have a road-show-run which ran for more than a normal length of run in any town. There would be a hiatus of maybe six months and then there would be a run at regular prices. And after that it would start its regular run through the subsequent-runs in the smaller towns and so forth." Some exhibitors, however, were wary of roadshows. "They were good but we weren't always that hot for roadshows because of the terms," remembered Georgia-based circuit owner Carl Patrick. "We always were worried about the precedent we would set for the next picture." This concern proved justified. In time, distributors would come to attach the 90/10 roadshow split of profits to all prestige pictures.

Higher film rentals meant higher ticket prices for patrons during the early television era, when theatres were struggling to stem the erosion of their audience. During the late 1960s and early '70s the film industry

Theatres of an earlier era played movies continuously during operating hours. Kermit Theatre, Kermit, Texas. *Roger Rice*

Richmond's Broadway Theatre had men and women attend separate showings of "Some Wild Oats" due to the film's "strong graphic lecture on questions of social hygiene." Children under 16 were not admitted. *Virginia Historical Society*

ation of a tradition that harkened back to the nickelodeon days, when exhibitors like William Fox and Marcus Loew also entered production to guarantee a steady supply of pictures for their theatres. A key difference some 60 years later was the enormous capital required to finance even a modest production.

Two of the most ambitious new production concerns were the Exhibitors Production and Distribution Cooperative (EXPRODICO), which was supported with funds and publicity by the National Association of Theatre Owners, and the Theatre Owners Film Cooperative (TOFCO). Both organizations ultimately failed, however, due to inadequate financing. Acting independently, a number of large theatre circuits and wealthy exhibitors — including General Cinema, United Artists Theatres, Mann Theatres, Metropolitan Theatres head Sherrill Corwin, and Plitt circuit chief Henry Plitt — successfully completed a number of pictures, but their efforts generated nowhere near the number of movies required to meet the needs of the nation's

entered a phase of mergers with corporate conglomerates. The studios thus became part of giant business enterprises that also operated insurance companies, parking lots, record companies and music publishers. Profits were the corporate goal and cost-cutting became the order of the day, so the studios found themselves making drastic cutbacks in production and shifting their emphasis to film distribution.

Facing the severest product shortage yet, exhibition waged a determined campaign to encourage new sources of production. Theatre owners embraced a growing number of foreign films, they contributed to the American Film Institute's student training programs and they supported the efforts of former studio-affiliated theatre circuits to enter production. They also rallied to raise money to produce films themselves in a continu-

picture-starved theatres. (Of all the exhibitors making films during this period only Corwin could claim credit for delivering a certified box office hit; he played a major role in producing "The Poseidon Adventure," one of the biggest moneymakers of 1972.) The severe shortage of top-rated films created a classic seller's market that allowed distributors to set stiff terms for theatres seeking to rent their pictures.

During this turbulent period, theatre owners faced the added challenge of blind bidding. Blind bidding required an exhibitor to formally bid for the right to show a film before the exhibitor ever had a chance to see it. The practice of buying a film sight unseen goes back as far as the mail-order exchange business that served nickelodeons in the early 1900s. The later system of block booking films, which began with the advent of feature films, also involved contracting for films without a prior screening. The practice had been outlawed by the courts in 1940 as part of the temporary consent decree rendered in the Justice Department's original anti-trust case against the major studios. However, the prohibition against blind bidding was not included in the final judgement of the *United States v. Paramount et al.* case in 1948 because the practice was not in use at the time. The later use of blind bidding was much more onerous to exhibitors because of the very high film terms that were prevalent at that time.

Distributors were "selling" their films this way in large part because the escalating costs of filmmaking were often matched by the high costs of film advertising and promotion. Distributors were now launching national advertising campaigns on TV, reaching millions with word of the latest "must see" film. The high costs of television advertising triggered a shift to wide release patterns. With wide releases, studios could take immediate advantage of the public's TV-heightened aware-ness of a film. This form of releasing films was more expensive for distributors, who had to produce hundreds of extra film prints. With costs going up all around, distributors turned to blind bidding and hefty cash advances to secure additional financing to underwrite a picture's expensive production and promotion.

Decrying the practice of blind bidding as "buying a

pig in a poke," exhibitors complained that they were forced to blind bid because of the era's film shortage. If they resisted the practice, they would end up without the necessary major releases required for their screens. Given only a brief script summary and the names of the producer, director and cast, exhibitors found themselves risking huge sums in cash advances and minimum guarantees bidding against each other for the chance to

Exploitation film, "Devil's Harvest," purported to be an expose of the marijuana racket. Gaiety Theatre, Oklahoma City, Oklahoma. *Roger Rice*

exhibit a picture. When pictures fared poorly at the box office, theatre owners were left with the losses. Exhibitors complained that blind bidding was similar to a car dealer asking a customer to buy an expensive car without a test drive and without seeing it. A brochure might be provided listing the car's engine specifications and some fancy prose on its road-handling ability, but there was no photograph or clear indication of just what the buyer was getting. On top of that, the customer was required to make a sizeable, non-refundable down payment. Distributors, on the other hand, claimed the system was a fair way to share the risks of filmmaking. They also argued that they needed to guarantee advance play dates for their pictures, often before the films went into production, to secure financing.

In the late 1970s the National Association of Theatre Owners launched an aggressive campaign to legislatively outlaw the practice of blind bidding. Facing a formidable foe in the Motion Picture Association of America, whose president Jack Valenti had strong ties in Washington, NATO decided not to seek a federal ban. Instead the exhibitor organization under the leadership of then-president A. Alan Friedberg decided to take the fight to the grass-roots level, where the influence of its members was strongest. NATO drafted a model bill that outlawed blind bidding and assisted its members with passage at the state level. The costly campaign, waged state-by-state, was an enormous success. By September 1982, 24 states as well as the territory of Puerto Rico had enacted anti blind bidding legislation. With almost half of the states having banned blind bidding, distributors largely dropped the practice.

Even with the elimination of blind bidding, exhibitors still faced difficult film rental terms in the form of guarantees, advances and extended playing time. While few members of the moviegoing public might have an interest in how films are licensed, the effects show up in every theatre. Higher film rentals result in higher ticket prices and even higher prices for concessions.

As stated above, up to 90 percent of a theatre's box office gross (after deduction of the house nut) is returned to the distributor during the first weeks of a picture's release. The distributor's percentage decreases the longer a picture plays. A distributor can also seek minimum terms that include cash advances and guarantees. A guarantee is an upfront cash payment against film rentals to be earned by a picture. If a film does poorly, the exhibitor loses the guarantee. An advance, on the other hand, is different. If a film fails to earn back the amount of a cash advance, the distributor owes this amount to the exhibitor. A theatre often must also guarantee a certain number of weeks of playing time for a film without regard to the film's success.

Lacking a seal of approval from the Production Code, films such as "Child Bride" did not play the conventional theatres catering to mainstream audiences, but found a niche in the so-called exploitation houses of the big city. *Jack Tillmany*

"A Child is Born" exploitation film, Freeport Theatre, Freeport, Texas. *Alvin Svoboda*

A distributor's insistence on extended runs underscores the importance of the modern multiplex. A multiplex operation can put a hit picture in its largest auditorium or feature it on more than one screen, satisfying the crowds that flock to see it. On the other hand, the multiplex operator also has the option of moving a poorly-performing picture to a small theatre to play out its contract, freeing up the larger auditoriums for the next crop of new releases. Industry veteran Joel Resnick recalled that during the early days of twin theatres distributors didn't know what to make of them. The distributors, said Resnick, would say things like, "People aren't going to go to the movies like that. They are going to want to go to the old-fashioned theatres which they're used to, with 1,000 seats. Here you are only offering 250 seats or 300 seats in the theatre and you can't do

Triple bill at San Francisco's Pix Theatre. *Jack Tillmany*

any business.

"It was very hard convincing people in the beginning to accept the fact that these were anything but secondary sub-run theatres that should play behind all the big old exclusive theatres," remembers Resnick. "You had to get the distributor to understand that these multiplex theatres could do business, that even though you had much less seats in those theatres, you could do a lot of business with them by playing a picture on more than one screen if necessary. The concept of taking the theatre to a person's backyard — that he didn't have to drive 20 miles to go to a movie or 15 miles, he could do it driving two or three miles — means he would go more often."

High film terms rise even higher in a competitive bidding situation; that is, where two or more theatres in the same area or zone want the same picture. In order to avoid competitive bidding, exhibitors devised a strategy that decided in advance which theatre would exclusively negotiate for the right to exhibit a given picture. The practice was called "product splitting" and it worked in a number of ways. Some exhibitors divided films by distributor. In some instances exhibitors would divide them on a film-by-film basis. "So we would sit down and make an agreement and we would split the pictures," explained Pennsylvania-based circuit owner Ted Manos. "And the way that we would split them was very fair. For instance, if there were 10 pictures available at a certain time, I would split those and put five on each side. But I would try to balance them fairly because *you* would have the choice of which pictures you wanted, you see what I mean?"

Given that the ratio of hit films to losers stays about the same over time, one theatre might choose by lot to negotiate for all of Paramount's films, while a second theatre would exclusively negotiate for Universal's product. In another variation, exhibitors would draw lots to determine who got the first choice of upcoming pictures. Or exhibitors might pour over the list of all upcoming new releases and decide which movies each will show. Manos said exhibitors would choose "by the stars and by the synopsis of the story, and by who made the picture and who produced the picture and so on and so forth. You had a fair idea. Nobody can tell what a picture's going to do. The only people that know what a picture is going to do are the patrons. The public is the one that decides that."

Split agreements had been in use for decades. Splits became especially prevalent after the 1948 Supreme Court decision that outlawed block booking. During the mid-1970s, distributors began to complain that product splits were a form of price fixing. Exhibition felt sure that they were within the law as they had relied on statements made by representatives of the Department of Justice that indicated that product splits were lawful as long as all exhibitors were allowed to participate and distributors acquiesced in the practice. Various court decisions also upheld the practice.

It therefore came as a bombshell in 1977 when the Justice Department issued a statement that it considered product splitting a "per se" violation of the anti-trust laws and warned exhibitors that they would face *criminal* prosecution if they continued the practice. After several test cases that resulted in different results, the courts ultimately upheld the Department of Justice's position, and product splitting by exhibitors was abandoned as a way to buy film.

"The relationship between exhibition and distribution has always been one of love and hate. Exhibitors love distributors for the wonderful films they provide, but they hate the fact they are forced to pay for those films. The issue of buying and selling film will always

be one of contention between exhibition and distribution, as it really involves who is going to get what share of the box office pie. Fortunately, in the recent past, exhibition and distribution have learned to work together to see how to enlarge the entire pie. Then the argument can begin over how to split it," concluded NATO president William F. Kartozian.

San Francisco's quintessential "grind house" the Strand, boasted "top entertainment at bottom prices." *Jack Tillmany*

Chapter 11

IN THE EYE OF THE BEHOLDER

Ever since the days of the peepshow, social reformers have targeted moving pictures as a menace to public morality. In 1894, the operator of an Atlantic City kinetoscope parlor caused an uproar with a film of an exotic dancer who bared an ankle or two. With a title more scandalous than anything seen through the viewer, "Dolorita and the Passion Dance" was promptly pulled to avoid a confrontation with local authorities. In 1896, Edison's release of "The May Irwin Kiss," the screen's first close-up of an amorous encounter, drew a storm of protest. 1897 marked the first court action involving a moving picture when a New York judge banned "Orange Blossoms" for showing a bride preparing to disrobe on her wedding night. Moviegoers were thus spared the barest glimpse of flesh in a film the judge decried as "an outrage on public decency."

Censorship became more organized in the nickelodeon days. Theatre attendance was booming and it became impossible to ignore the huge social impact of movies. Social reformers, the clergy and various pressure groups became alarmed and argued that the content of movies had to be controlled for the public good.

The first municipal censorship law in the country was passed in Chicago in 1907. It required police inspection and licensing of all films shown in that city. The police chief was empowered to withhold a permit if he judged a film to be "immoral" or "obscene." The following year the mayor of New York, under pressure from Protestant churches, temporarily shut down the city's 550 nickelodeons, ostensibly for safety inspections.

In 1909 10 New York State civic organizations sponsored a citizens' film evaluation group to evaluate films that became known as the National Board of Censorship and later, the National Board of Review. The organization was initially formed to discourage official censorship of motion pictures and gained the support of many exhibitors who wanted to blunt the hostility of reform groups and limit the danger of legal action and the threatened loss of licenses. The board succeeded in enlisting the cooperation of the powerful Motion Picture Patents Company and a few independent producers who agreed to submit their films for advance review so any offensive footage could be cut before release. The board objected to gratuitous acts of

Since the the "X" rating was not copyrighted, some distributors of exploitation films used the letter's association with explicit sex as a way to attract audiences. *Allen Michaan*

Edison's 1896 release of "The May Irwin Kiss" was the screen's first amorous encounter and it drew a storm of protest. *Academy of Motion Picture Arts and Sciences*

crime or violence, indecency, immoral behavior or the mere suggestions of them. The National Board of Review issued a seal of approval which consisted of the words "Passed by the National Board of Review" which would appear in the picture's main titles. The influence of the board's approvals lessened with the creation of a growing number of local censorship boards.

During the early teens, efforts at government control over movies moved from the city halls to the statehouses. Pennsylvania became the first state to approve a film censorship law (1911), followed by Ohio and Kansas (1913), Maryland (1916), New York and Florida (1921), Virginia and Massachusetts (1922), Connecticut (1925), and Louisiana (1935). As early as 1915 an attempt was made to pass a federal censorship law but the effort failed. There were numerous prohibitions against obscenity between 1912 and 1940. A federal statute banned interstate trade in any film containing a prize fight — a law that had its origins in the racial violence that was stirred by the 1909 Jeffries-Johnson fight.

During the 1920s the motion picture industry took its first steps to monitor itself after a series of highly publicized scandals involving major Hollywood personalities rocked the nation. The scandals reinforced the public's negative image of Hollywood as an unseemly land of high living and loose morals. The public outcry over perceived off-screen and on-screen immorality convinced filmmakers that some form of government control was imminent. The motion picture community moved swiftly to forestall any efforts toward federal censorship. In 1922, in an effort to curb the worst abuses, the industry formed the Motion Picture Producers and Distributors Association (MPPDA). Hollywood tapped Will H. Hays, the widely-respected former chairman of the Republican National Committee who served as the postmaster general during President Harding's admini-

stration, to head the watchdog organization and restore public confidence in the movie industry.

The Hays Organization, as it came to be known, experimented with a series of voluntary guidelines that comprised a form of self-censorship. In 1924, it asked members to submit a summary of any proposed films for review in order to receive advance guidance about possible objections that might arise. A stricter code enacted in 1927 identified a list of 11 "don'ts" and 26 "be carefuls" for producers to follow. Despite these industry attempts at self-restraint, the guidelines were strictly voluntary and widely ignored. During the early 1930s, the MPPDA faced increasing public pressure to adopt a formal code of self-censorship. In 1934, the National Legion of Decency was created and threatened a nationwide crusade against immoral films. The darkest hour came when Catholics in Philadelphia boycotted all theatres and enlisted widespread public sympathy to its cause. Faced with the potential threat of a nationwide boycott movement supported by millions of citizens, Hollywood took the issue of film content seriously.

In 1934, working under the guidance of Martin Quigley, Motion Picture Herald publisher and leading Catholic layman, and Jesuit professor Daniel A. Lord, the motion picture industry adopted the mandatory Production Code that covered production, advertising and exhibition. Administered by the Production Code Administration, the Code's stiff penalties bolstered compliance with its mandates. The fine for releasing or exhibiting a movie without the Production Code seal of approval was $25,000. Producers had to submit scripts in advance of production and were told what to cut in order to obtain the all-important Production Code seal. The code censors looked at crimes, sex, vulgarity, obscenity, profanity, costume (or lack thereof), dances, religion, locations (notably the bedroom), national feel-

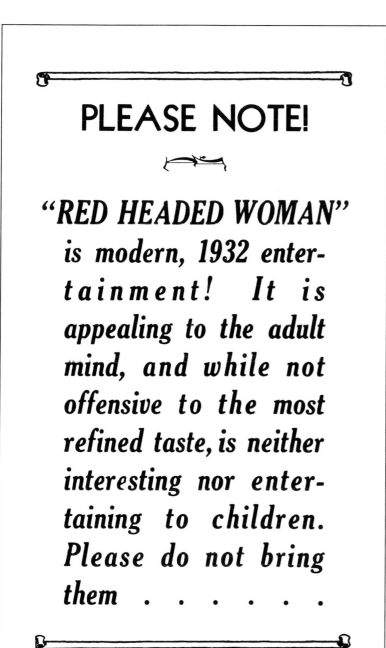

PLEASE NOTE!

*"RED HEADED WOMAN"
is modern, 1932 enter-
tainment! It is
appealing to the adult
mind, and while not
offensive to the most
refined taste, is neither
interesting nor enter-
taining to children.
Please do not bring
them . . . . . .*

ings, titles and repellent subjects such as torture. The guiding principle for violence came to be known as the "Law of Compensating Values." Characters could be violent and terribly evil throughout the film as long as they met proper punishment for their crimes before the credits rolled. The rules made for predictable "happy" endings where the bad guys would always lose to the good guys in the final reel. Despite this lack of on-screen realism, the Production Code worked remarkably well long after Will Hays left Hollywood. When Will Hays retired in 1945, he was succeeded by Eric Johnston, former president of the U.S. Chamber of Commerce. Soon after, the former Hays Organization was renamed the Motion Picture Association of America (MPAA).

Theatres played a central role in Code enforcement. Under the Code, the movie theatres owned by the studios — and these included the largest, most successful first-run theatres in the country — refused to screen any film that lacked the Production Code seal of approval. Independent theatre owners tied to long-term block booking contracts with the studios didn't have much room for independently-produced films. The bottom line was, without the Code seal, a movie could not be commercially successful.

During the 1940s Howard Hughes, maverick engineer, film producer and future owner of RKO, posed the first serious court challenge to the production and advertising codes of the Motion Picture Association. At issue was the film "The Outlaw" starring the voluptuous Jane Russell. Hughes launched an intensive publicity campaign for the movie even before production started. Provocative shots of Jane Russell appeared in the nation's newspapers and magazines and conferred upon her instant celebrityhood. When the finished film was submitted to the Production Code Administration, Hughes was told it could not be approved because of

This lobby advertisement from 1932 is an example of early efforts by exhibitors at self-regulation. *George Aurelius*

"the countless shots of Jane Russell, in which her breasts are not fully covered." Hughes made some revisions but balked at making several other cuts required for Code approval. The ensuing controversy only served to heighten interest in the film. Hughes eventually relented and removed the objectionable footage to earn a seal of approval.

By the time "The Outlaw" was finally ready for release, 20th Century Fox, the film's original distributor, had canceled its agreement. On February 5, 1943, "The Outlaw" debuted at a single San Francisco theatre. Area billboards displayed provocative poses of Jane Russell and the advertising campaign created a public furor. The publicity campaign fueled record-breaking attendance for "The Outlaw" for ten straight weeks. Early in 1946, United Artists, which was not a MPAA member at the time, agreed to release the film nationwide. Once again Hughes launched a massive and equally flamboyant and suggestive promotional campaign for the film. In an unprecedented move the Motion Picture Association moved to withdraw its previously-granted seal of approval. Hughes sued, charging anti-trust violations, restraint of trade and denial of free expression under the First Amendment. Hughes lost the case and, after exhausting all appeals, Hughes Productions was required to return the certificate of approval and delete the Production Code seal from all prints. Since the Production Code's $25,000 fine no longer applied to exhibition, a number of theatres were willing to screen "The Outlaw" without a Code seal and the film proved a hit.

Judged overall, the Production Code's method of self-censorship remained effective for nearly 20 years. Beginning in the early 1950s, however, the Code faced increasing defiance from its members. The first to break ranks was noted director Otto Preminger, whose 1953 comedy "The Moon is Blue" earned a "Condemned" rating from the Legion of Decency for its light-hearted treatment of adultery. In 1955, then-member United Artists resigned from the MPAA over its refusal to grant a Code seal for Preminger's "The Man With the Golden Arm," a film dealing with drug addiction. Despite the absence of a Code seal, both films attracted crowds and set the stage for other challenges to the Code. MPAA members, pledged not to release a film without a Code seal, began to distribute unapproved films through subsidiaries.

During the 1950s, the entire issue of motion pictures and censorship was cast in a new light by the nation's highest court. In 1952, in a celebrated case involving an Italian-made film called "The Miracle," the U.S. Supreme Court curbed the power of state and municipal censors when it brought motion pictures under the protection of the Constitutional guarantees of free speech and free press under the First and 14th Amendments. The decision helped to strike down local censor boards and allowed the MPAA's Production Code to eventually relax some of its controls on film content. By

1956, Code prohibitions against depictions of interracial marriages, drug use and prostitution were lifted. During the 1960s many of the Code's provisions seemed out of date in the face of mounting social change. Seeking to reclaim audiences that had defected to television, and facing competition from a growing number of foreign films not bound by the restrictions, filmmakers sought further relaxations in the Code to permit the production of more explicit films. Critics of the Code began to press for some form of classification system to replace the Code's system of self-censorship. A form of rating system, it was argued, would offer the public guidelines on a film's content while allowing for freer expression on the part of the filmmaker.

In the spring of 1966, the MPAA selected as its new president Jack Valenti, former presidential assistant to Lyndon Johnson. Valenti was confronted with a major challenge to Code restrictions by Warner Bros., one of the industry's most powerful studios. At issue was the film production of Edward Albee's award-winning play "Who's Afraid of Virginia Woolf?" which contained profanity and other language clearly forbidden by the Code. In a series of concessions, Warner Bros. agreed to certain cuts in the film and the MPAA got the studio's agreement to advertise the film with the printed caution, "Suggested for Mature Audiences." In a significant move at the theatre level, Warner Bros. inserted a clause in its film contract that prohibited exhibitors from allowing anyone under 18 to see the film unless accompanied by a parent. These innovations foreshadowed the later adoption of an industry classification and ratings system.

While the film industry and the nation's theatres were adjusting to a changing social climate, the forces of conservative morality were on the move. "Prior to the Code being established by the industry," remembered Florida-based exhibition veteran Arthur Hertz, "we did one because we had the concern. And being in the Deep South, where there was a very strong Bible Belt feeling, we were getting a lot of flak from people saying that we were putting stuff on the screen that wasn't fit for the family and kids. So we went ahead and put our own code in, in order to alert people as to whether they should be concerned about sending their kids to a picture or not. And it worked well."

Undeterred by the Supreme Court's extension of Constitutional protection to movies, social reformers and guardians of the public's welfare turned to the nation's obscenity laws. Both state and federal rulings had consistently denied any protection to obscenity under the First and 14th Amendments. Thus the issue of obscenity became a primary battleground at the local level. Theatre owners soon found themselves caught in a tangle of lawsuits, their livelihoods threatened by the fickle pronouncements of local film review boards and obscenity ordinances. On April 22, 1968, two Supreme Court rulings set the stage for a major overhaul of the industry's system of self-censorship. In *Ginsberg v. New*

Marquee illustrating the "R" rating. *NATO*

York, the high court ruled that material that was not obscene for adults might be obscene for children. In *Interstate Circuit v. Dallas* the court declared that a classification system for films could be constitutional if guidelines were clearly defined. Taken together, these two decisions opened the way for every city or state to devise its own classification code. The potential maze of conflicting local ordinances and criminal penalties posed a grave threat to the entire motion picture industry. Veteran East Coast exhibitor Julian Rifkin, who served as president of the National Association of Theatre Owners from 1967 to 1969, remembered, "A few of us, a very few of us I might say, saw tremendous danger, terrible danger, as far as the theatres were concerned. I don't know if you know the concept of a 'chilling effect.' A chilling effect is one where you are afraid to do something because you don't know whether it is right or wrong. You don't do anything. So here you have the chilling effect on 18,000 theatres in the country who don't know whether they can play a picture or not, or whether they are going to be arrested or not."

Theatre owners were galvanized for action. Some 70 percent of all the theatres in the U.S. had earlier put aside their long-held rivalries and united in 1966 as the National Association of Theatre Owners (NATO), a new organization that represented a merger of the U.S.'s two largest existing exhibition associations. Led by Rifkin, the exhibitors called for immediate action. MPAA president Jack Valenti agreed that decisive action was the way to avoid a sudden proliferation of state and city classification boards.

In an unprecedented show of cooperation between two often adversarial sides of the film industry, NATO and the MPAA forged a consensus on an industry-sponsored film rating system. Industry leaders recognized that any film industry system of classification required the support of church groups to succeed. "Jack and I and a couple of others really barnstormed the country for the next months," remembered Rifkin. "We spoke to PTAs, civic groups, legislative groups, anytime we could get five people together that were opinion makers, we would pitch the ratings system and what it should be and we discussed it with them.

"From the very beginning I got the church people involved. I said that we need the imprimatur of the church people. It has to have the aura of respectability. This was a very important factor in talking to legislators of each community. Don't forget the basic reason for

having this was to avoid legal classification and to eliminate being arrested for pornography."

On October 7, 1968, a mere six months after the Supreme Court's ruling that local film classification systems could be legal, the film industry's new motion picture rating system made its debut. According to the new system, the industry would no longer approve or disapprove the making of any film. Rather, it would shift its focus to giving parents advance information to help them decide whether a particular film is suitable for their children to see. The original plan worked much as it does today. Films were rated according to four categories: "G" for general audiences, all ages admitted; "M" for mature audiences, parental guidance suggested; "R" for restricted, those under 16 must be accompanied by an adult parent or guardian; and "X," no one under 16 admitted. The "M" was later changed to "PG" — parental guidance suggested — and the age limit for "R" and "X" was raised to 17. With the introduction of the voluntary system, the Production Code Administration was replaced by the newly-created Classification and Rating Administration (CARA).

CARA is comprised of seven members who serve for an indeterminate period of time. CARA's chairperson is selected by the MPAA president. The chairperson, in turn, selects the other six members to serve on the ratings board. Other than the X designation (which in 1990 became the registered NC-17), all MPAA rating symbols are registered with the U.S. Patent and Trademark Office and may not be self-applied by producers or distributors.

Since the MPAA's "X" rating was not copyrighted, some distributors of exploitation film used the letter's association with explicit sex as a way to attract audiences. Self-assigned "XXX" ratings began to appear on marquees. For some independent exhibitors with thea-

tres in decaying downtown areas, this approach spelled a way to stay in business. The VCR revolution of the 1980s and the emergence of video rental stores spelled the end for most X-rated, adults-only theatres, as former patrons of these theatres could now enjoy the most explicit adult fare in the privacy of their homes.

The rating system has successfully addressed the issue of helping parents evaluate the content of movies. However, the spectre of censorship and the desire by certain groups to monitor or censor movies has not abated. "I'll describe an example of just how narrow these people can think," said exhibition veteran Tim

Warner. "We fought a battle in Montana against a bill. It was introduced by a state senator who was against pornographic films. I went to see him, to see if I could build some sort of understanding. He says he is just totally against pornographic films playing in the town and that he saw a pornographic film last night in Helena, which is the state capital of Montana. I said, 'Well we own all the theatres in Helena and we don't play pornographic films.' And he says, 'Well you're a liar because I saw it with my own two eyes.' And I said, 'Well what film did you see?' and he says, 'The Towering Inferno.' I asked him what was pornographic about it and he answers 'There are two people in there that embraced and kissed that weren't married.' And so, the definition got pretty narrow in some of these marketplaces."

In its continuing effort to remain responsive to the informational needs of parents, the motion picture industry's rating system was modified in 1984 to divide the PG category into two groups. The new designation of "PG-13," parental guidance suggested for children under 13, was formulated in response to the intense level of action-adventure violence that marked "Indiana Jones and the Temple of Doom." The new rating alerts parents to a film's heightened level of intensity, which perhaps could be disturbing for some children.

In 1990, the ratings system dropped its infamous X rating and replaced it with a new designation of NC-17. The new designation was also developed to address the creative concerns of filmmakers who felt that the X rating, which meant no one under 17 admitted, had taken on a meaning practically synonymous with "pornographic" and that of course meant box office death. The NC-17 rating was designed to allow filmmakers to create adult-themed films while still alerting parents to the fact that the material is not suitable for anyone under 17.

In a further effort to serve parents, CARA began providing in 1992 concise written explanations describing why a particular film received its PG, PG-13 or R rating. Concerned patrons may obtain this information by calling their local theatre, or requesting this information at the box office.

By the time of CARA's 25th anniversary in 1993, it was evident that the rating system had forged an enduring partnership with the public it was designed to serve.

What Everyone Should Know About The Movie Rating System.

GENERAL AUDIENCES

G

Nothing that would offend parents for viewing by children.

G GENERAL AUDIENCES
All Ages Admitted

PARENTAL GUIDANCE SUGGESTED

PG

Parents urged to give "parental guidance." May contain some material parents might not like for their young children.

PG PARENTAL GUIDANCE SUGGESTED
SOME MATERIAL MAY NOT BE SUITABLE FOR CHILDREN

PARENTS STRONGLY CAUTIONED

PG-13

Parents are urged to be cautious. Some material may be inappropriate for pre-teenagers.

PG-13 PARENTS STRONGLY CAUTIONED
Some Material May Be Inappropriate for Children Under 13

RESTRICTED

R

Contains some adult material. Parents are urged to learn more about the film before taking their young children with them.

R RESTRICTED
UNDER 17 REQUIRES ACCOMPANYING PARENT OR ADULT GUARDIAN

NO CHILDREN UNDER 17 ADMITTED

NC-17

Patently adult. Children are not admitted.

NC-17 NO CHILDREN UNDER 17 ADMITTED

Chapter 12
YEARS OF TRANSITION

"It's just like the kitchens didn't put the restaurants out of business. People leave their own kitchens to go to somebody else's kitchen in order to have a good meal." — Myron "Mike" Blank on the impact of television on movie theatres.

The postwar years marked the start of a tumultuous period of upheaval for the movie industry. In 1946 the nation's booming box office reached a historic peak of 80 million admissions a week, with some estimates citing as many as 90 million. Beginning in 1947, however, movie attendance began a steep decline that extended over several years. By 1953, ticket sales had plummeted to one-half of their postwar peak. Profound social change and the emergence of television were cited as the primary reasons for the decline.

The end of World War II unleashed the public's pent-up demand for durable goods, which had been in short supply during the war. When the U.S. economy returned to civilian production, the nation went on a buying spree. Sales of big-ticket items like cars, refrigerators and washing machines reached record levels. Of all purchases, the most significant for its social impact was that of a single-family home. Attracted by low-interest mortgages from the Veterans Administration and the Farmers Home Loan Administration, an increasing number of Americans followed the road signs and highways to new tracts of affordable housing in the suburbs. Coupled with this outward migration came the baby boom, a rise in the American birth rate that continued until 1964.

The expenses of a new home and a growing family limited the amount of money that young couples could spend on entertainment. Listening to the radio remained popular, as did such neighborhood entertainment as miniature golf, bowling and backyard barbecues. What had the most significant effect on movie attendance, however, was the fact that suburbs, with their expanding populations, were taking people farther and farther away from downtown areas, where most of the large, first-run theatres were located.

By the early 1950s, a gradual but steady decline in moviegoing had given way to a virtual free fall. In 1953, movie attendance plummeted to almost one-half of its post-war peak. By contrast, sales of television sets had been increasing steadily since 1948; by 1954, more than half of all U.S. households had TVs. By the end of the decade television would invade 90 percent of the country's homes, and in the process manifest a potent force

Offering air conditioning and a double feature, the Duke Theatre competed with television's home appeal. *Wagner-Zip Change Inc.*

Following the dictum "if you can't beat 'em, join 'em," The Byrd Theatre, Richmond, Virginia, kept a television set in the lobby. *Frank Novak*

First-run theatres owned by Paramount, Fox and RKO competed for audiences in downtown Portland. *Act III Theatres*

Television's early miniature screen still meant big competition for the nation's movie theatres. *Ron Krueger*

that redefined American mass entertainment. It is hard to imagine from today's vantage point a time when every home didn't have a television.

"When TV first came in, not everybody really could afford a television set," remembered Boston-based exhibition veteran Carl Goldman. "If you were in an apartment building and one particular neighbor bought a TV set, he would invite his neighbors in on particular nights, Milton Berle night or what have you. They all sat in this apartment looking at this thing, and they just

didn't go out. Then as the prices came down somewhat, more and more people started buying televisions and of course the rest is history. Now, practically every household has at least one set if not more."

Before the film industry adjusted to the reality of television, it faced the disruption caused by the government's successful anti-trust suit against Hollywood's eight leading film companies: The Big Five (Paramount, RKO, Warner Bros., Loews/MGM and Fox) and the Little Three (Columbia, Universal and United Artists). The suit, alleging illegal restraint of trade, was first filed by the Department of Justice on July 20, 1938. The government's principal objective was to ban producers and distributors from owning theatres. After a decade of litigation, in 1948, the Supreme Court issued an historic ruling that abolished block booking, fixing theatre admission prices, maintaining unreasonable clearances, and other restrictive industry practices. The case was then sent back to the trial court for final adjudication. Between 1948 and 1954, through a series of con-

sent judgments, the five major studios were each split into two parts, a production-distribution company and a separately-owned theatre company. The divorced theatre circuits were then allowed a period of time to sell off a number of theatres to assure competition in the marketplace. In some cases this amounted to as many as half of a circuit's theatres.

The complicated details of the Paramount case and the individual judgements that were entered against the defendants are interesting grist for attorneys and others to ponder. For the casual student of motion picture theatre history, however, only a broad understanding of the case is required. In essence, the final decisions of the Paramount case changed the structure of the American film industry as it had operated since the late 1910s. No longer would the major studios hold a monopoly on the production, distribution and exhibition of movies.

Two of the defendants, Paramount and RKO, by agreeing to divest their theatre circuits in advance of the trial court's mandate, earned an advantage over the other three studios. After divorcing their theatres, RKO and Paramount were not restricted from later re-entering exhibition, and the divorced theatre circuit in each case was not enjoined from re-entering distribution. The other integrated studios, however — Warner Bros., Loews/MGM and 20th Century Fox — were not only required to sever ownership of their theatres, they faced the additional burden of securing court authorization before re-entering exhibition. Their divorced circuits, likewise, had to seek court approval before re-entering distribution and in addition, they were required to secure court approval to build or acquire theatres in the future.

The so-called Little Three defendants — Columbia, Universal and United Artists — were not restricted from owning theatres since, at the time of the court decree against them, they did not own any theatres. These distinctions within the Paramount case would become important many years later when fully-integrated production-distribution-exhibition companies emerged again in a vastly changed motion picture industry.

As a result of the Paramount decrees, independent theatre owners of the late 1940s and early '50s looked forward to wider access to films, lower rental costs and the opportunity to expand into new markets. The decision allowed new circuits to emerge and it was these new

circuits that were the first to tap the potential of developing suburban areas.

The practical benefits of the Paramount case, however, were far less than many exhibitors anticipated. In fact the timing of the decision, a full decade after the government's case was filed, couldn't have been worse. Independent theatre owners hardly had a chance to savor their victory before the entire motion picture industry was rocked by falling attendance and the ad-

Studio-owned RKO Theatre.
Allen Michaan

161

vent of television.

Television emerged as a viable technology during the 1930s only to have its development slowed by the manufacturing restrictions of World War II. Following the war the production of television equipment resumed, as did the broadcast of regular daily programing. The film industry's overall reaction to television was mixed. The major studios were blocked legally from network ownership. However, some studios such as Paramount, were investing in television stations from the medium's infancy. Others took a wait-and-see attitude; it was hard to judge, after all, how long this "technical novelty" would last. The potential audience was limited to specific geographic regions during an FCC-imposed freeze on new station licenses between 1948 and 1952. "Television didn't explode onto the marketplace; it came on gradually," explained former South Carolina exhibitor Charles Trexler. "It came on kind of slow and as a result of that, it was not as much

of a problem as we anticipated it might be." In addition, the first television receivers were expensive, with postcard-size screens. "TV was relatively crude," remembered Maryland-based circuit owner Irwin R. Cohen. "Not a lot of people had television sets, they were only black and white, and if they were 10 inches they were big." Another problem was reception. In many areas the best one could hope for was fuzzy black and white pictures. "Television didn't all come in at once," noted Louisiana-based veteran Teddy Solomon. "For instance, New Orleans had a station way before Baton Rouge did. It hurt the theatres in New Orleans some but the reception wasn't that good in Baton Rouge, so it didn't kill the theatre business there. People were still going, just not as much as before television."

"A lot of people in the business were crying doom," remembered veteran Illinois exhibitor George Carroll. "While a lot of us had the feeling that it was a very small screen, and there was so much lost in it. Although it was free, people still had to put up with all the commercials and stay in the house. For instance, they're cooped up all winter back here in the East and they're ready to get out of the house for outside entertainment. Most people were worried about it, but it was like crying wolf. I won't say it didn't hurt some theatres, it did. There was a lot of the smaller town theatres that it hurt very much. In fact a lot of the smaller theatres did go under because of television. But the larger towns, very few of them were hurt."

As the nation was slowly getting used to the idea of television, Paramount and RCA pursued research that would transform television technology into a movie house experience. Both companies envisioned theatres that would continue to offer feature films along with the added attraction of "theatre television," big-screen presentations of late-breaking news and major sporting

Theatre television on the big screen at the Fabian Palace Theatre. *Harley Lond*

events as they happened. "The theatres had closed-circuit television," noted Southern California-based circuit owner Bruce Corwin. "The big fights — Rocky Marciano, Archie Moore, Sonny Liston, Muhammed Ali's first fights, Floyd Patterson — all those fights had their very early beginnings in our downtown theatres on a big screen."

As early as 1948 Warner Bros. and 20th Century Fox demonstrated their versions of theatre television using the RCA system, but it was Paramount that had most fully explored the new technology, testing it between 1948 and 1951 in the theatres of its formerly affiliated Balaban & Katz circuit, which was at the time Chicago's dominant theatre chain. Critics applauded the effort but the experiment proved an expensive failure. The additional revenue generated by theatre screen presentations of the World Series, Big 10 football games and championship boxing matches — all in the days before the widespread availability of TV — didn't cover expenses, and the experiment was canceled. In other experiments during 1952 as many as 100 movie theatres presented some form of theatre television, but the idea never took off. The movie industry would soon move toward other more dazzling technology to compete against the living room TV.

After the Paramount decision, studios were no longer required to produce enough pictures to meet the film needs of their formerly affiliated theatres. Under the guaranteed film rentals of the old block-booking system the studios functioned like assembly-line factories, turning out a constant supply of premium "A" pictures in eight weeks and the cheaper "Bs" in six. But the Paramount decision now required distributors to rent their films on an individual, picture-by-picture, theatre-by-theatre basis. All pictures produced now had to be of sufficient quality and merit to stand on their

RKO Orpheum Theatre, St. Paul, Minnesota. *George Aurelius*

own. The end of theatre control and the ban against block booking, coupled with declining audiences, resulted in cutbacks in the number of feature films released by the major studios. When the widespread availability of television further ravaged box office tallies in the mid-1950s the studios instituted more drastic cuts in production. Competition among theatres for fewer films resulted in higher film rentals. Theatre owners, caught in a squeeze between higher costs and falling ticket sales, continued to cling to the belief that nothing could replace the unique experience of the movie theatre. The coming years tested their mettle, their showmanship and their very ability to survive. Exhibition rose to the challenge and joined the rest of the film industry to offer audiences more color, bigger screens, better sound and an array of astonishing visual effects.

Chapter 13
HIGH, WIDE AND SPECTACULAR

Beginning in the 1950s Hollywood retrieved and reworked existing technology to give moviegoers an experience they couldn't replicate with television. Audiences were wooed back to the theatre with — among other things — thrilling widescreen projection, lavish epics and stereo sound.

For sheer novelty, Hollywood's most memorable experiment of the time was 3-D. While standard motion pictures showed a flat two-dimensional image with height and width, 3-D movies added the startling illusion of depth. The idea of adding a third dimension to the movies was not a new one. During the late 1800s, the popular hand-held stereoscope gave viewers the illusion of three dimensions as they stared at two almost identical still photographs. A primitive form of 3-D movies was shown at the Paris Exposition in 1903. Other experiments with 3-D followed but, like so many other technical processes related to filmmaking (color, sound, panoramic screens), it was dismissed as little more than an interesting novelty until a slump in business forced producers to seek out any kind of gimmick that might help reclaim lost audiences.

The 3-D process of the 1950s required two synchronized projectors that displayed identical scenes shot from two slightly different angles. The pictures were projected through Polaroid filters and superimposed on the screen. Early 3-D systems required movie audiences to wear special disposable paper glasses with polarized lenses. The glasses fused the separate images into one picture of three exciting, realistic dimensions. In exchange for the trouble of fumbling with glasses, movie audiences experienced thrilling visuals that appeared to jump right off the screen. The successful release of Arch Oboler's "Bwana Devil" in 1952 started the 3-D fad. The highlights of this low-budget melodrama included spear-throwing African bushmen; moviegoers screamed and ducked for cover as the movie's deadly javelins seemed to fly into the audience. The movie proved so profitable that the other major studios soon rushed their own projects into 3-D production. When other 3-D pictures started arriving at local theatres the public flocked to them to experience the sheer thrill of cowering under an onslaught of knives, arrows, dripping

Advertising slick. *Dan Harkins*

A capacity crowd filled San Francisco's fabulous Fox Theatre for the presentation of "The Robe" in wide-screen CinemaScope. *Jack Tillmany*

wax, hatchets, rubber balls, rock slides, can-can dancers and stampeding animals.

"Bwana Devil" was produced with a process called Natural Vision, but other competing 3-D systems soon emerged with names like Depth-O-Vision, Stereo-Cine and True Stereo 3-D (the major studios chose the more

"Amazing! Startling! Astounding!," that's how theatres promoted 3-D. *Jim Emerson*

prosaic names of Columbia 3-D, Warner 3-D and Universal 3-D for their competing systems). Most of the 3-D systems were technically similar and required the use of polarized filters, two projectors and the ubiquitous viewing glasses, which often featured the distinctive one-green-and-one-red cellophane lenses. The cost of converting a theatre to 3-D was modest, ranging be-

tween $2,000 and $3,000, and theatres jumped at the chance to get in on the craze.

Because early systems kept a theatre's two projectors in constant operation, the presentation of 3-D movies required an intermission for reel changes. Audiences that had been half scared out of their minds no doubt welcomed a time-out at the snack bar before witnessing a film's concluding barrage of 3-D projectiles. From a projectionist's point of view, early 3-D movies provided constant aggravation. The two projectors had to be perfectly synchronized. If the speed of one machine was off even a fraction, the result was a screenful of blurred images that gave the audience headaches. If one of the films broke the operator had two choices: either replace the missing number of frames with black film or cut out the same number of frames from the good reel. Audiences, for their part, typically did not like wearing the glasses. "That's right," said veteran Kansas exhibitor Leon Hoofnagle. "We tried 3-D in the 1950s and there was 'House of Wax' and several pictures that were quality films. But people did not like the glasses."

Horror films were ideally suited to 3-D and one of the most popular was 1953's "House of Wax," starring Vincent Price and a cast of wax-dipped corpses. This well-crafted film was the exception among more hastily-made and cheaply-produced 3-D films. Despite the early surge in 3-D popularity, the novelty craze seemed to wear out its welcome within a year of its debut. All 3-D movies released during the summer of 1953 fared poorly at the box office. Audiences returned to 3-D the following year for Universal-International's fright-filled "Creature from the Black Lagoon." The hit horror film scored with a beauty-and-the-beast story infused with the appeal of its part-human, part-fish, part-alligator, part-turtle title character affectionately known as the "Gill Man." The movie's sequel, "Revenge of the Creature," was released in 1955 as the first 3-D picture to use a single-projector system, a welcome technical advance that eliminated problems with synchronization and audience headaches.

Moviegoers eventually tired of the low-budget, gimmicky nature of 3-D movies. By the summer of 1955 the 3-D craze was over, although from time to time the process has been revived on a limited basis for a new generation of movie fans. In 1970, 3-D was used to propel a soft porn feature called "The Stewardesses" to

box office stardom. The early 1980s saw 3-D return briefly for a spate of comedies, westerns, gory slasher movies and horror sequels such as "Friday the 13th 3-D," "Amityville 3-D" and "Jaws 3-D." Technical advances in newer 3-D systems meant the end of the funny paper eyeglasses and the amusing sight of a uniformly-bespectacled audience.

If 3-D could not save movie theatres from the audience-draining pull of the TV set, there were other gimmicks to try. "Wide-screen" became the industry

3-D feature, plus a prize fight at the Fox Theatre. *Jack Gunsky*

The Creature from the Black Lagoon makes a personal appearance at the Broadway Capitol Theatre. *Patrick Miller*

that was actually three screens in one. The curved screen was designed to capitalize on the effect of peripheral images and create the feeling that the audience was *in* the picture, at the center of the action. To heighten the sense of realism the system also used multitrack stereo sound.

The original Cinerama process was invented as "Vitarama" by Fred Waller for the 1939 New York's World Fair. The first Cinerama feature, "This is Cinerama," opened at the Broadway theatre in New York on September 30, 1952. The two-hour travelogue caused such a sensation that the New York Times covered it as front page news. The film's opening sequence took the audience on a breathtaking roller coaster ride with the camera positioned in the front car. The unnerving effect thrilled audiences at every twisting turn and stomach-wrenching drop.

Audiences flocked to experience the novel widescreen effects, keeping "This is Cinerama" playing in New York for more than two years. Extended presentations ran nearly as long in Detroit, Chicago, Philadelphia, Washington, D.C., Pittsburgh, San Francisco, Boston, St. Louis, Minneapolis, Hollywood and Dallas. The backers of the film were rewarded with a gross of more than $20 million.

The Cinerama process was genuinely thrilling although less than perfect. If focus and alignment weren't exact, the mammoth screen showed distracting faint lines where the three projected images joined together on the screen. Nevertheless, Cinerama gave theatre patrons an exciting visceral experience that more than made up for any technical problems. Film sequences with dog sleds, hydrofoils, stagecoaches and gondola rides all placed the theatre patron in the center of the action. The position of the camera and the curved-screen's use of peripheral vision made every scene feel

"Revenge of the Creature" was the first 3-D picture to use a single projector system. *Patrick Miller*

Mammoth theatre marquee announced the latest Cinerama feature. *NATO*

watchword for an array of filmmaking techniques and projection systems that delivered high, wide and mighty images that dwarfed the typical 16-foot by 20-foot theatre screen of the day.

Appearing almost simultaneously with the debut of 3-D was a wide, panoramic screen format called Cinerama. Cinerama featured a three-camera, three-projector process that, instead of overlapping the three film images the way 3-D did, projected them side-by-side. The system required a huge wall-to-ceiling curved screen

Cinerama" was presented as a special roadshow event with advance ticketing, reserved seating, a limit of two shows per day, an extended run and higher ticket prices.

The success of "This is Cinerama" led to a second well-received production, "Cinerama Holiday," in 1955, but subsequent releases in the format fared poorly at the box office. Travelogue films, even triple-screen, grandiose versions, had limited appeal. The first Cinerama movie with a plot didn't appear until 1962 with the release of "The Wonderful World of the Brothers Grimm" (followed later that year by the epic western "How the West Was Won"). "It's too bad that they ran out of product," lamented veteran New Jersey exhibitor Paul Peterson. "It was almost like found money in the bank every week. That's how good it was." Cinerama survives today as a specialty tourist attraction found in major metropolitan areas.

The most successful of all the new screen processes

Nuns in search of paradise. Clairidge Theatre, Montclair, New Jersey. *Paul Petersen*

Full screen Dimension 150 format. *John Lowe*

like a personal experience.

Cinerama was not for every theatre. It was clearly a specialty process and one that was never envisioned as a cure all for the failing box office. A Cinerama theatre had to be outfitted with special projectors, each requiring a separate booth and projectionist, a multitrack sound system and a huge screen, all at a cost of between $50,000 and $100,000 per theatre. Cinerama's expensive installation and size requirements automatically limited the system to movie palaces in major cities where a theatre could draw from a large population. "This Is

developed to combat the arrival of television was CinemaScope. The economical wide-screen process used an anamorphic lens during filming to squeeze a wide-screen image onto conventional 35mm film which was then "unsqueezed" using an anamorphic lens during projection. The result was an extraordinary image that was two and a half times wider than its height. CinemaScope publicity releases boasted, "You see it without

special glasses," an obvious reference to one of the drawbacks of early 3-D systems.

The wide-screen system was invented by Frenchman Henri Chretien in 1927 and was based on his research for tank periscopes during World War I. When 20th Century Fox bought the rights for CinemaScope in 1952, studio chief Spyros Skouras aggressively championed the virtues of the system as the salvation of the industry. Unlike 3-D and Cinerama, CinemaScope's

"Throw Away Your 3-D Glasses," exhorted this lobby display for CinemaScope. *Chuc Barnes*

Roadshow engagement of the "King and I." *John Lowe*

Sound racks and projector for Cinerama. *Paul Petersen*

simplified process offered a spectacular visual experience without the need for gimmicky glasses or the expense of new projectors and extra projection booths. The public's first look at CinemaScope came in 1953 with the highly successful release of "The Robe," which also featured stereophonic sound. Fox made the commitment to release most of its features in 'Scope and, to hasten its acceptance by theatres, offered licenses for the process to other studios to assure a steady flow of CinemaScope pictures. The success of "The Robe" was followed by the CinemaScopic box office hit "How to Marry a Millionaire," laying to rest most doubts about the system's commercial viability. The other leading studios (with the exception of Paramount, which was developing a competitive wide-screen system) soon began releasing their own pictures in CinemaScope.

Exhibitors found only one drawback with the CinemaScope system and that was Fox's insistence that such features be presented with stereo sound. During a time of grave economic uncertainty in the industry, the added

Ultravision — yet another wide screen format. *NATO*

TODD A-O film projector.
Harley Lond

a single camera with four lenses and, like CinemaScope, required only a single projector. The first film to be shot in Todd-AO was the 1955 hit musical "Oklahoma!" The second Todd-AO feature was the Academy Award-winning "Around the World in Eighty Days," a globe-trotting, cast-of-thousands spectacle that featured numerous cameo performances by more than 40 well-known celebrities. The Todd-AO system ended with the untimely death of its chief promoter, Mike Todd. "'Around the World In Eighty Days' launched a whole

expense of a new stereo sound system accounted for half of CinemaScope's $20,000 installation cost. After Fox dropped the stereo sound requirement in 1954, however, CinemaScope became more affordable and medium-size and smaller theatres joined the rush to wide-screen splendor. By November 1954 one survey indicated that nearly half the theatres in the country were equipped to show CinemaScope. The size of America's movie screens was changed forever.

These successes encouraged the development of other wide-screen formats. Paramount introduced VistaVision, RKO had SuperScope, there was Technirama, Magnascope and more. Todd-AO, named for producer Mike Todd and American Optical, was another promising wide-screen format. The system used 65mm film in the camera that was transferred to 70mm for projection on a wide, curved screen. Todd-AO used

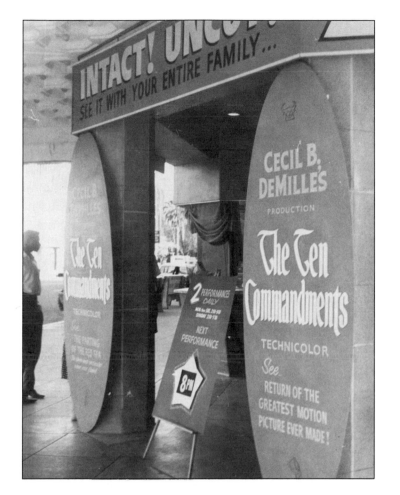

Hollywood rediscovered the epic with the likes of "Ben Hur," "Spartacus," and "The Ten Commandments." These colossal "event pictures" with "casts of thousands" usually played roadshow engagements in specially selected theatres. Heavily promoted and capitalizing on the appeal of big name stars and foreign locations, these roadshow pictures revitalized the movie-going experience.

"We had to make the transition from having all these movies to having *films*," remembered Maryland-based circuit owner Paul Roth. "By that I mean we could take a picture and play it for a week and play it as a single bill and get into a whole different kind of presentation merchandising. It caused a lot of us to learn a different kind of promotion, exploitation. When we started with CinemaScope, that was a helluva answer to television, with that big screen and the stereophonic sound. Then

Roadshow engagement of "The Ten Commandments," two performances daily. Paramount Theatre, Phoenix, Arizona. *George Aurelius*

Exhibitors successfully utilized group sales to guarantee sold-out performances. *Paul Petersen*

segment of what the industry could do — a highly specialized picture with extremely good sound," recalled veteran circuit owner Stanley Durwood. "And of course it was a 70mm print or a 65mm print, so you had a big picture with high fidelity. The sound was as high a fidelity as anything we have today, with maybe five huge sound horns behind the screen. We had reserved seats, 10 shows a week. It was just remarkable. It blew the lid off a number of things."

Seeking to exploit the new wide-screen technologies,

Shakespeare goes Technicolor.
John Lowe

CinemaScope — the modern
miracle you see without glasses.
Embassy Theatre, Reading,
Pennsylvania. *Eugene Plank*

"The King and I," "West Side Story" and of course, "The Sound of Music," then the highest-grossing picture in history.

Taking a cue from the unprecedented success of "The Sound of Music," the studios began pushing other family-oriented, big-budget musicals like "Camelot," "Star!" "Dr. Doolittle," "Funny Girl," "Oliver!" and "Hello Dolly" into production. Despite good intentions all of these films failed to deliver on their promotional superlatives. The fact that the public had overwhelmingly rushed box office windows to see "The Sound of Music" had little bearing on their interest in other high profile, star-packed musicals. Their often lukewarm receptions proved once again how few guarantees there are when dealing with fickle audience taste.

Deciding among the various wide-screen formats available was a dilemma faced by hundreds of theatre owners. While audiences enjoyed the new wide-screen look of the movies, most couldn't tell one system from another. Exhibitors, meanwhile, were vexed by the profusion of expensive wide-screen systems with different lenses, projectors and screen sizes; it was up to them to decide which formats would be the most appealing and long-lasting. By the end of the 1950s the film industry was anxious to decide upon a low-cost, single standard for film production and exhibition.

The eventual winner was Panavision, a system of equipment and lenses that eliminated the distortion problem associated with even superior wide-screen systems. By the late 1960s Panavision cameras and equipment became the industry standard. Ultra Panavision and Super Panavision would soon follow.

Color became an important part of the technical revolution that swept moviemaking in the 1950s. Until the 1960s, television could only offer black and white images, so color remained exclusively a big-screen fea-

there was the three-projector system, Cinerama, and other things that came along that were real presentation events. Instead of more movies, more flicks, we had to learn how to book *that* kind of film and how to advertise it and how to turn moviegoing into more of an event."

The disastrous box office disappointment that was "Cleopatra" turned Hollywood's attention away from the historical epic to the more tried and true formula of the hit Broadway musical. Audiences were enchanted by wide-screen feature adaptations of "My Fair Lady,"

A big breakthrough in color movies came with the introduction of the two-color Technicolor system during the 1920s. The color was an improvement over previous systems even though the color wasn't natural-looking because the process used shades of red and green but omitted the blue range. In 1932, Technicolor perfected a three-color process that was used in Walt Disney's animated short, "Flowers and Trees."

The process, although expensive, proved popular with audiences and producers began to insert color

Theatre staff taking reservations for the roadshow engagement in Denver of "Those Magnificent Men in Their Flying Machines." *Ralph Batschelet/Beverley Carlson*

AMC President Stanley Durwood, recognizing the added promotional possibilities of roadshows, changed the canopy and entrance to the Capri Theatre with every new picture. *American Multi-Cinema, Inc.*

ture for more than a decade. Some of the earliest moving pictures featured individual frames of hand-painted or hand-tinted color. Evidence of hand-tinting has been found in restored versions of "The Great Train Robbery," notably a red hue around the gun the outlaw fires at the camera. Tinting whole scenes was far more common. Many silent films featured blue tints for night scenes, red-orange hues for passion or other fiery emotions, and yellow and green tints for other scenes.

Over the years a number of attempts were made to introduce color to movies. The Kinemacolor system, first exhibited in the U.S. in 1909, is recognized as the first commercially successful natural color film process. Kinemacolor's two-color additive system involved filming and projecting pictures through colored filters at 32 frames per second. By the mid-teens the process was discarded, largely because audiences complained that the color hurt their eyes.

scenes into their black and white films. "Becky Sharp" (1935) was the first all-color feature film made with Technicolor's three-color process. The high cost of the Technicolor process restricted its use to a small percentage of Hollywood's "A" list of top features during the 1930s and 1940s.

The coming of television accelerated the commercial need for color films on the big screen. Frustrated by Technicolor's high cost and the company's insistence on controlling all aspects of color productions, the studios pushed for the development of more economical systems. Eastman Kodak introduced Eastman color negative and print film in 1950. The film was immediately successful and it soon became the industry standard. Today's film credits list patented names such as

Roadshow presentation at the Cine Capri Theatre, Phoenix, Arizona. *George Aurelius*

"Color by Deluxe" or "Technicolor" which refer to companies that process movies that are invariably printed on Eastman color film.

Efforts to attract theatre audiences entered the shadows realm of the improbable during 1959 and 1960 when two systems introduced the concept of synchronized smell to the movies. AromaRama was invented by Charles Weiss in 1958 and used a theatre's air conditioning system to filter scents into the theatre auditorium. Different scents accented different scenes, and an auxiliary air purification system was required to remove each scent before the next one arrived. The cost of installing the smell system ran between $3,000 and $7,500 per theatre. The first and last feature released in AromaRama was "Behind the Great Wall," a documentary on China released in 1959. The film featured the odors of incense, sour wine, fireworks, construction work, tigers and horses.

Equally short-lived was Smell-O-Vision, originally called Scentovision. This version required the installation of pipes to bring odors to individual theatre seats. Showman Mike Todd saw a demonstration of the system in 1954 and was intrigued by its potential. After his tragic death in a plane crash, his son, Mike Todd, Jr., carried the idea to completion.

The sophisticated system used electronic tones on a separately running soundtrack to trigger an automated system that could dispense up to 30 different scents at precise moments in the film. The trick was clearing the air to avoid the olfactory equivalent of Mulligan's stew. The process was used on only one feature, "Scent of Mystery" which debuted at Chicago's Cinestage on June 12, 1960, accompanied by the smells of garlic, tobacco, coffee and other scents. The picture was later defumed and released without Smell-O-Vision as "Holiday in Spain."

Fearful that systems like AromaRama and Scentovision could yield terrifying consequences should they fall into the wrong hands, many expressed anxiousness at the announcement that underground director John Waters had developed his own synchronized-smell system, which he dubbed "Odorama." Debuting with the filmmaker's 1981 feature "Polyester," Odorama employed scratch-and-sniff cards that simulated smells that were sometimes intentionally not altogether pleasant. Like AromaRama and Scentovision, Odorama was retired after only one feature application, but still gladdens the hearts and memories of many.

Despite Hollywood's creative arsenal of widescreen, stereophonic color spectaculars, movie attendance continued to decline. To make matters worse, Hollywood had already opened its library of older film titles to television. "It was devastating," remembered veteran Midwestern exhibitor Herb Brown. "I can remember one time when a TV station came out with 'Red River' starring John Wayne. This was a big picture on TV and they took out a two-page ad in the newspaper. It all but buried the theatres. The theatres did absolutely no business when it played that night."

The release of more recent films to television had been held up by concerns of the Screen Actors Guild over TV residual payments for its members. Once this union problem was resolved, the studios were free to offer their newer, post-1948 pictures for broadcast. Hollywood's movie floodgates soon opened, delivering a stream of more recent feature films to television. Neighborhood theatres and drive-ins that had depended on second-run and third-run films were left high and dry with no pictures to screen.

Faced with the discouraging prospect of more recent movies on television, exhibitors organized as the American Congress of Exhibitors (ACE) with the expressed

3-D mask. Portions of Warner Bros.' 1961 movie "The Mask" were filmed in red and green 3-D. Audiences were instructed when to don the "Magic Mystic Mask" for added thrills. *Alvin Svoboda*

intention of buying up the backlog of existent studio films to keep them off the airwaves. It was a bold plan, but doomed to failure. Because of lucrative television licensing agreements, the studios had learned to hold onto the ownership of their film libraries, and as a result could not be persuaded to sell their valuable titles.

The encroachment of television caused many exhibitors to categorize the 20th century's sixth decade as "the dark '50s." The good news for exhibitors, however, was that TV wasn't the only product that enjoyed new and wide-spread popularity after World War II. There was also the automobile.

Chapter 14
DRIVE-INS

"You can't imagine what a thrill it was to get up on the roof of the projection booth and look around at the 1500 - 2000 cars parked — the families, kids playing, people running back and forth. It was excitement. It was life, activity, it was show business." — Julian Rifkin on the Drive-In

*T*he innovation of the drive-in theatre resulted from the backyard tinkering of an auto-products executive. Imagine the amount of Whiz Auto Products one could sell, mused Richard M. Hollingshead, Jr., if you offered the motoring public a special venue — a deluxe service station, complete with adjoining restaurant and outdoor movies. Why not add a Hawaiian Village theme and disguise the gas pumps as palm trees? One tweak of creative inspiration in a different direction and Hollingshead could have launched a forerunner to the modern-day theme park. Luckily for movie fans, however, Hollingshead abandoned the idea of tropical motif service pumps and held fast to the idea of outdoor movies that could be enjoyed from the comfort of one's car.

Hollingshead's brainstorming came after careful consideration of market forces. He asked himself, what products would be the last that people would give up? He reasoned the answers were food, clothing, cars and movies, in that order. He was impressed with all the cash business his neighborhood theatre enjoyed. He next pondered the main reason people gave for *not* going to the movies and he arrived at the conclusion that people

didn't always want to get dressed up to go out. The idea of watching movies from the comfort and privacy of a big, roomy sedan intrigued Hollingshead and he set out to design an outdoor automobile theatre.

Hollingshead must have cut quite the comic figure sitting in his car night after night with a whirring Kodak

A list of suggestions for enjoying the drive-in experience. *Pacific Theatres*

Duncan Drive-In, Duncan, Oklahoma. *Roger Rice*

Pacific's Lakewood Drive-In Theatre, Lakewood, California. *Pacific Theatres*

the wheels of the second car until he achieved an elevation that allowed the driver in the rear vehicle to see over the car ahead to an unobstructed screen. Hollingshead then calculated angles and designed a system of dirt ramps arranged in terraced rows. This became the core of his drive-in theatre patent.

He then launched the construction of the world's first permanent drive-in theatre, located just outside the city limits of Camden, New Jersey. On the night of June 6, 1933, the aptly-named Automobile Movie Theatre, the marquee of which simply read "Drive-in Theatre," debuted to the public and attracted a sizeable opening night crowd. Some no doubt were lured by the sheer novelty of the undertaking; a good number of others had been given free passes.

Over the next 10 years, some 100 drive-in theatres emerged to encourage a novel new form of moviegoing, but it was not until the nation's postwar era, however, that the drive-in gained widespread acceptance by audi-

Fountain Valley Drive-In, Fountain Valley, California. *NATO*

Marquee. Twin screen drive-in theatre. *Wagner-Zip Change, Inc.*

Drive-in theatre operators promoted the special appeal of seeing a movie in the comfort of your own car. *Pacific Theatres*

projector balanced on the hood. As he watched the movies on a makeshift screen nailed to a tree, Hollingshead analyzed the potential problems of an outdoor car theatre. He even went so far as to rig up a set of sprinklers to simulate rain so he could gauge the impact of showers on the screen image. A portable radio set up behind the screen helped him envision the placement of a loudspeaker system.

Hollingshead realized that cars parked in front of each other would obscure the view of the screen. He experimented with a pair of cars and put blocks under

ences.

From the very beginning, the outdoor car theatre promoted itself as a tempting alternative to conventional "hardtop" theatres. Usually located on large tracts of vacant land outside city limits, the drive-in boasted cooling night breezes during hot summer months, absence of urban parking problems, and no dress code of any kind. "It made no difference what type of film you had on the screen in a drive-in," remarked veteran New England exhibitor Carl Goldman. "People came."

American cities had not been designed with the automobile in mind and by the early 1930s the joy of car ownership was tempered somewhat by inadequate parking and an increasing number of traffic-clogged streets. The spectre of hungry parking meters, which began appearing along city curbs, only made going to an in-town movie theatre more aggravating. By 1938 film industry trade articles lamented the negative impact of parking problems on the movie business. The new *drive-in* theatre, on the other hand, promised a parking space and theatre seat all in one.

Summertime was traditionally the slowest period for moviegoing due to the sweltering discomfort of un-air-conditioned theatres. While movie palaces during the 1920s offered air-cooled relief, early air-conditioning units were huge pieces of equipment and too expensive for smaller theatres. The Carrier Corporation introduced compact and more affordable air conditioning systems in the early 1930s and theatres gradually began investing in the cooling equipment. Movie houses that couldn't afford it during the uncertain economic years of the Depression simply shut down until the fall. Drive-ins, on the other hand, promised movies under a cool star-lit sky in a pastoral setting, a no-doubt alluring image compared to staying home with a noisy electric fan.

"Wish We Had This Car in the PARLOR"

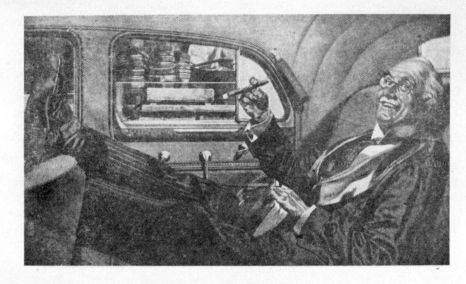

YOU CAN'T TAKE IT INTO THE PARLOR WITH YOU
BUT YOU CAN TAKE IT INTO THE DRIVE-IN

OUR FRIEND IS NOT SO DUMB. FOR THE SOFTEST, MOST COMFORTABLE SEAT AROUND MANY A HOME IS IN THE CAR OUT IN THE GARAGE

Movies and Motors Are The World's Greatest Entertainers

There is much in common between the automobile and motion picture industries, neither was dreamed of a few short years ago . . . if you would have dropped in on Thomas A. Edison fifty years ago at his laboratory in West Orange, N. J. you probably would have found him dividing his time between experiments on the phonograph, his pet project at that time, and a photographic device with which he hoped to show objects in motion. However it was not until he received strips of flexible film in long pieces from George Eastman two years later was he able to perfect his invention of the Kinetoscope. This device ran fifty feet on a spool bank and the spectator who looked through a peep hole saw figures in action.

About this time Henry Ford was working on his first automobile. Yet both now share the glory of freeing human beings from the shackles of time and distance. In his car a man can travel farther and more comfortably in an hour than his grandfather could in a day . . . and now you can enjoy the movies in the privacy and comfort of your own car and witness the major moving pictures in a most comfortable and unique manner. It is not necessary to split up theatre parties and the cushioned seats of automobiles offer more comfort than the average movie theatre.

And what's more entertaining than a snug ride on the soft cushions of your family car and enjoying the movies at a drive-in where you drive directly into the theatre and see the show from your car. It costs no more to take your car in with you and the problem of parking your car is entirely eliminated.

Just like being at home. Bring the Children—For the little tots we always have a cartoon comedy, and the baby can play or take a nap on the rear seat while mother and dad enjoy the picture—The DRIVE-IN is truly the Family Theatre.

183

Typical car speaker. *Pacific Theatres*

Rare photo of early blast speakers without volume controls, San-Val Drive-In, Burbank, California. *Pacific Theatres*

Art-Deco style speakers at Southern California's Olympic Drive-In Theatre. *Pacific Theatres*

And then there was the appeal of a drive-in's informality. In an earlier era, moviegoing and most other evening social activities (short of a barn dance) called for "dressing up." Viewing a movie from the privacy of your car, however, meant more casual dress was acceptable. "When the drive-in came along, nobody was going to see you anyway. One of the great advertising themes was 'come as you are,'" recalled veteran drive-in theatre owner Julian Rifkin. Early promotional literature for drive-in theatres stressed this informal convenience. Patrons could return from the beach or golf links and go directly to the drive-in theatre without first going home to change. Touting the safety, comfort and convenience of watching a movie from the inside of one of Detroit's finest, early promotional materials targeted the elderly, the disabled and the overweight, potential moviegoers who up until this time may have avoided the indoor theatre.

For all of its appeal, the early drive-in had its problems, first and foremost being the poor quality of its

sound. Giant foghorn speakers mounted atop the screen tower blasted the film's dialogue to reach the farthest car in the back row. Unfortunately, as bad as the sound was, there was nothing to keep it from traveling down the road to neighboring towns, where irate citizens implored the local authorities to enact and strictly enforce noise ordinances. Many a drive-in operator found himself hauled into court on charges of

disturbing the peace. "Seattle's Midway Drive-In was built before World War II and had a big speaker on top of the screen tower," remembered West Coast circuit owner Michael Forman, "and they'd get, usually on the weekends, or sometimes during the week, they'd get tickets for noise. So they would pay the ticket and keep showing the movie."

In bad weather patrons had to roll up their windows, which then blocked out the movie's sound from the

of the revolutionary speakers was postponed until after the war.

Technical problems aside, it would be hard for any analyst looking at early drive-ins to predict the boom in outdoor theatres that would occur following the end of World War II, — but boom they did. Drive-ins offered an affordable way for many entrepreneurs to enter exhibition. "The original screens were put up quite cheaply," remembered Boston-based exhibition veteran Malcolm Green. "They weren't even metal then. They were built on telephone poles and it was not metal facing. It was plywood, covered with reflective material. The only thing they spent any money on was grading for the ramps. You couldn't take raw land and expect to have cars drive over it with rain and so forth, and have anything but a quagmire. The refreshment stands and projection booths were built about as cheaply as you

Aerial view of the concession stand and playground, Beltline Drive-In, Grand Rapids, Michigan 1959. *John "Jack" Loeks*

Olympic Drive-In, Los Angeles, California. *Pacific Theatres*

tower speakers. The screen speakers also posed problems of sound synchronization for the back car ramps. Audiences would see a villain get shot and then hear the gunshot afterward.

To eliminate these aggravations, some drive-in owners experimented with individual speakers placed between every two cars. Another idea was to mount a speaker on each car's front bumper. Still another approach was to bury speakers in the ground and cover them with metal grills, allowing the sound to emanate upwards to fill a car's interior. All these systems were a decided improvement over the blast speaker approach to sound, but all were crippled by the same technical drawback: The speakers lacked volume controls that moviegoers could adjust.

In 1941 RCA pioneered a breakthrough with the development of in-car speakers with individual volume controls. Due to wartime restrictions, the manufacture

could build anything. Just the four walls with a cut-out for the light."

The end of World War II meant the lifting of wartime restrictions on gasoline, tires and automobile production and a prosperous nation hit the road. "Fundamental to the growth of drive-ins was the nation's newfound love affair with the automobile," explained Mary Ann Grasso, executive director of the National Association of Theatre Owners. "America became car crazy. A Sunday drive became the ultimate carefree expression of personal freedom." "It's no pleas-

Mission 4 Outdoor Theatres, San Antonio, Texas

Ronnie's Drive-In Theatre, St. Louis, Missouri. *Ron Krueger*

ure getting in the car today. In those years, it was," remembered Pennsylvania-based circuit owner Richard Fox. "Besides, you had to show everybody that you had a car."

America's obsession with automobiles, combined with the lure of a night out at the movies, proved an irresistible combination. "Everybody bought a car and people just liked to drive around," explained Green. "There was a whole freedom there. It was because of the many new roads and the development of new housing farther out — land was not that expensive — that drive-ins began to develop."

On January 1, 1946, there were 102 drive-ins theatres in the U.S. Three years later there were about 1,000. There were more than 3,000 in 1954; 4,000 in 1958. It seemed that drive-ins couldn't be built fast enough. Their popularity proved to be one of the few bright spots for exhibition in an era of declining ticket sales precipitated by the rise of television and the post-war population shift away from cities. As in the heyday of nickelodeons, drive-ins could be opened with modest capital and be expected to earn sizeable profits.

Bad weather proved less of a problem for drive-in theatres than might be expected. Enterprising exhibitors tackled the elements with a variety of innovative approaches. Fog was the only meteorological culprit that could automatically shut a drive-in down. "We had rain guards that would fasten over the windows. We had car heaters," explained Oregon-based exhibition veteran Larry Moyer. "The rain guards were a plastic visor that went over the windshield and kept the rain off your window so you didn't have to keep your windshield wipers going. We built our first drive-in in 1959 where we put in electric car heaters. We sold these rain visors for $2 and they were reusable. You could roll them, they had wire arms that stuck out and strings with a suction

cup on it that would stick to the hood of the car to keep the wind from blowing the rain visor off."

"We wired every speaker with 200 amp service and got these huge, ugly heaters that we would rent out at the box office for $1 or $2," remembered Fox. "They would plug into the speaker pole and turn on the heat so the car would keep warm during the winter. Looking back, it sounds so ridiculous, but, oh, I was so excited. We could stay open year-round." "In Montana, we did

Bluemound Drive-In, Brookfield, Wisconsin. *Larry Widen*

Paul Krueger (in suit) at the box office entrance to St. Louis' Ronnie's Drive-In which promised to stay open during any type of weather. *Ron Krueger*

offer one drive-in year round," remembered exhibition veteran Tim Warner. During the winter we had in-car heaters. I couldn't believe the people. As I look back, they were out of their minds to come out there!"

Drive-in exhibitors made families the focus of their operations and this emphasis was apparent in all of their promotions. "We never charged for children because we always made a play towards the family," explained Los Angeles-based exhibitor Jerome A. Forman. "We always had baby bottle warmers in the snack bar. We used to have milk available so they could fill up their bottles and warm them for the kids."

"People remember coming and bringing their kids in pajamas and that was very true," added cousin Michael Forman whose company oversees one of the largest drive-in circuits in the U.S. "You'd see these little kids walking around with their bunny pajamas with their bunny feet on with one bag of popcorn. That was the backbone of the business."

The family orientation also extended to programming. "We used to see people, the same young families week after week, come to the drive-in because that was their night out for entertainment," explained Jerome A. Forman. "They'd bring their children and we always put on two or three cartoons first, so the kids could watch the cartoons. Then the families would put the kids to bed in the back seat or on air mattresses if they had a station wagon and then the adults, the parents, would sit and watch the rest of the show. That was the whole thrust of what we did." Drive-in operators are credited with realizing the full profit potential of the concession

stand long before their indoor counterparts. "Families would go to a drive-in and eat their supper out there," explained veteran Southern circuit owner T.G. "Teddy" Solomon, "...while generally in an indoor theatre they'd just maybe come in and buy a bar of candy or maybe a box of popcorn or a cold drink." Some drive-ins offered mobile vending carts that brought refreshments to the patrons. Most expanded the range of choices available from the snack bar, moving on from soft drinks, candy and popcorn to ice cream, hot dogs, hamburgers and later pizza and nachos. "In those days families liked to go out and have hot dogs, hamburgers, popcorn and that sort of thing," recalled Paul Petersen. "The drive-in was a very likely place to go for that. Families could buy the kids pizza or what-

Buffeteria 50 — concession service on wheels. Boxoffice. Courtesy of John Lowe

Interior view of drive-in concession stand, Orange, California. Pacific Theatres

ever. All before the fast food restaurants came up on the highway."

Despite the limited 15-minute intermission period allotted for the majority of snack bar sales, owners could reasonably expect 35 to 40 percent of their gross receipts to come from concession sales. "They would run in and buy popcorn and hot dogs and pizza and egg rolls and all this stuff," recalled Fox. "Concessions was a really big business and the market was fantastic."

Drive-ins, boasting 500 to 2,000 cars, had to service a large volume of concession patrons in the limited 10- to 15-minute intermission. Cafeteria-style operations became the rage and were crucial to the success of the larger drive-ins. By 1953, nearly half of all drive-ins boasted the cafeteria method, a speedy form of self-service.

Drive-in operators successfully used a number of strategies to get their customers salivating. On-screen trailers of food items, clever reminders that it was time to stretch and have snack or a cool drink, were standard intermission fare.

A properly juggled schedule could also enhance concession sales. Each intermission began with an announcement that the concession stand was open and ready for business. During the 15-minute intermission the concession stand was a flurry of activity as hungry patrons converged on the counter to purchase a second feature's worth of goodies. A carefully timed an-

nouncement would let the straggler know there were a mere "three minutes," "two minutes," "one minute" left before the start of the next show. If that didn't work, the theatre owner allowed for some filler programming of cartoons, a newsreel or short subjects to allow the latecomer a little more time for food purchases. To insure that people would not leave the concession line when the feature began, some operators installed speakers in the concession area so patrons could hear a film's soundtrack.

Early drive-in snack bars were run by concessionaires. The enormous success of drive-in concession sales

Cedar Valley Drive-In Theatre. Rome, Georgia. *Donald Idarius*

Concession Stand, South Twin Drive-In. Late 1950s. *Ron Krueger*

before the movie — while hopefully making several trips to the snack bar.

Theatre operators seized on countless ways to create a full evening of lively entertainment. "We had playgrounds, and playsets and swing sets," explained Fox. "We had music for intermission and bands. I mean we made it a real family-type thing. It competed with television in a way that the downtown theatres could not."

Parents and adults could find wholesome relaxation with horseshoe pitching, shuffleboard, miniature golf and even game nights that featured musical chairs and three-legged races. Simple stages were built in front of the screen tower to present a variety of live entertainment. There were talent shows and baby contests, and prize drawings. Drive-ins also featured dance parties, boxing matches, circus performers, animal acts and even car stunts. Operators could cheaply rent a cagefull of monkeys or a litter of rabbits for the season, or go to the extra expense of offering a petting zoo with tame

Western art and neon decorate screen tower of the Gage Drive-In. *Pacific Theatres*

Typical cafeteria style concession stand, Ronnie's Drive-In, St. Louis, Missouri. *Ron Krueger*

prompted major concession companies, such as Berlo Vending and later Ogden Foods, to underwrite the cost of new drive-in venues. "When somebody wanted to build a drive-in theatre," explained Fox, "they would loan the individual money in exchange for the contract to run the concessions for the theatre."

The gimmicks and promotional stunts often associated with drive-ins grew out of the natural obstacles they faced. When long summer days forced late starting times for films, the savvy operator launched a myriad of special activities to entice families to come early and enjoy an extra hour or two of inexpensive entertainment

barnyard animals.

In 1956, a drive-in theatre owner could order a basic set of playland equipment for as little as $600. More elaborate set-ups might include such exotic equipment as trapeze bars, flying rings, climbing bars and even a "wave stride," that rotating circular platform that children propel by gripping the handrails and pushing with their feet.

In some areas, "super kiddielands" emerged adjacent to the drive-in property. These full-fledged playgrounds operated as a separate entity during the day and charged a separate admission price. This lucrative addition became a way for the theatre owner to make extra income during the day.

The idea of the drive-in church service originated during the 1950s. As a gesture of community goodwill, drive-in operators made their facilities available for outdoor Sunday services during the warm summer months.

When indoor movie attendance went into a nose-

dive following the rise of television, exhibitors joined Hollywood in offering such technical innovations as Cinemascope, Cinerama and 3-D in an effort to reclaim some of their lost audience. Some drive-ins also adopted this new technology but the overall effect was marginal. The ozoners simply could not match an indoor theatre's projection or sound quality, but their owners didn't worry. Cars still lined up at the ticket booth at dusk, eager for an outdoor evening's worth of entertainment.

During the 1960s drive-ins started to reflect changes in the world around them. In 1967, nationwide Daylight Saving Time went into effect. "Do you know what really killed the drive-in theatre?" asked Denver-based former circuit owner Bob Tankersley. "What started them on their downward road was Daylight Savings Time. I used to go to drive-ins a lot, but I'm not going to go out and start watching a movie at 9:30 or 10 o'clock

Concession stand, Terrace Drive-In, Casper, Wyoming. *Charles G. Manley*

CinemaScope comes to the drive-in. Ronnie's Drive-In, St. Louis, Missouri. *Ron Krueger*

The swap meet became synonymous with daytime drive-in operations. Simi Drive-In, Simi, California. *Metropolitan Theatres*

The drive-in held special appeal for youngsters. *Barbara Stones*

use as swap meets." "The theatre part of it is successful, and the swap meet part is also successful," agreed Southern California-based circuit owner Bruce Corwin. We use the drive-in today as a swap meet on Sundays where people come; it's a garage sale. And that's a family activity too. Bring the kids, the kids play in the playground, and the snack bar is open all day long."

When suburban indoor theatres invaded the drive-in's territory they competed head-on with the outdoor theatre's most promotable assets. The new indoor theatres offered the same convenient locations, with more creature comforts. They boasted comfortable seating, air-conditioned auditoriums, no mosquitos, plus (usually) first-run films and vastly improved sound and projection technology.

As the standard of social etiquette relaxed everywhere, a dress code of casual and informal attire, (once a feature nearly exclusive to drive-ins) became the prov-

and sit through a double feature." In addition, the baby boom tapered off, leaving fewer families with infants to appreciate the drive-in's affordable refuge. When the drive-in audience changed, operators often switched to screening R- or X-rated films, intermixed with race car movies, low budget horror and science fiction fare. The kiddie rides and playgrounds slowly disappeared, along with the young family audience. In a changing world they also became the victims of high insurance premiums and the threat of lawsuits.

"More recently swap meets have become a mainstay of drive-in theatres," explained Jerome A. Forman. "Swap meets, which are like flea markets, really became quite a boon in the '70s and '80s and we have used many of our drive-in sites that are still operating for daytime

ince of theatres everywhere. When shopping centers and fully-enclosed malls entered the scene, they gradually took over the drive-in's role as a community social center. A trip to the mall meant meeting friends, shopping at dozens or even hundreds of stores under one roof, dinner at a nice restaurant and the chance to take in a movie. Drive-ins began to close when their acres of once-undesirable land became more valuable. The suburbs had grown to meet the drive-in's perimeter fence and those vast plots of essentially cleared land close to nearby highways and residential areas proved irresistible to developers. Former bean fields purchased at low market prices after the war were now worth millions of dollars; who wouldn't take the offer to sell? "Land values became very, very expensive, and industries, or other types of developments would come along and make you an offer that you just couldn't resist," explained New England-based exhibitor veteran Carl Goldman. "Consequently you sold your land, you sold your theatre."

In 1958, the industry claimed a peak of 4,063 drive-ins; by 1993 number of ozoner screens had dropped to 870. Outdoor theatres often became shopping malls;

when moviegoers lost their drive-ins they often gained suburban multiple-screen theatres, which were frequently built on what used to be drive-in land.

The final blow to many a drive-in operation was the advent of the VCR. "The final nail in the coffin," said

North Avenue Outdoor Theatre, Chicago, Illinois. *Wagner-Zip Change, Inc.*

Aerial view, Orange Drive-In, Orange, California. *Pacific Theatres*

Tankersley, "was the videocassette market. What used to go to the drive-in, the second-, third- and fourth- run, that is now the one that goes to the video store. That's the one that really killed them."

Drive-in theatres that survived embraced the industry's widespread pattern of multiple screens. While single-screen outdoor theatres still do business, most drive-in acreage has been reshaped to accommodate numerous screen towers.

All that being said, news of the drive-in's extinction has been greatly exaggerated. "The moviegoing habits of Americans have changed substantially over the past 15 years," explained William F. Kartozian, president of the National Association of Theatre Owners. "This has resulted in a great reduction in the number of drive-in theatres — but that reduction has leveled off dramatically since 1990 and the drive-ins that exist today are alive and well and thriving. Also, even as the number of drive-in screens has declined, the number of motion picture theatre screens in the U.S. has increased substantially. You might say that your local drive-in didn't disappear — it was simply replaced by a suburban mall theatre where you can 'drive-up' instead of 'drive-in.'"

Phoenix's Indian Drive-In Theatre featured a "walk-in" seating section and children's playground in front of the screen tower. *George Aurelius*

Horse-in at Colorado's Centennial Drive-In. *Ralph Batschelet/Beverley Carlson*

Twin drive-in screens in suburban Denver. *Ralph Batschelet/Beverley Carlson*

Chapter 15
ART HOUSES

*I*n its purest definition, an "art house" is a theatre that caters to a specialized audience of film lovers, those who embrace movies as a serious art form akin to dance or literature. First established during the 1920s, the art house or "little cinema" movement focused on avant-garde and critically-acclaimed films that fell well outside of Hollywood's commercial mainstream. In its more modern incarnation, an art house specialized in first-run foreign films or in revivals of well-known American movies or in the presentation of obscure independent product. Whatever the actual format, art houses owe their success to a loyal audience segment that seeks out alternative programming. While art houses represent a small percentage of the total number of American movie theatres, they have a disproportionate influence on the development of American cinema. Innovative filmmakers of successive generations often received their earliest education in film style and content at the local art theatre.

Symon Gould is credited with launching the art house movement in the U.S. with the founding in 1925 of the International Film Arts Guild in New York. He inaugurated regular Sunday screenings of art films at Manhattan's George M. Cohan and Central theatres. In 1926, the Guild organized a retrospective of films by the acclaimed German director Ernst Lubitsch and also put together programs of American classics (such as D.W. Griffith's "Birth of a Nation," and "Intolerance") at the Cameo Theatre on 42nd Street. Public response

Many art houses specialized in foreign language films. *Wagner-Zip Change, Inc.*

Stanford Theatre, Palo Alto, California. *Tom Paiva*

Seattle's Seven Gables Theatre, Washington. *Landmark Theatres*

was strong enough for Gould to establish in 1927 the Film Guild Cinema, later renamed the 8th Street Playhouse, and the Film Art Cinema in Philadelphia.

During the 1920s and 1930s, American-made avant-garde films found a home in a growing network of art theatres, galleries and amateur film clubs. The little cinema movement gave filmgoers a chance to sample artistic pictures that otherwise would not be found on local theatre screens. The nation's economic woes during the 1930s forced the closure of most art theatres, and in the years just prior to World War II only a handful of U.S. theatres were presenting European or avant-garde films.

Following the war, American audiences showed a revived interest in foreign films, particularly British movies. The late 1940s and early 1950s saw a number of theatres devoting their screens to British spy capers, mysteries and sophisticated romances.

In 1947, Amos Vogel organized a film society called Cinema 16 in New York City. Describing itself as the "Off-Broadway of the cinema," the film group sponsored programs of social documentaries, controversial adult films, experimental movies and international classics. As similar film societies grew in number, exhibitors were only too happy to convert theatres to an art policy to meet the growing demand. By the end of the 1940s the Motion Picture Herald reported nearly 300 art theatres operating throughout the country.

An art house is defined by its programming, and the number of these specialty theatres in the U.S. fluctuates in response to changing audience interest and product availability. By 1952 there were an estimated 470 art houses in the country and up to 1,500 theatres booking foreign films on a less regular basis. Typical art house cinemas were located in major cities or in smaller towns near college and university campuses. "The Eighth

Street Playhouse," recalled Irving Ludwig who used to manage the venue, "was classified as a neighborhood theatre. Its operation intrigued me. I remember when it had an art gallery there. I served coffee. I made a tie-up with someone from Philip Morris and they gave me packages of two cigarettes which I offered to patrons. I was very, very selective in the shorts program, so I had a good balance between the feature and the short subject that went with it."

The art house trend was like the drive-in trend, a bright spot for exhibition in the turbulent postwar era. Theatre owners were relieved to discover an avid group of serious film fans who blithely ignored the homogenizing inroads of television on public taste. Switching to an art house policy kept many theatres from closing their doors. Also, as the public turned more and more to televised news broadcasts, many newsreel theatres evolved naturally into art house cinemas.

During the 1960s, the first American generation raised with television came of age. For most of these viewers the entertainment box in the living room had

Art house fans converged on the Elite Theatre's box office. *Sam Feldman/ Peggy Keating*

San Francisco's Mandarin Theatre, one of many theatres in San Francisco's Chinatown catering exclusively to Chinese audiences. October 1934. *Jack Tillmany*

always been there, or so it seemed, and it held no particular sense of novelty or fascination. But movies! They were gems to be discovered and savored. New movies, old movies, foreign films, message films, the offbeat, the bizarre. It was all part of a growing interest and appreciation of film as an art form, in particular among the nation's college students. They discovered the appeal of art houses as previous generations had. "We had a good following because patrons enjoyed the atmosphere, the selection of programs, the offbeat attractions, which other theatres didn't have patronage for," recalled Ludwig. "A young lady would ask them if they would like coffee and offer them cigarettes. It was a nice experience for them."

Ever since Thomas Edison introduced the 20-second peepshow as the latest novelty for amusement parlors, filmmaking in America has always been geared more toward business than art. For most of the public, movies were pure entertainment, a chance to get out, relax and share in some on-screen excitement. Begin-

ning in the 1960s a wholesale shift in attitude about American films occurred. Movies were somehow taken more seriously and elevated to the status of "film literature." Film appreciation courses and fully accredited film departments proliferated across American college campuses. Scholarly film journals emerged to dissect the aesthetic hidden in Hollywood's mainstream work. National weekly news magazines added film critics to their staffs to explain filmmakers' symbols and hidden meanings. And, just like the directors, actors and actresses that they reviewed, these film critics soon enjoyed a celebrity status of their own.

Among the avid film fans of this era were future movie directors George Lucas, Francis Coppola and Martin Scorsese, film school students and ardent movie buffs who found both inspiration and an education in film style and content at their local art house theatres.

Other directors, influenced by art cinema, also joined the wave of what became known as the "new Hollywood" of the late 1960s and early 1970s. Film historian David Bordwell described how freeze-frames, slow motion and ambiguous narrative were adapted by filmmakers such as Stanley Donen, Dennis Hopper, and Robert Altman, among others. The modern filmmaker's familiarity with classic Hollywood film styles opened the opportunity for them to parody or revitalize such classic genres as the western or the detective thriller.

By 1966 some 600 theatres regularly presented European films, the fare most commonly associated with the art cinema. To the art house patron foreign film directors like Truffaut, Fellini, Godard, and Bergman were household names. The works of such acclaimed directors as India's Satyajit Ray and Japan's Akira Kurosawa also had wide appeal.

The art house often presents a series of films grouped

Director's film series were popular programming at art houses. *Wagner-Zip Change, Inc.*

Interior of art house lobby fashioned after Parisian sidewalk. Trans-Lux Theatres, 85th St, New York City. *Richard Brandt*

around a common theme. For example, a theatre could elect to play three filmed Greek tragedies: "Electra," "Antigone," and "Oedipus Rex." While these movies

Oakland Paramount Theatre, Oakland, California. *Donald Idarius*

Varsity Theatre, Palo Alto, California. *Tom Paiva*

Interior concession stand, The Mayan Theatre. *Landmark Theatres*

The Mayan Theatre, Denver, Colorado. *Landmark Theatres*

may be difficult to promote individually, when presented together under the banner of a "trilogy" they become a special draw. Likewise, a series of French comedies, British spy capers, Japanese epics or Hollywood femme fatale films — be they current pictures or

retrospective titles — can find its way onto an art house screen.

The art house operator is limited only by his imagination. Among the most popular film festivals are those that feature a particular director such as Francois Truffaut, Alfred Hitchcock or Charlie Chaplin. Other programs might feature the award winners from the Cannes Film Festival or the New York Film Festival, or films produced by a particular company. Programs as diverse as a Janus film festival of classics, the films of Humphrey Bogart, the classics of film noir, and an opera series have

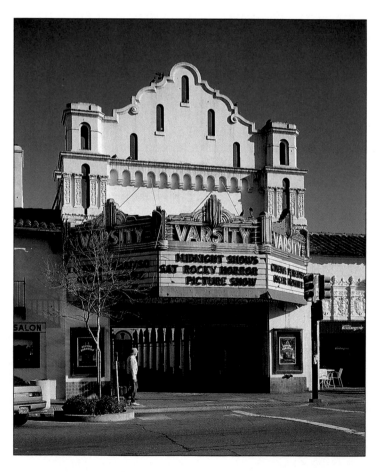

all proved popular with art house audiences.

The art house owner has another advantage over the conventional operator — if a series is successful, it can be brought back on an annual basis. In addition, since the theatre owner does not have to rely on current titles to create a successful bill, he has a certain flexibility in developing programming that the mainstream operator does not.

Catering to their audience's sophisticated knowledge of film, art house cinemas regularly publish detailed program notes, and calendars, and send mailers detailing their offerings to special interest groups. In addition, pairing a film with a lecture or evening of conversation is yet another way art house cinemas sometimes satisfy their patrons' intense interest in cinema.

All is not serious, however, on the art house circuit — just ask any fan of "The Rocky Horror Picture Show." "Rocky Horror" was an abysmal failure in 1975 in its initial box office release. The following year it opened as a weekend midnight movie and began a sustained run in more than 200 theatres across the country. Many of these art house cinemas featured the cult favorite for 10 to 15 years or more. People began going to their local "Rocky Horror" theatre dressed as the film's characters. During the show, most of the audience will typically recite treasured bits of dialogue along with the movie's actors. Midnight screenings of the film helped theatre owners make extra money at a time when the theatre would normally be closed. Advertising expenses were minimal as film fans discovered the picture by word of mouth.

The habit of midnight movies evolved during the 1960s with screenings that centered around filmed rock concerts, Halloween titles, and dusk-to-dawn film marathons. In 1982 an estimated 600 to 1,000 theatres na-

tionwide ran regularly scheduled midnight movies on weekends. Some midnight movies like "Rocky Horror," have evolved into ritualistic events, luring many of the same people back weekend after weekend.

In the 1980s, some suggested that the rise in popularity of the VCR would put specialty theatres out of business. As exhibition's first century drew to a close, however, new filmmakers were drawing new audiences to the art house. The 1990s saw a flowering of interest in a broad range of new foreign language and alternative films, including: "Howards End," "Mediteranneo," "Like Water For Chocolate," "The Player," "Indochine," "Much Ado About Nothing," "Wild At Heart," "Drugstore Cowboy," "My Own Private Idaho," "Slacker," and of course the phenomenally successful "The Crying Game." Specialty films such as these became in the 1990s the trademark of the art house cinema — largely replacing the traditional revival house or strictly foreign language fare that graced art house marquees in years past.

Arizona-based exhibitor Dan Harkins and loyal followers of "The Rocky Horror Picture Show." *Dan Harkins*

In the '50s, Berkeley's Northside Theatre offered free espresso. Some 40 years later it had a snack bar offering exotic and expensive imported candies but the coffee refills were still free. *Jack Tillmany*

"The contemporary art house audience is very diverse," explained Stephen Gilula, president of the sprawling specialty house chain Landmark Theatres. "It is comprised of 'baby boomers' who as college students in the 1960s were weaned on revival house fare and foreign films; older audiences who appreciate the literary or traditional art films such as 'Enchanted April,' or 'Howards End'; members of the 'X' generation, those 20-year-olds who identify with young alternative filmmakers; as well as gay audiences who have found a voice in such films as 'My Beautiful Laundrette,' 'My Own Private Idaho,' 'Longtime Companion' and others.

"While obituaries for art theatres have been written every few years," noted Gilula, "they have never died, they have just continued to change and evolve in response to the continual shifts in audience interests and tastes as well as new directions and innovations in international and American independent filmmaking. The definition of the art theatre continues to change. No longer can a theatre survive solely on revival or retro-

spective programming since video fulfills much of that demand. The expansion and contraction of the number of art theatres is due primarily to changes in the availability of product rather than declining audience interests. New "waves" of film, first from Europe, then from Australia, Britain, and American independents have brought successive surges in media and audience interest. The result has created the modern successful art house, one that caters to a broad, diverse audience by presenting an eclectic mix of films from many sources.

"The current interest in specialty films is unprecedented in my 20 years in the business," said Gilula during the summer of 1993. "So it is okay to file away the obituaries for another day."

L.A.'s Nuart Theatre with typical art house programming.
Landmark Theatres

The Surf Theatre, San Francisco, California. 1968.
Jack Tillmany

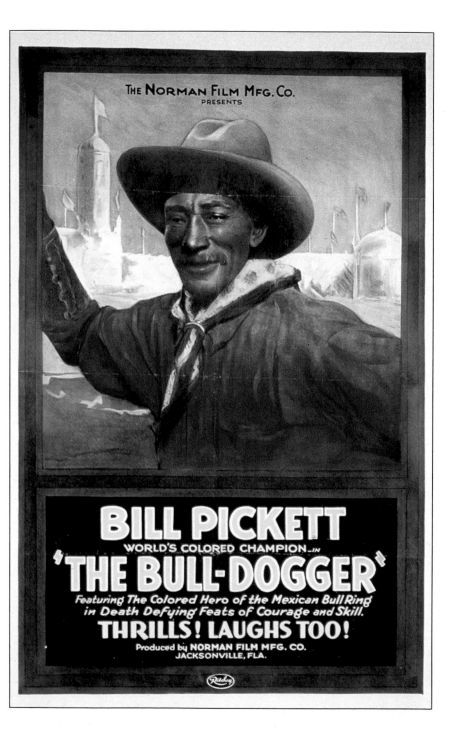

Chapter 16

BLACK THEATRES/BLACK MOVIES

Prior to 1964 and the enactment of the nation's landmark Civil Rights Act, millions of black Americans experienced the movies in segregated or blacks-only neighborhood theatres. Compounding this situation was the parade of negative black images that graced the screen. From the time of Edison's earliest moving pictures, scenes of watermelon-eating blacks were followed by a succession of equally exaggerated stereotypes. Unlike white patrons who enjoyed a range of screen portraits that included dashing heroes, beautiful maidens, cowboys, sheriffs, gangsters, teachers, mothers, cops, society ladies and priests, black audiences saw themselves reflected only in comic or subservient roles. They witnessed a succession of movie slaves and servants, confidantes, handymen and porters — all passive, excessively cheerful, irresponsible or dimwitted one-dimensional caricatures. These characterizations, some made even worse when portrayed in the earliest moving pictures by white actors in burnt-cork make-up or blackface, bore faint resemblance to the everyday lives of black Americans and mirrored none of their strengths or aspirations.

The eventual development of black movie theatres gave rise to an independent black cinema movement, one that treated black audiences to positive film images of people much like themselves. The continued existence of segregated theatres, whether dictated by law in the South or created by housing patterns or entrenched local custom, meant that these positive screen images were enjoyed as part of a moviegoing experience differ-

Audience at Santee Cinema in St. Stephens, South Carolina. *Christine Funk*

Rex Theatre for Colored People, Leland, Mississippi, 1939. *Library of Congress*

Lithograph, 1923. Bill Pickett in "The Bull-Dogger." *Library of Congress*

Motion Picture Poster, 1939. "Lying Lips," Micheaux Pictures. *Library of Congress*

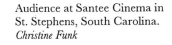

ent from that enjoyed by the majority of Americans.

From the earliest days of moving pictures, the South was a segregated society. Movie theatres fell under the same statutes that had legally separated the races at legitimate theatres since 1883. Failure to comply with these race laws could mean stiff fines for both the offending patron and theatre owner alike. Thus it was that black Americans, who held movie tickets in their hands just like the other paying customers, were routinely directed to cramped theatre balconies or the less desirable seats down front and to the side of the screen.

In some areas audiences were segregated by time. Movie houses held special screenings for blacks during off hours, long after the theatre had closed for white audiences. These were the first "midnight movies" and these late night shows became a common practice throughout the South. In some instances, racial atti-

tudes were so entrenched that blacks still faced restricted seating arrangements at these shows.

In small rural communities some moviehouses operated with a split-week policy offering movies for whites and blacks on different days of the week. In rare cases, small Southern theatres achieved segregation by erecting a curtain or simple barrier down the aisle. The segregated balcony was by far the most common way to separate the races. In larger theatres this might actually be a second balcony, referred to in South Carolina as "buzzard roosts" and "peanut galleries." While white patrons entered the theatre through its front doors and had their choice of orchestra seats, blacks were directed to exterior staircases leading to the balcony. "A lot of the big, big theatres that had been stage show houses, opera type houses, had a balcony and then what we called the 'peanut roost,' a second balcony above that," elaborated former Mississippi-based exhibitor Ad Orkin. The only entrance to it was a steel stairway, up the side of the building. Scare you to death to climb up there. When you get up there and look down, you'd think you were on Mars, it was so far down to the stage. And that's where the blacks went."

If refreshments were available, blacks were restricted to separate concession areas set up on the exterior stair landings or in the balcony corners. Refreshments were limited and might consist of a few choices of candy. "We usually had a separate staircase with a big open window that you could sell concessions through, or the concessions stand was backed up to the staircase and available to both areas, but was still segregated," remembered veteran Texas exhibitor John Rowley.

"Now [some of our black theatre] concession stands were kind of novel," remembered Orkin. "The concession stand was open at both ends, one end was for street

The Dixie Theatre, Ohio, circa 1927. *Cincinnati Historical Society*

traffic to come, we had stools and a counter. The other end of it is where patrons went into the show. And the prices were so cheap they could do better at the theatre than they could at the restaurants."

During the first decade of the 20th century black vaudeville theatres spread throughout the larger cities of the South. These variety houses presented an entertaining mix of vaudeville, burlesque, musical comedy — and eventually, movies. "At the Howard Theatre for example," explained veteran Virginia-based exhibitor Seymour Hoffman, "we had all of the big name bands appear at one time or another. There was Charlie Barnett, and Cab Calloway, Duke Ellington and Woody Herman." Black theatres with a movies-only policy emerged next. By 1910, there were an estimated 100 black theatres where patrons could enjoy movies only or see pictures in combination with variety shows. "During the days of the black theatres we had traveling stage shows made up of one person and the one person would be a movie star," recalled Orkin. "Lash LaRue did a lot of these, Dizzy Gillespie, we played him and Fuzzy St. John. I don't remember his real name, he was Lash LaRue's sidekick. We'd put them on between every show starting at noon. The shows were at two, four, six, eight and 10 o'clock and we charged extra admission for the stage show."

William Foster's production of a series of black film shorts in 1910 Chicago marked the beginning of a black cinema movement. His efforts were built upon by a group of independent black filmmakers who were determined to make pictures that more accurately portrayed the black experience. The release of D. W. Griffith's "Birth of a Nation" in 1915 proved a flashpoint for black filmmaking efforts. Critics hailed Griffith's monumental Civil War epic as a cinematic masterpiece of great emotional power. Nevertheless, it contained some of

Abandoned cafe and movie theatre had separate doors for "white" and "colored." Shot somewhere in northeast North Carolina. *Library of Congress*

the most extreme racial stereotypes ever found on film. The picture earned the dubious distinction of being the first American-made feature film to provoke nationwide calls for censorship. The newly-organized National Association for the Advancement of Colored People (NAACP) spearheaded a crusade of black organizations and sympathetic whites to have the film banned outright. Failing that, opponents of the picture sought to eliminate the most objectionable scenes. Pickets surrounded theatres in major cities where the picture opened and there were scattered reports of stink bombs planted in theatres and eggs thrown at the screen. On the whole, protests against "Birth of a Nation" proved ineffective and the epic-length feature played as an enormously successful roadshow presentation for years.

In the years following the film's release, a growing number of production companies were organized to

Crowd leaving Chicago's Regal Theatre. 1941. *Library of Congress*

try, black-cast film companies were an important legacy for generations of black filmgoers. Black-cast or so-called "race films" were the first to present non-stereotypical, positive film roles for blacks. Sadly, the talent and creativity found in this separate black cinema were rarely seen by the general public.

One leading black production company was the Lincoln Company, whose first feature, "Realization of a Negro's Ambition," was a drama set against the backdrop of black middle-class society. Its success spawned other features and Lincoln eventually established exchange offices in cities with a sizeable number of black theatres. Within two years, the company opened booking offices in Omaha, Chicago, New York, Philadelphia, Washington, D.C., Atlanta, St. Louis and New Orleans. The Lincoln Motion Picture Company is credited with establishing the first national booking organization for black theatres. The company typically licensed films for a weekly rate of $400. Theatres in smaller cities that couldn't afford to pay for a week's run were serviced by two traveling salesmen. After Lincoln's advance man previewed a new film for a prospective customer and scheduled a playdate, a second company rep would arrive some weeks later with the picture and stay to collect the company's share of the gross receipts.

The best known of all the early independent black cinema companies was the Micheaux Film Corporation, founded in 1918 by Oscar Micheaux as the Micheaux Film and Book Corporation. The company produced several adaptations of its founder's many novels and stayed active until 1940. As John Kisch and Edward Mapp explain in their book "A Separate Cinema," "On his tours Micheaux approached white, Southern theatre managers and owners, often persuading them to show his black films at special matinee performances for black audiences or at special late

produce black-cast films presenting positive black images. The first was the Lincoln Motion Picture Company established in 1916 in Los Angeles. Between 1910 and 1950, an estimated 150 film companies were established with the specific intent of producing black-cast feature films. Producers targeted their efforts toward the segregated theatres of the South and the increasing number of black ghetto theatres in the North. Of the total number of these black film companies, roughly a third were owned by blacks. With a handful of notable exceptions, most failed to achieve even modest success. The companies that managed to produce one or two films before folding were the lucky ones; fully one quarter of these companies failed before completing even a single picture. Yet, despite their limited success when measured against the mainstream motion picture indus-

shows for white audiences interested in black camp."

The audience for black-cast films grew rapidly between 1915 and 1923 while producers continually struggled with the basic problems of financing, production and a haphazard distribution system that often overlooked many potential exhibitors. The budding black film industry faced its hardest times in the mid- to late 1920s because most theatres catering to whites refused to book black-cast films. Out of 1926's estimated 20,000 American movie theatres, only a few hundred would play an all-black production. The limited income derived from ghetto theatres and Southern theatres with midnight shows for blacks was not enough for most production companies to survive. The added expenses dictated by the coming of sound also hurt black-cast film companies. Many were forced to limit their productions to silents or part-talkies.

The shortage of black-cast films meant that theatres catering to black audiences filled 80 percent or more of their programs with last-runs of standard Hollywood fare and an endless succession of B westerns and action films. "The pictures were not available to the colored theatre until after they had played their first run in the white theatres, moved on to the drive-ins, and after the drive-in then we could take the pictures," remembered Orkin. Teddy Solomon recalled that black theatres typically featured programming originally produced for white audiences. "We ran action pictures like westerns on Saturday and Saturday night," said Soloman. "Films with Gene Autry, Roy Rogers, and Hopalong Cassidy, those pictures not only appealed to the white population, they also appealed to the black population in the black theatre. During the week we would have more of an action type picture in the black theatre rather than a Shirley Temple or something like that."

During the 1930s the number of movie theatres on the "race circuit" grew to nearly 600, including those houses that played to integrated audiences. Midnight movies for blacks at white Southern theatres grew in popularity in the 1930s and '40s, adding to the number of theatres that presented black-cast films.

Black theatres had never grown in sufficient number to meet the needs of the entire population they were intended to serve. Before the start of World War II, a growing number of theatres in the South opened their balconies to blacks, thereby expanding the opportunities for Southern blacks to go to the movies. "Sometimes we had black balconies and sometimes only one-half of the balcony would be black and the rest would be white," remembered veteran Georgia-based circuit owner Carl Patrick. "If you sat in the balcony you only paid 25

Regal Theatre, Chicago, 1941.
Library of Congress

cents. If you sat downstairs you paid 35 cents."

Hollywood's attempt to make a "cross-over" film that would appeal to white and black audiences resulted in the 1929 MGM production of "Hallelujah," a black-cast musical directed by King Vidor. The film's release met with unanticipated resistance from Northern exhibitors who worried about attracting a larger-than-usual number of Negro patrons to their theatres.

In Pittsburgh, the film never played at the first-run Loews theatre that typically showed most MGM product. It was instead booked into a smaller house where local custom dictated that blacks were not welcome. In other cases, the studio refrained from advertising the film in local black newspapers until it played at a black neighborhood theatre.

In New York City, "Hallelujah" was booked into a major theatre on Broadway and uptown in Harlem on the assumption that blacks would remain in their neighborhood to see the film. When a group of blacks ventured downtown to see the film during its opening week, they were told that the show had been sold out, a fact betrayed by the subsequent sale of tickets to white patrons. It was an incident that underscored the nervousness of Northern theatre owners who sought to discourage any large-scale mixing of the races.

Exhibitors' nervous reception of "Hallelujah" and its weak performance at the box office convinced the major studios to abandon for the time being any similar productions featuring black leads. Outstanding black performers such as Ethel Waters, Bill Robinson, Dorothy Dandridge, Ossie Davis, Ruby Dee and Lena Horne were relegated to minor roles or musical numbers that could be easily cut out to satisfy censor boards in the South.

Southern censors routinely employed a form of "racial editing" to delete film scenes that showed blacks in anything but comic or subservient roles. This form of censorship was formally prohibited by the Supreme Court in 1952 when it extended the guarantee of free speech to motion pictures. Even when Southern censor boards were at their most strident in opposing positive black depictions in mainstream Hollywood films, they didn't bother to review black-cast films, deeming them unimportant. Audiences fortunate enough to see these pictures, however, were exposed to an absorbing variety of fully-drawn black film characters.

During the 1920s and 1930s an increasing number of black Americans streamed north and pursued opportunities in the nation's industrial centers. As the trend continued, an increasing number of black movie theatres opened. The number of black movie houses in the U.S. grew from 232 in 1937 to 430 in 1942 and then to 684 in 1947. Many of these were theatres that had "turned" black as previous waves of immigrants left neighborhoods and were replaced by the arriving newcomers from the South. Facing changing audience needs, the owners of some of these venues turned to film production themselves to increase the flow of black-cast films for their audiences.

The postwar years brought a new sensitivity to Hollywood and audiences saw some improvement in the on-screen portrayals of blacks in films released by the majors. At the same time, black moviegoers became more selective and gradually lost interest in black cinema's hastily-made, technically-inferior, low-budget movies. In 1953, operators of black theatres reported to the industry trade paper Variety that "standard Hollywood fare generally met the demand of black audiences."

Even the informality of drive-in theatres brought scant relief from segregation for black moviegoers. At many drive-in theatres the farthest ramps were reserved as "colored sections" with their own adjacent yet separate concession buildings and restroom areas.

By the late 1950s the country was slowly recognizing the inequities of segregation, whether it was enforced by law or established through custom.

As the population of the nation's largest cities became increasingly black due to the flight of middle-class whites to the suburbs, theatre owners were among the first to integrate their businesses. "I don't think we approached the city government," recalled veteran East Coast circuit head Richard Brandt. "We did this through the black churches, and through the exhibitors. I remember talking to the other exhibitors in town and telling them what I was going to do, and asking them if they would follow suit if everything worked out okay. I was able to get in touch with a local Negro pastor who seemed to have some influence in town and I suggested to him that he bring some Negroes into the theatre and break the barrier and let people know we've done it. We didn't have any major protests, we had a few little ones. But anyway, it worked."

By the start of the 1960s, the civil rights movement was already sweeping the country and among the first people to feel its effects were exhibitors, remembered veteran Virginia-based circuit owner Sam Bendheim. "We had gotten a telegram from the Justice Department, from Bobby Kennedy, asking us to appear at a meeting in his office. When we got there, there were 25 to 30 other exhibitors from throughout the South. He was both soft and firm at the same time. He sort of sat back in his chair comfortably and just spoke the whole time about what the President wanted for the country, and what he expected of us, and that the day had come, that what was being done was wrong. At that time, the state of Virigina had a law that prevented integration, and any violation of it, you were subject to severe penalties. So in essence he told us 'you'll break the state law.'" "We didn't do anything, we didn't say anything," remembered Virginia-based theatre owner Jerry Gordon. "When a black person came up to buy a ticket, we sold it to him. Pretty soon word got around and a few more blacks would come and that was really the beginning of integration."

The passage of the 1964 Civil Rights Act outlawed segregated theatres. Theatres in black ghetto areas continued to operate for a time in local neighborhoods while larger downtown theatres gradually absorbed the majority of America's black film patrons.

Early demonstration against segregated theatres. Rialto Theatre, Phoenix, Arizona. 1953. *George Aurelius*

Chapter 17
MOVIES IN THE 'BURBS

W hile the nation's postwar downtown areas and their once magnificent theatres faced decline, all that was new and booming was in suburbia. Initially serving as "bedroom communities" for the nation's central cities, America's suburbs soon became places where people both lived and worked. When regional shopping centers emerged to cater to this growing population, theatres were not far behind. "The industry moved to where the public was," said Maryland-based circuit owner Irwin R. Cohen. "As new shopping centers developed in the late '40s and early '50s, after World War II, theatres went into them. They were still building 800-seat theatres, and they were single screens."

The first suburban theatres, located in or near these new shopping malls, offered the best of what the popular suburban drive-ins offered, with some important bonuses. They too were conveniently located, they boasted acres of free parking, they were informal, they were inexpensive, they catered to families — plus, they offered comfortable seating in a mosquito-free, temperature-controlled environment, with a better picture and better sound. "People liked to shop in their own neighbor-

hood," reminded Virginia-based theatre owner Jerry Gordon. "They still do today."

The number of suburban shopping centers grew from a few hundred in 1950 to nearly 3,000 by 1958, and more than 7,000 by 1963. Shopping centers became a fertile spawning ground for a new generation of moviehouses. Located in the heart of suburbia, these new theatres were the picture of convenience, the new watchword of value for modern Americans. For exhibitors, the emphasis was on a streamlined, economical operation tailored to new audience realities. The oversized and architecturally-ornate designs of the past were abandoned in favor of smaller theatres of more functional design.

Former movie palaces were now dismissed as cavernous barns. Now aged and badly in need of refurbishing, many of these once magnificent picture palaces were doomed by a falling number of patrons and the rising cost of upkeep. Gone were the days when crowds packed the massive auditoriums or milled expectantly through huge, ornate lobbies. Gone too were usher spill cards and hand signals to track any available seats.

Exhibitors rallied public support to fight pay TV. Roth's Americana Theatre, Annandale, Virginia, circa 1967. *Paul Roth*

Sparse audience attendance forced the closure of many movie palaces. *John Lowe*

Many downtown movie palaces resorted to science fiction and horror flicks to hold an audience. *Allen Michaan*

Demolition of the Paramount Theatre, St. Paul, Minnesota. 1965. *George Aurelius*

These impressive buildings now stood half-empty during showtimes. A large part of the downtown theatres' former audience stayed home.

During the 1960s many urban neighborhoods gradually deteriorated and whole populations left the cities for outlying areas. "People didn't go downtown anymore," remembered veteran East Coast exhibitor Bernard Myerson. "All the urban areas were destitute. I wanted to have theatres out where the bedrooms were, out in the suburban areas. Of course people wouldn't leave downtown, go home and have dinner, and then come back downtown again. But if they had a movie theatre 10 minutes away from where they lived, they would go there."

Downtown theatre owners valiantly tried to appeal to the downtown audience that remained. In some cases this meant catering to Spanish-language audiences. "Little by little we became a Spanish-oriented market," remembered veteran Southern California exhibitor Morton Lippe. "Sunday afternoon in downtown Los Angeles was incredible. It was like a mall on Broadway of Spanish speaking people. They enjoyed the film. They liked to come and bring their whole family. It was a wonderful experience for us."

As the decade progressed, more and more marquees of stately downtown houses blazed with the titles of cheap action thrillers, horror and sci-fi tales, and "adults only" pictures. In the end, many of the country's beloved downtown movie cathedrals faced the wrecking ball. Too cavernous to be converted to other uses, these adored theatres were sacrificed for their prime real estate value. Sadly their land could be more profitably used for parking lots or building sites than for palaces.

The evolution of the traditional single-screen movie theatre into today's modern multiple-screen cinema complex began on July 12, 1963 when American Multi-Cinema, then known as Durwood Theatres, opened the Parkway Theatres in Kansas City's Ward Parkway Shopping Center. The Parkway One featured 400 seats; the Parkway Two held 300. The twin theatres shared a common box office, lobby, projection booth and concessions stand.

Credit for the world's first multiple-screen, shopping center movie complex goes to Stanley Durwood, then president of the theatre company that his father, Edward D. Durwood, had founded in 1920. By the early 1960s,

Baltimore's Century-Valencia Theatre was an early "twin" theatre built as separate movie palaces with no common areas or staff. The Moorish-styled Valencia was built upstairs from the Spanish Gothic Century. *Irwin R. Cohen*

San Francisco's Haight Theatre ended its life as a neighborhood second-run theatre in 1964. *Jack Tillmany*

Durwood Theatres was a small company whose holdings included some drive-ins in Kansas City and other cities in Missouri and Kansas. The chain had recently expanded into shopping center theatres and young Stan Durwood envisioned twin theatres as a way to increase business.

The idea of twin theatres had been tried at different times in exhibition history, but Durwood is generally acknowledged as the first to introduce the concept into a shopping center. The Parkway Theatres debuted with the coup of a hit first-run feature, "The Great Escape," starring film idol Steve McQueen, playing on both screens. The combination of a hit movie, the added convenience of extra show times and the sheer novelty of the twin idea captured the public's attention. Durwood next booked different films in each auditorium and watched as the Parkway twin succeeded beyond all expectations.

Within months Durwood opened two other twin theatres and then a triple. In 1966 the company opened the world's first four-theatre complex; in 1969 it opened a six-plex in Omaha. General Cinema Corporation, another drive-in circuit that had recently switched its emphasis to shopping center theatres, also embraced the concept of multiple-screen theatres. Other circuits would follow. Exhibition's multiple-screen theatre revolution had begun.

During the shopping center boom of the 1960s, developers used extensive marketing research to pinpoint areas of greatest suburban growth. Former regional theatre circuits that forged alliances with major developers soon found themselves criss-crossing the country opening multiple screen theatres in shopping malls all across the U.S.. These new national circuits each boasting hundreds of theatre screens emerged as the powerful successors to the theatre chains once oper-

ated by the Big Five motion picture studios.

Early twin theatres were not without their problems. Critics decried them as cramped "shoe boxes" or "cookie cutter" theatres devoid of any architectural imagination but others did not share this opinion. "The theatre became much more intimate, and we felt more

Twin cinemas in the suburbs. *John Lowe*

Eastland Theatre, the first theatre built in the Southern California suburb of West Covina boasted one thousand seats. *SoCal Cinemas*

First suburban theatre in Phoenix, Arizona, 1945. *George Aurelius*

This streamlined suburban theatre has no marquee and no front displays, only a neon sign, a "reader board" and floodlights. Cine Capri Theatre, Phoenix, Arizona. 1966. *George Aurelius*

Short-lived attempt to franchise movie theatres failed. The franchise opportunity offered by Jerry Lewis Cinemas came and went in the early '70s. *Jack Tillmany*

desirable," recalled veteran East Coast exhibitor Julian Rifkin. "They weren't these big arks in which you would feel lonely. We felt very strongly, and I think the customers felt, that there was a small intimate theatre and you had people there and you felt one with the group. So, instead of saying small, boxy, let's say they were intimate."

Many of the troubles faced by these early mini-theatres, as the industry called them at the time, stemmed from design problems as the infant multiplex industry struggled through a period of trial and error. In the earliest multiplex designs, implemented before the advent of automated projectors, one projector booth served two or more screens. With the projector not properly aligned to any one of the individual screens, one side of the image looked larger than the other, an effect called "keystoning." Some of the early theatres had inadequate soundproofing and patrons experienced annoying sound leakage from adjoining auditoriums. Nothing could be more disruptive to the mood of a

romantic drama than hearing the bass rumble of starfighters from the space adventure next door. "I remember sitting in a twin theatre where I think 'Love Story' was on one side and that Steve McQueen movie was on the other, recalled Ohio-based exhibition veteran Russell J. Wintner. "Every time he'd go around a corner you'd hear the squeal of tires, just as Ryan O'Neal was going to kiss Ali McGraw. It was just really weird, like listening to squealing kisses."

The remodeling of movie palaces into multiple screen theatres — however wrenching to devoted fans of their original architectural splendor — gave many of these proud moviehouses a new lease on life and helped return them to profitability. "I don't think there is anybody who is really honest with himself that can say that twinning a theatre made a better theatre for the customer," reflected Russ Wintner, "We knew that they were bowling alleys, they were not fun places to go, and many times, sitting in a twin theatre, you'd get a crick in your neck because the seat was facing the center wall and you wanted to look at a screen that was now off to the right or left side of the old room."

Numerous innovations in the late 1960s provided the impetus that saw twin theatres leapfrog into six-plexes, eight-plexes and even ten-plexes. By the early 1990s exhibitors were housing as many as 24 screens under one roof, and multiplex design was becoming increasingly sophisticated. "The neat thing about the six-plex and the five-plex and the triple we were doing," remembered Wintner, "was that they were *designed* to be multiplex theatres. We used the information that was available in those days to provide customers with a much more pleasing atmosphere."

The single most important revolutionary breakthrough occurred with the introduction of the xenon bulb, a gas-filled vacuum lamp that emits a brilliant and

constant light for movie projection. Its introduction in the mid 1960s marked the most significant improvement in projection lighting since the carbon arc replaced limelight.

To fully understand the impact of the xenon bulb, it's helpful to first understand the limitations of carbon arc lighting. Carbon arc light had been used reliably for film projection since the first decade of the 20th century. A burning carbon stick cast a bright light but only burned for a few minutes before it sputtered out. With

the coming of longer films improvements were made and the life of the carbon stick was extended to 20 minutes. When movies exceeded this length "change-overs" and the 2,000-foot reel were born. Since the carbon had to be replaced several times during the standard running time of a 90-minute to two-hour movie, theatres had to install two projectors to avoid delays during the film presentation. Feature films were divided onto 20-minute reels to match the burning time of the carbon light. The projectionist was on hand to change reels, change carbons and clean out the resulting smoke and debris. Under a projectionist's expert supervision the change between reels would appear seamless to the audience, but carbon arc projection was far less than perfect. It flickered, changed color and required a projectionist in the booth at all times to maintain constant vigilance.

The xenon bulb, on the other hand, burned with consistent brightness for 1,000 hours or longer. The essential beauty of it was that it worked just like a regular incandescent light bulb that could be turned on and off. Once theatres could turn their projection light source on and off with the flick of a switch, revolutionary possibilities of automation had arrived, which in turn held the potential of a better film presentation. Previously the slightest miscue could result in changeover error. A word or two of dialogue might be cut off between reels. There might be a flash of light or, worse yet, the film would actually run out and the screen would go blank until the second projector got rolling.

Automated equipment eliminated these potential reel-change problems. Computer systems controlled projector functions, handled changeovers and alternately turned on and extinguished the xenon lamps in each. Systems also sounded a warning if a projector was improperly threaded, a light failed or the film broke.

The invention of the platter eliminated the need to use two projectors in showing a feature length film. *NATO*

The next technical revolution to transform the projection booth came with the development of huge film projection systems called platters that could accommodate all 12,000 feet of a standard-length feature film. Changeovers were eliminated altogether, allowing a single operator to run as many projectors as there were multiplex auditoriums. The touch of a button activated the projectors and maintained proper focus throughout the film's presentation. Advances in automation also made it possible to program the house lights, the opening and closing of the theatre curtains, and even the start-up of popcorn warmers at the refreshment stand. In time, a fully-automated system allowed the theatre manager to double as the house projectionist. He could still take on the time-honored role of starting the show with a flick of the switch, only now that switch was often located in a console off the lobby.

Just as the xenon bulb introduced an extraordinary new crispness to the projected film image, new developments in sound technology pushed the moviegoing experience to new realms of sensory delight.

With the advent of the 1974 adventure-thriller "Earthquake," Universal Pictures introduced a new process called "Sensurround." The film's seven-minute sequence depicting the destruction of Los Angeles was enhanced with low-frequency sound waves which were added to the soundtrack during the dubbing process. As audiences watched Charlton Heston and Ava Gardner scramble for safety, they would feel a rumble-like temblor effect. For the added cost of $500 a week, theatre owners could rent extra speakers and an amplifier to further heighten the sensory effect of rumbling destruction. The Sensurround sound system, which earned a special Academy Award, helped move "Earthquake" into the ranks of the year's biggest box office hits. Subsequent films released in Sensurround, however,

The world's first twin movie theatre built in a shopping center, the AMC Parkway 2, 1963. Kansas City, Missouri. *American Multi Cinema*

failed to generate the same box office excitement and the system was eventually abandoned.

The cinema sound barrier was decisively broken in 1975 with the introduction of Dolby stereo. The Dolby system provided high-fidelity stereo optical soundtracks on economical 35mm film prints. Previous experiments with multi-channel sound during the 1950s had proven prohibitively expensive, largely due to the high cost of producing magnetic sound prints and the expense of equipping theatres to present the handful of stereo re-

True Dolby stereo was introduced in 1975 with the release of the rock opera "Tommy," and came to be used in a number of subsequent movie musicals. Dolby came to wide public attention when it helped catapult George Lucas' "Star Wars" (1977) and Steven Spielberg's

leases that were available. Dolby prints, by contrast, cost nothing extra to produce and the equipment necessary for the system required little maintenance. The Dolby noise reduction system, meanwhile, made for a sparkling clarity of sound. Physicist Ray M. Dolby formed Dolby Laboratories in 1965 to develop noise reduction techniques for the music industry. Applied to movies, Dolby's noise reduction technique was first used on Stanley Kubrick's futuristic 1971 satire "A Clockwork Orange."

"Close Encounters of the Third Kind" (1978) into the box office stratosphere. The average cost to equip a theatre with Dolby sound was under $10,000, but the extra expense was typically counterbalanced by the extra patronage and customer satisfaction that it generated. By the end of the 1970s, 1200 theatres were equipped with Dolby sound.

Exhibitor interest in continually improving the moviegoing experience was further rewarded in 1983 with the introduction of the THX sound system developed by Lucasfilm, Ltd. The patented system included a special screen speaker installation, an improved surround system and a number of other technical refinements that gave audiences the sense they were in the middle of the screen action.

The issue of pay-TV was a prominent one for exhibitors during the turbulent 1960s and 1970s. The issue first surfaced in the late 1940s with a technology called Phonovision. This was a system which proposed to offer primarily first-run motion pictures prior to their release in theatres. Developed by A T & T, Phonovision used telephone lines to deliver movies directly to home television sets. Another system was developed by Zenith, a leading manufacturer of television sets. For the next 25 years, exhibitors kept a wary eye on the advance of pay-television experiments.

Beginning in 1968, the FCC sanctioned experiments of pay-television technology in a limited number of test markets. The action was vigorously opposed by exhibitor organizations, the television networks and proponents of cable systems. While "free" television had significantly altered moviegoing habits, it did not compete directly with first-run theatres. Pay-television, on the other hand, threatened to rob theatres of their exclusive access to first-run movies.

Exhibition waged a protracted and expensive legal

The Lenox Square Theatre opened in the first regional mall in the Southeast, circa 1963. *Bill Stembler*

campaign against pay-TV, first under the leadership of the Theatre Owners of America and then under the banner of its successor organization, the National Association of Theatre Owners. Theatre owners rallied public support to their cause under the slogan "Save Free TV." Theatre marquees and banners spread the word and petition drives encouraged the public's active involvement in the campaign to defeat pay-TV. During the summer of 1969, petitions containing 10 million signatures were collected and sent to Congress in the campaign to ban pay-television. All pay-TV tests conducted through 1969 proved expensive failures due to lack of public support. In 1973, after the FCC recommended that feature films be restricted from pay-TV systems for at least one year after their initial theatrical release, NATO called off its efforts to defeat the new medium. Still, newer potential threats to exhibition loomed just over the horizon.

Beginning in the late 1970s, "home entertainment" came to mean much more than radio, stereo systems and television broadcasts. The age of the videocassette

recorder dawned, followed closely by the nationwide launch of cable TV systems. Within a year of a picture's first-run release to theatres, a videocassette of the same movie would now routinely become available for rent at a burgeoning number of video rental stores. For the cost of one rental, an unlimited number of relatives, friends

Jose Theatre, San Jose, California, 1991. *Jack Tillmany*

Former home of the Newsreel Theatre (1938-65), Los Angeles' Globe Theatre led the trend of many downtown theatres and converted to Spanish language films. *Metropolitan Theatres*

Downtown theatres faced decline in the postwar years. Lorenzo Theatre, San Lorenzo, California. *Tom Paiva*

and neighbors could gather in a living room to see a top-rated feature film, albeit several months to a year after the film's initial release.

Cable television had originally been developed to bring television broadcasts to areas with poor broadcast signal reception. Before long, however, cable systems and satellite distribution services would emerge to add a broad range of non-broadcast programming, including movie channels that were available at an extra charge over the cable system's monthly subscription rate. Movies on cable were a decided improvement over their broadcast network counterparts. Cable ran pictures uncut, uncensored and commercial free.

In 1975 the Home Box Office microwave service went to satellite distribution. By offering subscribers feature films a few months after they had left the nation's theatre screens, HBO sparked a home entertainment revolution. Within five years, HBO's subscriber base grew from 300,000 customers to more than six million. By 1983, its number of subscribers had doubled to 12 million. In 1976, Viacom International, a leading supplier of television programs and owner of cable systems, launched Showtime to directly compete with Home Box Office. A proliferation of other movie services followed.

Despite competition from an expanded number of home entertainment choices, the movie theatre proved to be enduring. Audiences in the late 1970s rediscovered the pleasures of going out to the movies. The '70s brought the birth of the modern blockbuster and Hollywood rediscovered a potent audience — the youth market. Filmmakers targeted their new efforts squarely at the young — with enough spectacle and whiz-bang special effects to attract the occasional older moviegoer as well.

The blockbuster film, supported by multi-million dollar marketing campaigns, along with an onslaught of media exposure and a deluge of licensed product tie-ins, brought back the sense of moviegoing as an "event." Audiences turned out in droves and the era of the $100 million blockbuster was born. Visionary theatre circuits prepared to maintain the audience's newfound allegiance with a new generation of larger, upgraded, beautifully-designed theatre complexes.

229

Chapter 18

MODERN TIMES

"It's like taking aspirin. I figured if two was good, four would be twice as good." — Stanley Durwood on the development of the multiplex

*T*hroughout exhibition history, doomsayers have regularly predicted the demise of movie theatres. The dire forecasts began with the advent of radio, grew more pronounced when television arrived, and reached a negative crescendo of gloom when the triple threat of videocassettes, cable and satellite services reached full maturity during the 1980s.

To be sure, a full-blown revolution in home entertainment was underway. VCRs, costing some $1,200 when they were first introduced in the seventies, soon plummeted in price to less than $300. By the mid-1980s two-thirds of America's households owned a VCR, and the market was still growing. A proliferation of video stores emerged to flaunt thousands of movie titles for sale or rent on cassette. And then there was cable. By the late 1980s every cable system in the country had at least one movie channel, with more than 90 percent of the systems offering two or more. The pay-per-view concept also gained in popularity. Rather than paying a fee for a month's worth of premium movie channel programming, cable subscribers could instead pay a sepa-

rate, usually smaller fee for each special event or movie watched, much as they did at a movie theatre's box office. Laser discs debuted in the early 1980s as competition to the videocassette. Laser discs played back a superior video image and theoretically would never wear out, but disc players were generally much more

The concession counter of the Starship nine-plex in Lincoln, Nebraska. *Debby Brehm*

ACT III's Embassy 14, San Antonio, Texas. *Act III Theatres*

Modern discount theatre operation. Cinemark Movies 7, Tallahassee, Florida. *Cinemark*

expensive then VCRs, plus they lacked the VCR's ability to record.

Far from folding under the onslaught of these home entertainment systems, exhibition entered a stage of

dramatic growth that climaxed with a record 23,000 movie screens in place by the end of the 1980s. The expanded ancillary market for films generated a gold mine of new profits that studios promptly pumped back into increased production. After battling a drought of pictures for years, exhibition was enjoying a deluge.

Despite the competition from VCRs and cable, the moviegoing audience remained stable during the '80s with more than one billion tickets sold in the U.S. each year. What became abundantly clear was that all the new media depended on movie marketing and box office success to attract home audiences. Movie theatres retained the enviable position of launching a film in its first release. Despite a shortening of the "release window" — an industry term for that period of time between the end of a film's first run and the start of its subsequent release to ancillary markets — going to a movie theatre was still the only way to see the latest pictures with top stars. And of course, it was the only way *ever* to see a movie in the richness of detail and sound that the filmmaker originally intended, all while enjoying a shared emotional experience in a darkened auditorium full of people.

Mindful of the increasing sophistication of big screen televisions and home stereo systems, exhibition embarked on an aggressive campaign to upgrade screen presentation and all aspects of the moviegoing experience. Theatre complexes expanded into larger, more stylish showhouses. The 1980s saw a trend away from twin, triple and four-screen theatres to new and remodelled complexes featuring six, ten or more auditoriums. The multiple screen theatre had outgrown the shopping mall and increasingly emerged as a free-standing complex. "There are a number of reasons why theatres wanted to be free standing now," explained veteran Midwestern exhibitor Herb Brown. "First of all if you are in a mall generally you have certain constraints. The mall might want to close at 10 and then they start designating certain exits that will be available to your people when they get out at 11 or 12 or one in the morning. If you are doing business and you have a line or a big crowd, you don't want to be concerned about these people lining up in front of the mall stores."

Modern multiplexes saw plain-faced functional designs give way to those with more imagination, color and neon. Lobbies expanded to embrace huge, brightly-lit concession counters with an expanded array of snack choices. Seats became wider and more comfortable. "Probably the biggest improvement we've made in seating was the cup-holder arm rest," remarked veteran circuit executive Vincent Guzzo. "They didn't work at first. We couldn't figure out how to hold them on there. They were too wide and the seat bucket wouldn't come up or wouldn't go down. People would bang into them with their knees. We made them out of wood for a long time. They were expensive. We couldn't figure out a way to make all of the drink sizes fit. It was about a two year cycle before we got one that really worked."

Cleanliness and regular maintenance were re-emphasized; courteous staff service became a top priority. Showtimes were staggered with military-like precision to eliminate lines and maintain a smooth traffic flow at all times. The advent of computerized ticketing and credit card advance sales put a crowning touch of convenience on the whole moviegoing experience. "You stand in line and you see someone just scanning the board and you realize what's going on," said veteran Florida-based exhibitor Arthur Hertz of the multiplex experience. "It's like going to a smorgasbord and they'll see what appeals to them at the moment. There is a psychology to having a lot of small auditoriums playing a lot of pictures. If you are sold out of one, there are still

choices for people to come in and see something else. They're not usually going to walk away and say 'the hell with it, I'm going home.' They'll see something else."

The centerpiece of a successful multiplex is its focus on economies of scale. Multiple auditoriums that share a common parking lot, box office, lobby, restrooms and concession area reduce overhead expenses and generate more profit per square foot. Behind the scenes, theatre circuits pursued the economies of centralized purchasing and utilized computers to track inventory and pre-

AMC's Rolling Hills 6, Los Angeles, California. *American Multi Cinema*

vent spoilage.

The 1980s witnessed the birth of the mega-multiplexes, wondrous theatre complexes that put a new premium on style, service, comfort and screen presentation. In 1982, Canada's Cineplex theatre circuit, which had startled the industry three years earlier with the opening of the world's first 18-plex in Toronto, gained a foothold in the U.S. market when it opened the $3 million, 14-screen Beverly Center Cineplex inside a sprawling new upscale Los Angeles shopping mall. The sleek new complex was kept spotlessly clean, and included Perrier and Cadbury's chocolates among its concession choices. The complex would typically put a popular, well-advertised film on as many as three or four screens at a time, and cut back the number of screens as interest in the film declined.

Fueled by its North American successes, the company bought out a major Canadian chain to emerge as Cineplex Odeon. The company continued its expansion into the American market. In 1985 after buying out the Plitt circuit, Cineplex Odeon became, overnight, the fourth-largest theatre chain in the United States. Soon after it joined with MCA, parent company of Universal Studios, to build and jointly operate what was then the world's largest cinema complex. The 18-screen mega-multiplex, located adjacent to Universal Studios in Los Angeles, which could accommodate up to 6,000 patrons, opened in 1987. Some 38,000 patrons showed up for its July, 1987 opening weekend and the venue remains one of the most successful theatre complexes in the U.S.

But by the early 1990s, if you wanted to see the biggest theatre in the Western Hemisphere — 6,000 seats, spread over 20 screens, spread over 125,000 square feet of property — you had to first journey into America's heartland to an area not far from Motor City, U.S.A. There stood the Studio 28, a 20-plex owned by

Jack Loeks in Grand Rapids, Michigan. In the early 1990s prominent theatre circuits announced plans for even *bigger* mega-multiplex theatres. Mammoth 24-screen theatre complexes were set for construction.

In sharp contrast to the rise of super-colossal theatres came the 1980s phenomenon of the discount "dollar" house, a theatre that presented sub-run features at a

Interior, Loeks Studio 28, Grand Rapids, Michigan, Loeks Theatres Inc. *John "Jack" Loeks*

Concession stand, Cineplex Odeon Universal City Cinemas, Universal City, California. *Cineplex Odeon*

fraction of their first-run prices. The traditional audience for the dollar house is the audience on a low or fixed income: the elderly, the poor or the student. "There are many people in the country that can't afford more than a dollar for a movie ticket," explained Texas-based exhibition executive Randy Hester. His circuit operated dozens of dollar houses in the 1990s.

"We've always felt that there's a place for sub-run," said Virginia-based circuit owner Sam Bendheim III. "It is a different audience and this is our feeling: It does not take away from the first-runs because those people are not going to go anyway. We have found that we are bringing in people who haven't been to the movies in years because of the cost, because they have large families and they can't afford the whole experience, or because they're on fixed incomes. But they would rather see a movie in a theatre than rent a video."

Exhibition's business climate during the 1980s was marked by an intense phase of consolidation that saw a handful of companies grow to dominate the industry. "The consolidation took place for several reasons," explained exhibition veteran Joel Resnick, "One, the inherent fear of how we are going to do business in an atmosphere that wouldn't let us split. And two, theatre owners got offered deals they never dreamt they could get offered. Why not sell when you could get more money than you could ever make?" Regional circuits that had weathered decades of exhibition's struggles faced the choice of a lucrative buy-out offer or the difficult prospect of competing against the financial clout of a major national chain. Scores of these smaller circuits sold out, their theatres submerged into new corporate identities.

Beginning in 1986, the parent companies of major Hollywood studios began to enter exhibition by purchasing interests in national theatre circuits. But unlike the vertically-integrated studio-owned theatres of the 1930s and 1940s, theater chains owned or partially owned by studio parent companies are typically run by independent management teams and boards of directors.

As a result of the fierce competition for market share, some areas of the country were overbuilt with too many screens, turning once profitable venues into poor performers for the competing circuits. Saddled with debt from what one veteran exhibitor called the "feeding frenzy" to acquire theatres at prices many times their market worth, some of the major circuits faced a period of retrenchment at the end of the decade and began to raise cash by selling off some of their theatres, usually venues in smaller markets. As a result, some regional

Loeks Studio 28 adjacent to the Loeks Beltline twin Drive-In, Grand Rapids, Michigan, Loeks Theatres Inc. *John "Jack" Loeks*

Discounted movies show at the Beverly Theatre, Peoria, Illinois. *Donald Idarius*

Suburban 8-plex, Lexington
Theatre, Lexington, Kentucky.
Donald Idarius

United Artists' Scottsdale
Pavilions, Scottsdale, Arizona.
United Artist Theatre Circuit, Inc.

smooth. But I am convinced that after some 25 years in the business — and after being around, listening to and learning from men and women with literally thousands of years in the business — people will always want to go to the show. We are the Great American Date whether you are six, sixteen, or sixty-six. Nothing will ever replace the movie theatre," concluded NATO president William F. Kartozian.

With the dawning of the 1990s, American exhibition entered yet another era, and the industry found its focus turning increasingly inward. With the decline of the big-money acquisitions and mergers that only a few years before were such a common industry occurrence, numerous exhibition concerns began to renew their emphasis on customer service.

The industry's continued success in the early '90s soundly reflected its commitment to service. Having barely set foot into the new decade, exhibitors nationwide were aggressively introducing a slew of patron-friendly innovations.

Credit cards are now such a fact of life at moviehouses all over the world that many may find it difficult to believe that most moviegoers could only purchase their tickets with cash prior to 1989. The widespread introduction of plastic to the nation's box offices seemed a small innovation at the time, but it also quietly revolutionized the way Americans go to the movies. Many theatres that took credit cards were now able to offer film fans the option of buying tickets by phone. Another innovation allowed patrons to buy tickets from on-site ticketing machines using their ATM cards. The machines allowed purchases completely free of cash *and* credit; the debit was made directly to the moviegoer's bank account.

If Pacific Theatres' patrons needed cash and didn't know where to find an ATM, many of them could utilize

circuits that resisted the tide of consolidation would come to increase their screen totals and grow to greater prominence.

As the 1980s drew to a close, the long progression of the suburban theatre from shopping centers to shopping malls to giant stand-alone movie complexes reversed itself, but with a innovative twist. Movie theatres in major cities returned to specialized retail complexes that give the public a lively mix of retail shops, restaurants and a chance to go to the movies.

As the 1990s dawned, theatre circuits began to experiment again with the American moviegoing experience.

"Exhibition has come a long way in 100 years. The road has not always been straight nor has it always been

the circuit's new Patron Assistance Program. The service, which Pacific debuted in 1991, utilizes a concierge-like theatre employee called a "patron assistance coordinator" who can, among other things, disseminate information on upcoming attractions, movie showtimes, local restaurants, taxi services and ATM locations. The patron assistance coordinator can also make dinner reservations for a patron, call for a taxi, or page a moviegoer in case of an emergency.

The idea of expanding patron services caught on throughout the industry in many notable ways. SoCal Cinemas' Cinemapolis multiplex in Anaheim, California came to implement "The Screening Room" as a new way to entertain moviegoers before the lights went out. Every Tuesday evening moviegoers are met by a host or hostess who presents them with a menu from which items from the theatre's Cafe Bar can be ordered. The host then typically opens a discussion of the featured film or related industry topics. A female investigator spoke before the detective thriller "V.I. Warshawski," and a cancer specialist before "Dying Young." For "Fried Green Tomatoes" actress Kathy Bates visited the Screening Room.

One of the highest-profile customer programs of the 1990s began at the smallish Michigan-based Loeks-Star circuit, but found itself transferred to a national scale when Loeks-Star owners Jim and Barrie Lawson Loeks were named co-chairs of Sony's sprawling 900-screen Loews circuit. According to Barrie Loeks, employees at both circuits are encouraged "to think like owners," to seek out patrons who express the slightest bit of confusion or distress, and greet them with a warm welcome and, "Is there anything I can do for you?" It's a proactive approach that underscores their trademark "next-in-line" policy, which was designed to ensure that patrons never have to line up behind more than one other moviegoer. If a patron waits in line for more than three minutes for *anything*, or has the slightest complaint, he or she get a free Coke.

Michigan's Monroe Evening News business columnist Steve Gray gushed that the Loekses' customer service program offered "a glimpse of the service of the future...By the time the movie starts, you'll be wondering how they do it. How can this business get a crew of otherwise normal young people to be so warm and efficient?"

Short subjects, a staple of movie house programming in previous decades, returned to many cinema screens during the 1990s with an updated look. CNN-produced news features replaced the newsreels of a previous era, and circuits introduced various entertain-

One of the lobbies of the Michigan-based Loeks-Star circuit. *Loeks-Star Theatres*

SoCal Cinemas' Cinemapolis, Anaheim, California. *SoCal Cinemas*

Loews Village Theatre VII,
New York City, New York.
Loews Theatres

AMC's Union Station 9,
Washington, D.C. *American
Multi Cinema*

practices. Many within the movie industry believe that customer-oriented programs and services may elevate motion picture grosses to unprecedented heights. Dan Taylor, president of the Theatre Equipment Association, says he strongly believes that box office success is generated in large part by "the Disneyland-type experience these people are getting in their local theatres."

And yet, service isn't exhibition's only battlefield; technology is playing an increasingly important role in luring consumers to theatres. In fact, numerous existing technologies may well be offering a glimpse into the theatre of the future.

Digital sound, certainly, continues to revolutionize what theatre audiences are hearing. "We believe it will add a new dimension to the theatrical experience as it has the power to make movies a bigger and more complete sensory experience," noted Barbara Stokes of Optical Radiation Corporation, one of the first companies to develop a digital sound system for movies. "Digital sound will allow the filmmakers to draw the audience's attention to a specific part of the theatre where a soft, barely discernible whisper of footsteps will be coming out of the darkness. At the same time, they will be able to more realistically duplicate the explosive boom of cannon fire shaking the earth. And, of course, they will be able to reproduce all the subtle shadings of sound in between."

At least four different digital sound systems were making inroads into the motion picture marketplace as this book was going to press. Digital systems from Dolby Laboratories and Strong International were joined over the summer of 1993 by two new systems: Sony Dynamic Digital Sound debuted with the release of Sony subsidiary Columbia Pictures' "Last Action Hero"; Universal Pictures' Digital Theatre System made its bow with the release of Universal's megablockbuster "Jurassic Park."

ment shorts and music videos to keep audiences both informed and entertained before the featured attraction.

Exhibitors have never lost sight of the importance of customer service. Each era explores new approaches and innovations that soon become standard industry

Wehrenberg Theatres' Des Peres 14 (under construction) in Des Peres, Missouri. *Wehrenberg Theatres*

Concession stand, Act III, Broadway Metroplex, Portland, Oregon. *Act III Theatres*

In the visual arena, conventional larger-than-life movie screens may soon be supplanted by the larger-than-Godzilla variety.

IMAX, which employs gigantic 50-foot by 70-foot screens (on which it projects the images of equally gigantic reels of 70mm film), already has five-story-tall auditoriums spread throughout the United States, Canada and Europe.

Iwerks Entertainment, a leader in creating giant-screen theatres, ride simulation theatres and movie-based attractions for theme parks and world expos, has not only constructed even bigger, 60-foot by 80-foot screen auditoriums around the world, the company also boasts a 360-degree circular theatre that engulfs the audience with seamless images of foreign lands and exotic adventures.

Moviegoers who want to create the end of the film they're watching now can do so — at special auditoriums that allow such behavior. With the flip of an armrest switch, patrons sampled the interactive world of

"virtual reality" systems. A natural attraction for amusement parks, interactive systems debuted in a limited number of conventional movie theatres during the early 1990s to test the technology's appeal to mainstream movie audiences.

Motion control theatres also bloomed on exhibition's specialized border. Showscan Corporation decisively breaks the "passive audience" barrier by combining hyper-realistic screen images with synchronized motion simulator theatre seats. Showscan utilizes 70mm images projected at 60 frames-per-second, the upper threshold of the amount of visual information that the human eye can assimilate and perceives to be "real." For the moviegoer clinging to a moving theatre seat while being bombarded with thrilling 3-D-like images of incredible depth-of-field and resolution, the experience is nothing short of pure visceral excitement. Iwerks' simulator "thrill rides" transport audiences into illusionary adventures based on blockbuster movies like "RoboCop" and "Days of Thunder." George Orwell's prediction of movie theatre "feelies" made in the once-futuristic novel "1984" is now fact-based with these

leading-edge simulator film attractions.

Motion control theatres like these may sound incredibly futuristic and state-of-the-art, but the concept of combining motion control with motion pictures actually dates back to the earliest years of the 20th century. In 1904, Hale's Tours and Scenes of the World introduced moviegoers to the novelty of a theatre built to resemble a train car. Passengers gave tickets to a "conductor" and sat in authentic railroad seats to view projected scenic views from around the world. Built on rollers, the theatre's realistic visual effects were enhanced by the rocking motion of an actual train ride and

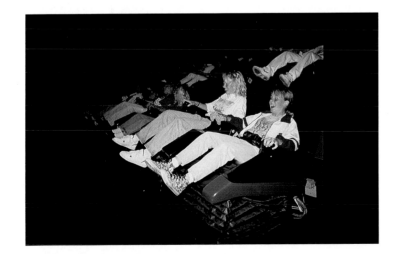

Showscan Corporation's "Showmotion Theatre" at Universal Studios' City Walk attraction in Los Angeles, California. *Showscan Corporation*

Iwerks motion simulator "thrill ride" for movie audiences. *Iwerks Entertainment*

Hollywood U.S.A. Theatre, Garland, Texas. *Cinemark*

sound effects. Clearly, the old adage of "the more things change, the more they stay the same" remains as true for exhibition as for other fields of endeavor. Motion picture novelties are updated, enhanced and imbued with the latest technical wizardry to deliver an ever more rewarding audience experience.

When the technological future of exhibition comes

Showscan auditorium, with synchronized motion simulator theatre seats. *Showscan Corporation*

United Artists' Greenwood Plaza, Englewood, Colorado. *United Artist Theatre Circuit, Inc.*

up, high-definition television, or HDTV, tends to come up as well. With HDTV, movie theatres may be able to pull movie-like projected images out of cables, videotape, laser discs, and satellite dishes. Rather than lessening or degrading a movie's images and sound — as today's standard "low-defininition" video technologies do — HDTV's sounds and images are expected to be indistinguishable from standard 35mm projected

film images, and may even feature considerably sharper pictures and audio.

How soon will we seeing HDTV? Perhaps very soon indeed. By 1990 representatives of a joint American-Japanese corporate venture had already announced that their two companies would soon be building a slew of HDTV theatres in China and the Soviet Union which would employ a projection system that utilized high-definition laser discs.

HDTV could bring a lot more than movies to theatres. During the 1950s, movie studios had experimented with the idea of inscribing electronically- televised images and sounds onto motion picture film in an attempt to renew people's interest in movie theatres during the rise of television's popularity. But as ingenius as this idea of running television shows on larger-than-life movie screens might be, technology lagged behind the idea. People *could* go to theatres to watch championship boxing matches or the World Series, but the pictures on the movie screens resembled those of a grainy and imperfect newsreel image.

HDTV, however, would allow theatres to play not only theatrical motion pictures, but also (perhaps at off-peak hours) satellite-transmitted concerts, spectator sporting events, and even continuing educational programs for professionals. With satellite technologies, a newly-reinvigorated exhibition industry could again find itself experimenting with the venerable idea of "theatre television." As the late Will Tusher of Daily Variety once put it, the high-tech, electronic systems of HDTV could transform movie theatres into "round-the-clock profit centers."

With high-tech color and sound, giant screens, and even futuristic ride-films and "Disneyland-type" customer service, theatres have come a long way since the nickelodeon days.

Will these new technologies make or break the motion picture theatre industry?

As noted earlier, pundits have been predicting the demise of the motion picture theatre virtually since the medium's inception. First the introduction of wireless radio was to have signaled the movies' death-knell; then the arrival of television; then home video and cable; and most recently pay-per-view. With family entertainment conveniently located in the living room of every American's home in the '90s, again the question is poised: "Who needs to drive out to a theatre to watch a movie?"

Well, actor Harrison Ford, for one. "Going to the movies is one of the last things we do together as a people, one of our last community rituals," Ford told Vanity Fair in a 1993 interview. "We enter a darkened room as a group of strangers and we all watch the same images up on the screen and we generally share the same reactions — the same emotions — to these images. If we are lucky, if the movie is good, we watch something that reminds us of our commonality and our humanity. That makes it very different from sitting at home watching a VCR by yourself or with one other person."

And, of course, Ford has perfectly distilled the enduring appeal of moviegoing. Almost everyone seems to agree that new technologies and the "freshness" of newly-released first-run films keep the moviegoing experience exciting, but it is the *sharing* of the out-of-home experience with others that makes it unique and irreplaceable.

Or, as Sony Pictures Entertainment chairman Peter Guber once explained, "We can expand our business to the farthest points of the earth, repeat movies in a dozen new formats and technologies, blaze new pathways into home entertainment, but there is no substitute for the shared emotion of going to the movies — the 20th century version of the tribal campfire."

The tribal campfire burns on.

The Minor Theatre in Arcata, California, remains completely unaltered, its auditorium the same as it was in 1914. A testament to the enduring pleasure of going to the movies.
David Jervis

George Aurelius

ACKNOWLEDGEMENTS

Publishing a book is very much a collaborative process. "America Goes to the Movies" is the result of scores of individuals who shared NATO's enthusiasm to record the history of American movie theatres. To all those individuals who supported our efforts by providing interviews, photographs and memorabilia, in addition to referrals and other important suggestions, NATO expresses its sincere gratitude and proudly lists them as contributors below.

Speaking personally, I want to acknowledge the contributions of all those authors whose diligent research helped me summarize nearly 100 years of exhibition history. And I am forever grateful to the many librarians of various institutions who helped make this material readily accessible to me. The background research for this book was augmented by more than 100 oral history interviews. Special credit goes to Linda Mehr, library director of the Academy of Motion Picture Arts and Sciences, and Barbara Hall, the Academy's oral historian for their guidance and helpful suggestions for NATO's extensive interview program. Judith Weaver Seegrove and the talented staff of Studio Transcription Services earn our appreciation for their timely and professional work. Thank you Paul Roth, John Lowe, Brad Tierney, Tom B'hend and Preston Kaufmann for research guidance and welcomed encouragement. I also want to express my personal gratitude to the NATO staff and others who were an integral part of this book's completion. My sincere appreciation to Jim Kozak for his superb editing and flair for design; to Jim Law for typesetting; to Steve Beland for the cover design; and to Michael Spatola for photography. Thank you Lisa Levinson, Daphne Sison, Terri Seifried and Helen Chen for your hard work and unfailing good humor. And thank you Bill Kartozian for your helpful guidance when the project needed it most. The idea for this book was conceived by Mary Ann Grasso and she deserves a large measure of credit for its completion. Thank you Mary Ann for your inspiration, encouragement and friendship.

— Barbara Stones

INDIVIDUAL CONTRIBUTORS

Lisa Abramowitz	William Benedict	Elbert Chance	Gus Eyssell	Kathy Gray
Meyer Ackerman	Byron Berkley	Helen Chen	J. R. Feehrmeyer	Albert Greene
Stanley Adelman	Tom B'hend	Corky Coble	Nat Fellman	Malcolm Green
Ben Adler	Myron Blank	Kathy Cobleigh	Jean Firstenberg	W.D. "Dave" Gross
Deanna Adnay	Randy Blaum	Elliot Cohen	James Folts	Eleanor Gudmundson
Shirley Ahlgren	Don Bloxham	Irwin R. Cohen	Jerome A. Forman	Jack Gunsky
Lane Allen	Petie Bogen-Garrett	Bruce Corwin	Michael Forman	Vince Guzzo
Yvette Arango	Anthony Bordonaro	Beth Cretors	Peter Frederick	Charles Hacker
Jess Armitage	Robert Bostick	Harry Curl	A. Alan Friedberg	Barbara Hall
Ted Arnow	Sharron Brandrup	Timothy, Cathy and Amy Dalke	Richard Fox	George Hall
Billie Aul	Matthew Brandt	H.A. Daniels	Christine Funk	Dan Harary
George Aurelius	Richard Brandt	James D'Arc	Darrell Gabel	Dan Harkins
Sharon Badal	Debby Brehm	James Deeter	Jere Gabriel	Dave Harney
Richard Baer	Roy Brewer	Virginia DeMaagd	Bill Gartley	Paul W. Harris
Linda Bailey	Brad Brown	Bernard Diamond	Stephen Gilula	Richard Herring
Nancy Baird	Herb Brown	Frank Diaz	Rich Given	Ruthie Herstein
Don Baker	Lou Brown	Kent Dickinson	Irv Glazer	Arthur Hertz
Chuc Barnes	Fred Brush	Ralph Donnelly	Carl Goldman	Randall Hester
Winnie Beane	Bill Burnett	Harry Dressler	Marvin Goldman	Rick Hidde
Larry Bearden	Herb Burton	Kristi Dunn	Charles Goldwater	George Hill
Steve Beland	Ross Campbell	Stanley Durwood	Evan Gordon	Russell Hoffman
Jack Belasco	Beverley Carlson	Ulmer Eaddy	Jerome Gordon	Seymour Hoffman
Charles Bell	George Carroll	Tom Elefante	Steve Grage	Oscar Holzhausen
Sam Bendheim III	Michael Chakeres	Jim Emerson	Mary Ann Grasso	Leon Hoofnagle

Sean Hughes
Derek Hyman
Donald Idarius
David Jervis
Willis Johnson
Emma Moyer Kane
Kathleen Karr
William F. Kartozian
John Kaufman
Preston Kaufmann
Peggy Keating
Paul Kelly
James Kenison
George G. Kerasotes
Albert Kern
John Kisch
Susan Kopman
Jim Kozak
Steven Krams
Ronald and Midge Krueger
Bill Lampe
Laura Lanfranchi
Maryanne Lataif
Jim Law
Paul Lazarus
Eric Levin
Brian Levine
Lisa Levinson
Norm Levinson
Arthur Levy
Bernard W. Levy
Peter Leyh
Sidney Lieb
M.A. Lightman
Weldon Limmroth
Morton Lippe
Lambert Little
John "Jack" Loeks
Louise Loepke
Jeff Logan
Harley Lond
Grant Loucks
John Lowe
Irving Ludwig
Mary Lyday
Dean Maccagnone
Ray Majewski
Karl Malkames
Charles G. Manley
George Mann
T.M. "Ted" Manos

Edward Mapp
George Maranville
Gene Marchu
Steve Marcus
Tom Martin
Juanita "Skeeter" and Paul Maxey
Nettie McDonald
Doris McHugh
Bill McMannis
Linda Mehr
Allen Michaan
Patrick Miller
William L. Miller
Leonard Mishkind
Tandy Mitchell
Ron Moore
Milton Moritz
Jeanie Morris
Harry Moyer
Larry Moyer
Marie Mulligan
Maureen Murphy
Bernard Myerson
Frank Novak
Bruce Olson
Richard Orear
Ad Orkin
Wayne Painter
Tom Paiva
Roger Palmer
Carl Patrick
Sperie Perakos
Paul Petersen
Eugene Picker
Ayron & Howard Pickerill
Katie Peck
Bob Pinkston
Eugene Plank
AnnMarie Price
Myron Price
Ralph Pries
Martin Quigley, Jr.
Sumner Redstone
Joel Resnick
Roger Rice
Paul Richardson
Harmon "Bud" Rifkin
Julian Rifkin
Tim Romano
Albert Rook
Larry Roper

A. Q. Roquervert
Diana Rose
Paul Roth
Robert Rothschild
John Rowley
Ralph Russell
M.W. "Bud" Saffle
Arthur L. Sanborn, Jr.
Bruce Sanborn
Henry Sampson
Eli Savada
Clyde Scarboro
Caroline Schaffner
G. David Schine
Truman Schroeder
Betty Schuler
Fred Schwartz
Muriel Schwartz
Richard Schwegel
Terri Seifried
Herbert Seitz
Robert Selig
Otto Settele
Ed Sharp
Ruth Shaw
Sam Sherman
Delmar Sherrill
Carol Signet
Alan Silverman
Maurice Silverman
Daphne Sison
Duane Sneddecker
T.G. Solomon
Michael Spatola
William Stembler
John Stembler, Sr.
Barbara Stokes
Pamela Stones
Frank Stryjewski
Robert Sunshine
Alvin Svoboda
Bob Tankersley
Phil Tardif
Dan Taylor
John Tegtmeier
Brad Tierney
Jack Tillmany
Kris Topaz
Charles Trexler
Ron Van Timmeren
Billie Turley

Marilyn Veditz
Tim Warner
Judith Weaver Seegrove
Sue Weddle
Lisa Welch
Larry Widen
Carey Williams
Kemmons Wilson
Chuck Winans
Russell Wintner
Woody Wise
Richard Wolfe
Don Woodward
Alan Wrobel
Anthony Yannatelli
Charlie Ziarko
Tony Zucker

RESOURCES

Academy of Motion Picture Arts and Sciences
Act III Theatres
Arkansas History Commission
B'hend & Kaufmann Archives
Beverly Hills Public Library
Burbank Public Library
Chicago Public Library
Cincinnati Historical Society
Cinamerica, L.P.
Circus World Museum
Coca-Cola USA
Colorado Historical Society
C. Cretors and Company
Decorators Supply Corporation
Eastman Kodak Company
Hoblitzelle Foundation
Hollywood Film Archive
Donald Idarius Collection
Jewish Historical Society
Karl Malkames Collection
Library of Congress
Loeks-Star Theatres
Loews Theatres
Metropolitan Cooperative Library System
Metropolitan Theatres
Missouri Historical Society
Museum of Repertoire Americana
NATO Archives, Brigham Young University

NATO of California
Pacific Theatres
Tom Paiva Photography
Pepsi-Cola Entertainment Group
Harry Ransom Center, University of Texas, Austin
Tim Romano, Historic Photo Service
SoCal Cinemas
Southern Regional Library, UCLA
Michael Spatola Photography
Tampa Hillsborough County Public Library System
Theatre Historical Society
Jack Tillmany Collection
United Artists Theatres
University of California at Los Angeles
University of the State of New York, Albany
Virginia Historical Society
Virginia State Library and Archives
Warner Research Collection
Wagner-Zip Change, Inc.
Wehrenberg Theatres
Western Kentucky University
Western Pennsylvania Historical Society
Larry Widen Collection

Boldly-stylized cut-out of James Cagney, as used in movie theatres circa 1934. *Eric Levin*

BIBLIOGRAPHY

BOOKS

Allen, Robert C. *Vaudeville and Film, 1895-1915: A Study in Media Interaction.* New York: Arno Press Dissertation Series, 1977.

Allen, Robert C. and Douglas Gomery. *Film History: Theory and Practice.* New York: Alfred A. Knopf, 1985.

Badal, Sharon. *The Big Screen: A Passionate Look at the Motion Picture Palace.* Unpublished M.A. dissertation, New York University, New York, 1991.

Balio, Tino. *The American Film Industry.* Madison: The University of Wisconsin Press, 1985.

Balio, Tino. *United Artists: The Company That Changed the Film Industry.* Madison: The University of Wisconsin Press, 1987.

Baxter, John. *Sixty Years of Hollywood.* Cranbury, N.J.: A.S. Barnes and Co., Inc., 1973.

Bergman, Andrew. *We're in the Money.* New York: New York University Press, 1971.

Bordwell, David and Janet Staiger and Kristin Thompson. *The Classic Hollywood Cinema.* New York: Columbia University Press, 1985.

Bowers, Q. David. *Nickelodeon Theatres, and Their Music.* New York: The Vestal Press, Ltd., 1986.

Bowser, Eileen. *Volume 2: The Transformation of Cinema 1907-1915.* New York: Charles Scribner's Sons, 1990.

Brownlow, Kevin. *The Parade's Gone By.* New York: Alfred A. Knopf, 1968.

Butsch, Richard. *For Fun and Profit.* Philadelphia: Temple University Press, 1990.

Carr, Robert E. and R.M. Hayes. *Wide Screen Movies.* Jefferson, N.C.: McFarland & Company, Inc., 1988.

Chase, Linda. *Hollywood on Main Street, The Movie House Paintings of Davis Cone.* Woodstock, N.Y.: The Overlook Press, 1988.

Coe, Brian. *The History of Movie Photography.* New Jersey: Eastview Editions, 1981.

Conant, Michael. *Antitrust in the Motion Picture Industry.* Berkeley: University of California Press, 1960.

Cook, David A. *A History of Narrative Film.* New York: W.W. Norton & Company, Inc., 1981.

C. Cretors & Co. *The First Hundred Years: 1885-1985.* Chicago: C. Cretors & Co., 1985.

Cripps, Thomas. *Black Film As Genre.* Bloomington: Indiana University Press, 1978.

Cripps, Thomas. *Slow Fade to Black: The Negro in American Film 1900 -1942.* New York: Oxford University Press, 1977.

Donahue, Suzanne Mary. *American Film Distribution, The Changing Marketplace.* Ann Arbor, Mich. UMI Research Press, 1987.

Edgerton, Gary R. *American Film Exhibition and an Analysis of the Motion Picture Industry's Market Structure 1963-1980.* New York: Garland Publishing, Inc., 1983.

Finler, Joel W. *The Hollywood Story.* New York: Crown Publishers, Inc., 1988.

Franklin, Harold B. *Motion Picture Theatre Management.* New York: George H. Doran Co., 1927.

Fulton, A.R. *Motion Pictures.* Norman, Okla.: University of Oklahoma Press, 1968.

Geduld, Harry M. *The Birth of the Talkies.* Bloomington: Indiana University Press, 1975.

Gomery, Douglas. *Movie History, A Survey.* Belmont, Calif.: Wadsworth Publishing Co., 1991.

Gomery, Douglas. *Shared Pleasures: A History of Movie Presentation in the United States.* Madison: The University of Wisconsin Press, 1992.

Gomery, Douglas. *The Hollywood Studio System.* New York: St. Martin's Press, 1986.

Green, Abel and Joe Laurie, Jr. *Show Biz: From Vaude to Video.* New York: Henry Holt and Co., 1951.

Grenz, Christine. *Trans-Lux: Biography of a Corporation.* Norwalk, Conn.: Trans-Lux Corporation, 1982.

Griffith, Richard and Arthur Mayer. *The Movies.* New York: Simon and Schuster, 1957.

Hall, Ben M. *The Best Remaining Seats.* New York: Crown Publishers, Inc., 1987.

Hampton, Benjamin B. *A History of the Movies.* New York: Covici Friede, 1931.

Hayes, R.M. *3-D Movies: A History and Filmography of Stereoscopic Cinema.* Jefferson, N.C.: McFarland & Company, Inc., 1989.

Headley, Robert Kirk, Jr. *Exit: A History of the Movies in Baltimore.* University Park, Md.: Privately published, 1974.

Hendricks, Bill and Howard Waugh. *The Encyclopedia of Exploitation.* New York: Showmen's Trade Review, 1937.

Huettig, Mae D. *Economic Control of the Motion Picture Industry.* Philadelphia: University of Pennsylvania Press, 1944.

Izod, John. *Hollywood and the Box Office, 1895-1986.* New York: Columbia University Press, 1988.

Jacobs, Lewis. *The Rise of The American Film.* New York: Harcourt, Brace and Co., 1939.

Jones, G. William. *Black Cinema Treasures: Lost and Found.* Denton: University of North Texas Press, 1991.

Jowett, Garth. *Film: The Democratic Art.* Boston: Little Brown and Co., 1976.

Kaufmann, Preston J. *Fox: The Last Word.* Pasadena, Calif.: Showcase Publications, 1979.

Kindem, Gorham. *The American Movie Industry.* Carbondale, Ill.: Southern Illinois University Press, 1982.

Kisch, John and Edward Mapp. *A Separate Cinema: Fifty Years of Black-Cast Posters.* New York: Farrar, Straus and Giroux, 1992.

Knight, Arthur. *The Liveliest Art.* New York: MacMillan Publishing Co., Inc., 1959.

Kobal, John and V.A. Wilson. *Foyer Pleasure: The Golden Age of Cinema Lobby Cards.* New York: Deliliah, 1983.

Koszarski, Richard. *Volume 3: An Evening's Entertainment: The Age of The Silent Feature Picture 1915-1928.* New York: Macmillan Publishing Co., 1990.

Lampe, William. *Frame by Frame in Huron.* Huron, S.D.: Privately published, 1982.

Leab, Daniel J. *From Sambo to Superspade: The Black Experience in Motion Pictures.* Boston: Houghton Mifflin Co., 1975.

Lewis, Howard T. *The Motion Picture Industry.* New York: D. Van Nostrand Co., Inc., 1933.

Macgowan, Kenneth. *Behind the Screen.* New York: Delacorte Press, 1965.

Margolies, John and Emily Gwathmey. *Ticket to Paradise.* Boston: Little Brown and Co., 1991.

Mast, Gerald. *A Short History of the Movies.* New York: Bobbs-Merrill Co., 1971.

May, Lary. *Screening Out the Past.* New York: Oxford University Press, 1980.

Mayer, Arthur. *Merely Colossal.* New York: Simon and Schuster Inc., 1953.

McGee, Mark Thomas. *Beyond Ballyhoo.* Jefferson, N.C.: McFarland & Company, Inc., 1989.

Murphy, Anne Marie. *Sit In Your Car - See and Hear The Movies.* Unpublished Ph.D Dissertation, University of California, Los Angeles, 1990.

Musser, Charles. *The Emergence of Cinema: The American Screen to 1907 Vol. 1.* New York: Macmillan Publishing Company, 1990.

Naylor, David. *American Picture Palaces.* New York: Van Nostrand Reinhold, 1981.

Naylor, David. *Great American Movie Theatres.* Washington, D.C.: The Preservation Press, 1987.

North, Joseph H. *The Early Development of the Motion Picture.* New York: Arno Press, 1973.

Pildas, Ave and Lucinda Smith. *Movie Palaces.* New York: Clarkson N. Potter, Inc., 1980.

Pratt, George C. *Spellbound in Darkness.* Greenwich, Conn.: New York Graphic Society Ltd., 1973.

Ramsaye, Terry. *A Million and One Nights.* New York: Simon & Schuster, Inc., 1926.

Ricketson, Frank H. Jr. *The Management of Motion Picture Theatres.* New York: McGraw-Hill Book Co., Inc., 1938.

Sampson, Henry T. *Blacks in Black and White: A Source Book on Black Films.* Metuchen, N.J.: Scarecrow Press, Inc., 1977.

Scott, Emory Frank. *One Hundred Years of Lawrence Theatres.* Mission, Kan.: The House of Usher, 1979.

Segrave, Kerry. *Drive-In Theatres: A History from Their Inception in 1933.* Jefferson, N.C.: MacFarland & Company, Inc., 1992.

Seldes, Gilbert. *The Great Audience.* New York: The Viking Press, 1950.

Sexton, R.W. and B.F. Betts. *American Theatre of Today.* New York: Architectural Book Publishing Co., Inc., 1927, 1930.

Sharp, Dennis. *The Picture Palace.* New York: Frederick A. Praeger Publishers, Inc., 1969.

Shipman, David. *The Story of Cinema.* New York: St. Martin's Press, 1982.

Sinyard, Neil. *Silent Movies.* New York: Gallery Books, 1990.

Sklar, Robert. *Movie-Made America.* New York: Random House, 1975.

Slide, Anthony. *The American Film Industry: A Historical Dictionary.* New York: Limelight Editions, 1990.

Sorensen, John. *Our Show Houses.* Grand Island, Neb.: The Hall County Historical Society Press, 1990.

Squire, Jason E. *The Movie Business Book.* New York: Simon & Schuster, Inc., 1983, 1992.

Stanley, Robert H. *The Celluloid Empire.* New York: Hastings House Publishers, 1978.

Stuart, Fredric. *The Effects of Television on The Motion Picture and Radio Industries.* New York: Arno Press, 1976.

Tarbox, Charles. H. *The Five Ages of the Cinema.* New York: Exposition Press, 1980.

Thorp, Margaret Farrand. *America at the Movies.* New York: Arno Press, 1970.

Thrasher, Frederic M. *Okay for Sound.* New York: Duell, Sloan & Pearce, Inc., 1946.

Vogel, Harold L. *Entertainment Industry Economics: A Guide For Financial Analysis,* 2d ed. New York: Cambridge University Press, 1990.

Wasko, Janet. *Movies and Money: Financing the American Film Industry.* Norwood, N.J.: Ablex Publishing Corp., 1982.

Widen, Larry and Judi Anderson. *Milwaukee Movie Palaces.* Milwaukee: Milwaukee County Historical Society, 1986.

Other Publications

Boxoffice

Film Daily Yearbook

Motion Picture Herald

Motion Picture News

Moving Picture World

NATO Encyclopedia of Exhibition 1978-1993

New York Times

Theatre Catalog

Variety

INDEX